A
WILDERNESS
ORIGINAL

A
WILDERNESS
ORIGINAL

◆ ──────────────────────────── ◆

The Life of
Bob Marshall

JAMES M. GLOVER

◆ ──────────────────────────── ◆

The Mountaineers, Seattle

THE MOUNTAINEERS: Organized 1906
". . . to explore, preserve and enjoy
the natural beauty of the Northwest."

© 1986 by The Mountaineers

Published by The Mountaineers
306 Second Avenue West, Seattle, Washington 98119

Published simultaneously in Canada by
Douglas & McIntyre Ltd.
1615 Venables Street, Vancouver, B.C. V5L 2H1

Manufactured in the United States of America

Cover photos: Background—forest grove in Great Smoky Mountains
National Park, Tennessee, © Pat O'Hara. Front inset—Marshall in the
early 1930s. Photo courtesy Bancroft Library, University of California,
Berkeley. Back inset—Jesse Allen, Marshall and Nutirwik (Harry
Snowden) in Alaska. From *Alaska Wilderness* with permission from George
Marshall.
Frontispiece—Marshall in the Quetico-Superior area, 1937. Photo by Sig
Olson.

Library of Congress Cataloguing in Publication Data

Glover, James M., 1950–
    A wilderness original.

    Bibliography: p.
    Includes index.
    1. Marshall, Robert, 1901–1939.   2. Foresters—
United States—Biography.   3. Conservationists—
United States—Biography.   4. United States.
Forest Service—Officials and employees—Biography.
5. United States. Bureau of Indian Affairs—Officials
and employees—Biography.   6. Wilderness Society—
History.   7. Forests and forestry—United States—
History.   8. Wilderness areas—United States—History.
I. Title.
SD129.M29G58   1986   634.9'092'4 [B]   86-18050

ISBN 0-89886-121-7
ISBN 0-89886-122-5 (Pbk.)

For George Marshall

Contents

	Acknowledgments	ix
1	"The Kind of Vision We Need Today"	1
2	An Activist Father	7
3	A Young Romantic (1901–1920)	15
4	Pond Seeker (1920–1924)	37
5	Bee Stings and Broiled Eggs (1924–1925)	55
6	Rocky Mountain Greyhound (1925–1928)	67
7	Baltimore Liberal (1928–1930)	99
8	Wiseman Winter (1930–1931)	119
9	Writer and Socialist (1931–1933)	141
10	The Wilderness Society (1933–1935)	159
11	Indians and Wilderness (1935–1937)	197
12	Back to the Forest Service (1937–1938)	215
13	Two Last Flings (1938–1939)	241
14	"He Never Rested" (1939)	267
	Notes	275
	Index	313

Acknowledgments

◆ ——————————————————————————— ◆

Nobody writes a book like this without a great deal of help from many different people and organizations. George Marshall and James Marshall—Bob's brothers—provided valuable advice, suggestions, and comments on my manuscript. They also granted permission to use various photographs and manuscripts without which the book could not have been done.

Paul Oehser, long-time Wilderness Society Councillor, scholar, humanitarian, and humorist, gave me tremendous encouragement when I was first beginning the study; he also directed me to a lot of information and offered excellent editorial advice on the manuscript. My folders marked Mable (Abercrombie) Mansfield, Neil Hosley, and Paul Schaefer are also very fat, an indication of the help and encouragement they provided.

I wish to thank the following for reading all or parts of my manuscript: Connie Carlson, Dick Cohen, Jim Ford, James P. Gilligan, Regina Glover, George Marshall, James Marshall, Roderick Nash, Paul Oehser, Kenneth Philp, and Woody Stroble.

Several publishers kindly gave me permission to use their materials. I am especially grateful to the University of California Press for permission to quote liberally from Bob Marshall's *Alaska Wilderness*. I also wish to thank the Estate of Robert Marshall for permission to quote from *Arctic Village;* Doubleday books and the Adirondack Mountain Club for permission to reprint an early photograph of Bob and George Marshall with Herb Clark, from *Peaks and People of the Adirondacks*, by Russell M. L. Carson; the Forest History Society for permission to quote from their oral history interview with Leo Isaac; and *Adirondack Life* for permission to re-use material from my articles, "The First Forty-Sixers" and "Louis Marshall."

I wish to thank the staffs of the following institutions for their generous and cooperative help: Adirondack Research Center, Schenectady Museum, Schenectady, New York; Adirondack Museum, Blue Mountain Lake, New York; American Jewish Archives, Cincinnati, Ohio; Dartmouth College Library, Hanover, New Hampshire; Denver Public Library, Denver, Colorado; Bancroft Library, Berkeley, California; F. Franklin Moon Library, State University of New York College of Environmental Science and Forestry, Syracuse, New York; Franklin D. Roosevelt Library, Hyde Park, New York; Harvard Forest, Petersham, Massachusetts; National Archives, Washington, D.C.; Region One Office of the U.S. Forest Service, Missoula, Montana; The Wilderness Society, Washington, D.C.; University of Washington Libraries, Seattle, Washington; University of Wyoming Library, Laramie, Wyoming; United States Office of Personnel Management, Washington, D.C.

I would like to thank Mary Falaster for a professional typing job on the final draft; Carol Kraus for tolerating my nightly and weekend use of her office at Southern Illinois University as I was finishing up the project; and Georgia Cromwell and Virginia Olmsted for loaning me photographs.

Most importantly, I wish to thank my wife Regina for her help and encouragement. During the time it took me to write this book, she completed several graduate courses, wrote a doctoral dissertation, carried a full-time teaching load, wrote several articles, counseled dozens of wayward college students, and produced a sustained yield of first-class cherry pies and chocolate chip cookies. But she still found time to tour the West with me in search of Bob Marshall and help me collect a lot of the data. Trying to thank her in a paragraph is like trying to describe the Bob Marshall Wilderness with a snapshot of the Chinese Wall—each gives only a tiny impression of what you feel and would like to express.

Jim Glover
Carbondale, Illinois

1
"The Kind of Vision We Need Today"

◆ ——————————————————————— ◆

The universe of the wilderness... is disappearing while most of
those who care more for it than anything else in this world are trying
desperately to rally and save it.

Bob Marshall, 1937

Around one o'clock on the afternoon of July 15, 1932, a young
builder of early-American houses named Paul Schaefer was carrying a movie camera toward the glacier-scarred summit of Mount
Marcy, highest peak in New York State's Adirondack Mountains.
A devoted conservationist in his off-work hours, Schaefer was
photographing both natural beauty and human destruction in the
Adirondack Park. The resulting film would be used to fight against
various proposals that Schaefer and others feared would destroy the
park's wilderness character.

As he made the last few steps onto the rounded summit,
Schaefer was met by a wiry Adirondack mountaineer named Herb
Clark. Clark, then in his sixties but still slender as a greyhound,
had for many years been a guide for the Marshall family, who
owned a cabin on Lower Saranac Lake. Clark was carrying a lunch
for thirty-one-year-old Bob Marshall, who, Clark explained, was
trying to see how many peaks he could climb in one day. Marshall
had begun his marathon hike at 3:30 that morning and had arranged to meet Clark for lunch on Marcy around one.

1

High above treeline, Clark and Schaefer gazed at the spectacular view as they waited for Marshall to appear. For miles in all directions, a jumble of rugged green ridges stood up in sharp relief against the deep blue of the clear summer sky. To the southwest, they looked almost straight down nearly 2,000 feet into a spruce-tangled ravine known as Panther Gorge.

Scanning the steep eastern slope, they now spotted a solitary figure emerging from the stunted subalpine firs about a half-mile below. As the figure came closer, Clark could tell that it was Marshall. The sturdy but slightly pear-shaped frame, the square shoulders, the wavy brown hair, and rapid gait were distinctive. As Marshall came closer they could see that he was wearing his customary loose-fitting blue-denim jeans, high-topped sneakers, and faded old cotton shirt.

Springing over boulders like a kid on a pogo stick, Marshall quickly reached the summit. He greeted Clark happily, for he considered the old guide one of his closest friends and greatest teachers. Then he walked over to Schaefer.

"I'm Bob Marshall," he said. A toothy smile came over his round, boyish face as he stuck out his hand. Had Marshall been in one of his frequent joking moods he might have let the hand go as limp as an earthworm just as Schaefer grabbed it. This was a favorite trick of his at formal dinner parties in New York or Washington, D.C., when he thought the protocol was getting a little too "stuffy." But on a mountaintop there were few pretentions to protest against, so he grabbed Schaefer's hand and gave it an exuberant squeeze.[1]

"His eyes reflected a great joy for living," Shaefer later recalled, "and his face was deeply tanned and ruddy with health."[2]

Marshall's face *should* have looked healthy. He had recently spent thirteen months exploring the uncharted wilderness of Alaska's Brooks Range and studying the frontier lives of the people who lived there. Prior to that, he had lived for three years in the Northern Rocky Mountains of Montana. There, while conducting tree-growth research for the U.S. Forest Service, he had spent his weekends indulging his passion for long-distance hiking.

2

Something around thirty-five miles in a day was usually enough for him in those western mountains, although he was known to go out after supper on a Sunday night to walk up and down the road if he needed another mile or two to make it an even forty for the day.[3]

Marshall sat down to eat his lunch, and Schaefer began telling him about some of the recent threats to the wild Adirondacks. He warned of a movement to allow cabins to be built in the park, then pointed westward toward Mount Adams.

"They're stripping Adams of its virgin spruce, clear to the top," Schaefer said. "And over there—see the burned lands of the Opalescent? It was a crown fire. It leapt Lake Sanford and the river and burned deep, clear to the summit of North River Mountain."

Marshall had no trouble picturing the places Schaefer was talking about. There was no place Schaefer could point to that he hadn't visited. Marshall, his brother George, and the guide who stood with him on Marcy today, Herb Clark, had been the first people to climb all forty-six of the Adirondack peaks over 4,000 feet high.

Schaefer's comments were disturbing. Marshall said, "Before I left for the Arctic they promised us there would be no more cutting above 2,500 feet elevation. Those are the most critical watershed forests in the Adirondacks."

Marshall was well-versed in such technical matters, for in between marathon hikes and Arctic explorations he had earned two forestry degrees and a Ph.D. in plant physiology. What concerned him now, though, was an issue that could never be solved by science. It had to do with beauty and history and ethics and the loss of something that could never be replaced.

Marshall began to pace around the summit, visibly upset. He had seen the same kind of whittling away at wilderness areas in Montana, Colorado, Washington, Oregon—wherever there was still any backcountry left to be whittled. He had already written an article for *The Scientific Monthly* in which he called for "an organization of spirited people who will fight for the freedom of the wilderness." Now it occurred to him again that some kind of nationwide wilderness organization was badly needed.[4]

Bob Marshall in the Cascade Range, Washington, 1929 (Photograph courtesy of The Bancroft Library, University of California, Berkeley)

"We simply must band together," he finally said to Schaefer, "all of us who love the wilderness. We must fight together—wherever and whenever wilderness is attacked."

They talked for a few more minutes, agreeing to keep in contact with each other. They shook hands again, and then Marshall loped off down the mountainside. (He frequently ran on the downhill slopes. It saved time and was also fun.)

At 10:30 that night Marshall finished his hike. It had lasted for

nineteen hours and he had climbed fourteen peaks, ascending a total of 13,600 feet.

The next day he sat down to write an account of his accomplishment. He had always enjoyed writing almost as much as mountain
climbing. Already he had published half a dozen articles in national
magazines and well over a dozen pieces in local publications. And
he was just now finishing a book about life in the far north, to be
called *Arctic Village*. An ardent socialist, he planned to share his
royalties from the book with the 127 Indians, Eskimos, and white
pioneers he'd written about.

In his diminutive, upright handwriting, he began to describe his
long walk: "Yesterday I ascended 14 Adirondack peaks. . . . [This]
would fit perfectly in a class with flagpole sitting and marathon
dancing as an entirely useless type of record, made only to be
broken, were it not that I had such a glorious time out of the entire
day. . . ."[5]

When the 2,000-word account was finished, he sent it off to the
Adirondack Mountain Club for publication in the club's newsletter, *High Spots*. Then it was time to start thinking about his next
project. He was soon due in Washington to write a section on recreation for the U.S. Forest Service's *National Plan for American
Forestry*. Perhaps he could use the assignment to strike a blow for
wilderness preservation.

Paul Schaefer, meanwhile, returned to his house-building business in Schenectady, New York. It was a long time before he saw
Marshall again, but memory of their chance meeting on the summit of Marcy lingered with him. He later recalled being "acutely
conscious of having met a dynamic personality."[6]

Schaefer was even more impressed when Marshall followed up
on his commitments to keep in contact and to organize a national
network of wilderness defenders. In 1935 Schaefer received word
that Marshall and seven others had formed an organization called
The Wilderness Society, dedicated to "battle uncompromisingly"
for wilderness protection all over the country. The society was just
one aspect of an unprecedented campaign to save wilderness that
Marshall had begun. His efforts would eventually influence the

fate of millions of acres of wildland from the Great Smoky Mountains to the Olympic Peninsula.

"Bob Marshall clearly saw the whole picture more than thirty years ago," Schaefer observed in 1966. "He had the kind of vision we need today."[7]

Schaefer referred to Marshall in the past tense because by 1966 it had been twenty-seven years since Bob Marshall, age thirty-eight, suddenly and inexplicably died while sleeping on a train.

2

An Activist Father

◆ ──────────────────────────────────── ◆

Any cause can be destroyed by a lackadaisical attitude toward it.

Louis Marshall

Any attempt to understand Bob Marshall must begin with his father. For it was through him that Bob acquired much of his humor, his humanitarianism, and especially his environmental activism. Louis Marshall was a brilliant constitutional lawyer, a prominent Jewish leader, and an eloquent champion of minority rights. He was also an ardent amateur naturalist and a staunch defender of wilderness in the Adirondacks.

When Bob was away from home during the last nine years of his father's life, Louis wrote him over five hundred letters. Bob responded in kind, taking special delight in relating funny incidents to his father. "Some of my letters," Bob recalled, "he would read to every unfortunate who came along. He enjoyed the amusing incidents so much."[1]

When Louis Marshall died in 1929, Bob told a family friend that he would especially miss his father's sense of humor and love of the outdoors—two of Bob's own outstanding qualities. "There was in the woods a tremendous natural tie between us," Bob wrote, "a bond which it is indeed painful to realize is broken forever."[2]

Louis Marshall's own father, Jacob Marschall, was a Jewish immigrant from Württemburg, Bavaria. He reached New York City

7

in 1847. According to Louis, Jacob arrived "with only a five franc piece, which he forthwith spent for peaches."[3] Louis also had a favorite joke about why Jacob changed the spelling of "Marschall" shortly after arriving: ". . . after being on a sailing vessel for nearly fifty days, during all of which time he was seasick, he crossed the 'c' out of his name."[4]

In New York, Jacob had a hard time getting started, even though he was willing to work hard. He tried peddling for awhile, but had his goods stolen from him while suffering from typhoid fever. Upon recovery, he found work helping to build the Northern Central Railroad but was cheated out of his pay when the contractor skipped town. Still undiscouraged, he worked his way up the Erie Canal to Syracuse, where he opened a hide, fur, and leather business. It was marginally profitable.[5]

Jacob married another German-Jewish immigrant, Zilli Strauss, in 1855. Louis, the first of their six children, was born on December 14, 1856.[6]

Louis's mother was self-educated. She encouraged her children to be scholars. When Louis was young, she had him read aloud to her while she did her housework. When she stopped to rest, she would have him recite as much as he could from memory.[7]

Louis attended German and Hebrew schools in the afternoons, when public school was over. By the time he finished high school, he was conversant in French, Latin, and Hebrew.[8]

At age eight he began keeping his father's books. "I became fairly expert in furs," he recalled. He also learned about cruelty and prejudice. From his parents he heard stories of brutal raids on unoffending Jews in the German forests. He learned that his parents' experiences in Germany "were of the most bitter kind, such as were little calculated to inspire love or tender recollections."[9]

Louis began speaking out against prejudicial statements of his peers and teachers. Once, in high school, he went to great pains to persuade a class that Shylock, in *The Merchant of Venice*, was "the only really human and consistent character in the play."[10]

After graduating from high school and serving a two-year apprenticeship in a law office, Louis enrolled at Columbia University's law school (then Dwight Law School). The law program was supposed to take two years. But Louis noticed that all of the first-year classes were given in the afternoon, while all the second-year classes were given in the morning. So he took them both in the same year. He passed all the required courses, but the school would not give him a degree because he had not put in the usual two years.[11]

The New York State Bar—showing more flexibility than the law school—admitted Marshall into its ranks in January of 1878. He joined the Syracuse firm of William C. Ruger, who later became chief justice of the New York State Court of Appeals.[12]

As a lawyer, Marshall regularly worked from nine in the morning till midnight, with time off only for meals. He became especially good at appellate work; between 1878 and 1894 he argued more than 150 cases before the New York State Court of Appeals. This success and his active involvement in the Syracuse Jewish community made him a prominent figure in the city. In 1891 he was part of a national delegation that asked President Benjamin Harrison to intervene on behalf of persecuted Russian Jews.[13]

In 1894 Marshall was invited by his Columbia classmate Samuel Untermyer, and another prominent attorney named Randolph Guggenheimer, to join their law firm in New York. With little left to accomplish in Syracuse, he gladly accepted, and the new partnership—Guggenheimer, Untermyer, and Marshall—was formed.[14]

After first arriving in New York, Marshall stayed with the Untermyers. One night, at the opera, he was introduced to Sam Untermyer's cousin, Florence Lowenstein. She was the daughter of Sophia Mendelson Lowenstein of New York and Benedict Lowenstein, a wealthy Bavarian immigrant who represented his family's business concerns in New York. She had been educated at The Normal College (now Hunter College) in New York. One of her sons has described her as beautiful and charming, but with "an almost Victorian, or Edwardian type reserve."[15]

Louis Marshall began seeing her regularly. They were married on May 6, 1895. They had four children, whose names, by order of

Louis Marshall (Photograph courtesy of the American Jewish Archives, Cincinnati Campus, Hebrew Union College, Jewish Institute of Religion)

birth, were James, Ruth, Robert (always called Bob), and George.

The Marshalls bought a brownstone house at Number 47 East 72nd Street. Louis joined the Metropolitan Museum of Art and began a personal collection of fine paintings. His manner remained unpretentious, even as his law firm prospered. According to Oscar Handlin, "He wore his clothes until they were shiny, rode the 'el' or the subway, and made a fetish of rescuing stamped envelopes for his own use. He never owned an automobile and saw but a half-dozen movies in his lifetime." This total disregard for the trappings of success was another quality he would pass along to Bob. [16]

Marshall soon became one of the nation's preeminent specialists in constitutional law. He eventually argued more cases before the U.S. Supreme Court than anyone except solicitor generals. Many of these cases were of major constitutional significance. [17]

Florence Marshall, meanwhile, devoted herself completely to her husband. Cyrus Adler, a family friend, wrote that "she merged her life absolutely with Louis's. She had a direct influence on his public career because he was high-tempered and at times stormy, while she was a soothing and restraining influence which undoubtedly aided him in becoming more friendly and companionable with hosts of men." Her personal interests included the education of young Jewish women and the work of certain Jewish welfare organizations.[18]

Louis became active in a wide variety of civic affairs. As president of the American Jewish Committee from 1912 to 1929, his efforts to secure Jewish civil rights became almost legendary. In a 1923 readers' poll by the *Jewish Tribune* to name the twelve most outstanding Jews in the world, he finished fourth. None of the three men who topped him in the poll—Albert Einstein, Chaim Weizmann, and Israel Zangwill—were Americans.[19]

Typical of Marshall's civil rights work was the case involving Melvil Dewey. Known as the founder of modern American library science, Dewey became state librarian of New York in 1899. He also happened to be head of a resort in upstate New York called the Lake Placid Club, and in that capacity was responsible for distributing a circular which announced that Jews were barred from the club. Outraged, Marshall and others in December 1904 submitted to the Board of Regents of the State University of New York a petition demanding Dewey's dismissal. Under mounting pressure, the board censured Dewey for his anti-Semitic sentiments and activities. Dewey finally resigned in February 1905.

Marshall was exultant. "I have succeeded in getting Dewey's scalp," he crowed to a friend. "The result is most gratifying." To those Jews who feared the matter would only stir up old conflicts, Marshall had a reply. Turning the other cheek was "an exercise to which we have been accustomed by the practice of centuries. It has, however, grown somewhat monotonous."[20]

At the same time, Marshall knew that Jewish rights could be guaranteed only if the rights of all minorities were protected. So he also took up the causes of Catholics, Indians, Japanese, blacks, and socialists. He often provided free legal counsel to groups whose civil rights he feared were being violated. He became active in the National Association for the Advancement of Colored People, declaring that nobody could protest the treatment of Jews in Russia who would not speak up for blacks in the American South.[21]

Marshall also found time to champion the cause of wilderness preservation in the Adirondack region. He became interested in this issue as a delegate to the New York State Constitutional Convention of 1894. At that convention New York City Democrat David McClure proposed a historic amendment to the State of New York's constitution. The amendment said that state-owned forest lands in the Adirondack and Catskill Mountains would remain wild forever. Timber harvesting would be strictly forbidden, and the state could never sell or transfer its ownership of these lands. More than 600,000 acres in the Adirondacks would thus be protected from any development.

McClure had introduced the amendment at the request of a group of New York City businessmen who were mainly concerned about watershed protection. New York's primary water source, the Hudson River, had its headwaters in the Adirondacks, as did several other major rivers important for commerce and human welfare. The businessmen feared that continued forest destruction in the Adirondacks would ruin their source of drinking water, fire protection, and transportation.[22]

Measures similar to McClure's amendment had been enacted by the state legislature in the past; but development interests had always persuaded the state's lawmakers to compromise them. A protection clause in the state's constitution would be far more effective, for it could never be modified without the direct approval of two-thirds of the state's voters.

Marshall, though not a Democrat like McClure (he was a lifelong Republican), supported the amendment. He became, by his own recollection, "most active in formulating the amendment and in securing for it what was practically a unanimous vote of the members of the convention." There were attempts to weaken the clause before it was passed. But "those who had given the subject careful study," Marshall observed, "were of the opinion that this was not a subject to be trifled with and that a rigid rule should be laid down and rigidly enforced."[23]

George and Louis Marshall at Knollwood (Photograph courtesy of the Adirondack Museum, Blue Mountain Lake, New York)

The new constitution was approved by the people of New York in November 1894. The Adirondack Forest Preserve now had strict protection that could not be undone by any agency or even the state legislature. The amendment was a major landmark in the history of wilderness preservation. And for the next thirty-five years, nobody fought harder to keep the Adirondacks wild than Louis Marshall. "Blister rust, canker and insects," he decided, "are infinitely less dangerous than homo sapiens, who, whether he takes the form of a lumberman, or a tax title exploiter, a vandal or a commercial hotelkeeper, is the real enemy of the forest."[24]

With that in mind, Marshall kept the public, legislators, law enforcers, and news reporters well informed of every possible threat to the Adirondack forest. In the early 1900s, timber thieves were still helping themselves to state-owned trees. Marshall—who had frequently taken up the cause of accused criminals—felt little compassion for these rogues. "I am not ordinarily in favor of Draconian measures," he told the Governor,

> but when it is considered that the destruction of the Adirondack Preserve would affect the water supply of the State, would diminish the flow of the Hudson River, destroy a health resort which is a boon to humanity, and alter our climatic conditions, no punishment can be too severe for those who thus menace the public welfare.[25]

Any person who would so destroy the forest, Marshall thought, was "as great an enemy of the public as one guilty of treason."[26]

An even greater threat to the Adirondacks in those years was fire. In dry seasons, sparks from railroads caused extensive fire damage in the Adirondacks. When that happened, Marshall's temper—and his acerbic pen—flared up in direct proportion to the intensity of the conflagrations. "What has the State done?" he demanded of the Forest, Fish and Game Commissioner. "It has lain by supinely and permitted the railroads which run through the forests to employ locomotives which are so many instruments of arson."

As for the railroad companies, they had "presented to view the continuous panoramas of forest graveyards, strewn with the blackened corpses of once noble trees." The net result, in Marshall's eye, was "the spectacle of death, death, on every hand, where but a few years ago the weary traveller beheld the beckoning finger of life."[27]

Marshall's interest in the Adirondack forest was permanently secured in 1900. That year he joined with some friends in purchasing a small tract of land on Lower Saranac Lake, in the heart of the Adirondacks. The place was to become immensely important to the Marshall family. It was especially so to their son Robert, who was born just a few months later, on January 2, 1901.

3

A Young Romantic (1901–1920)

My ideology was definitely formed on a Lewis and Clark pattern.

Bob Marshall, *Alaska Wilderness*

Bob Marshall spent the first and second grades, as he later said, "under the private teaching of an antiquated damsel named Rosenberg." After that, he attended the Ethical Culture School, across Central Park from his house. The school was a product of the Ethical Culture Movement initiated by the theologian-philosopher Felix Adler. Ethics were discussed for at least an hour a week in every grade, and students were encouraged to think for themselves.[1]

Throughout his career at the Ethical Culture School, Marshall was extremely shy. His classmates saw little to indicate that one day he would be a charismatic leader of an important environmental movement. One classmate, Ethel Wortis, remembered him as bashful and awkward, with a pale complexion and undefined physique. "Bob was so shy and not sociable even with his schoolmates," she recalled several decades later. "He did not dance as far as I knew and we never knew of his having a girl friend. He wasn't at all hostile, but quietly friendly. No one knew him really well, except that he played basketball and baseball on class teams and was known as an outdoorsman given to long hikes."[2]

15

The Ethical Culture School basketball team, 1918–1919: Bob Marshall is in the front row, far right. (Photograph courtesy of The Bancroft Library, University of California, Berkeley)

But every once in a while he would do something zany. Once, in a science class, the teacher was about to dissect a toad. Hoping to inject a little art into this inelegant operation, the instructor recited the following appropriate lines from Shakespeare's *As You Like It:*

> *Sweet are the uses of adversity,*
> *Which like the toad, ugly and venomous,*
> *Wears yet a precious jewel in his head; . . .*

The teacher then asked if anyone else knew of any verses about toads. Young Marshall said yes, he could think of one. He then recited several lines which he said were written by Robert Browning; in fact, he had conjured them up on the spot.[3]

Another time, for an ethics class, he purposely wrote an essay of incomplete sentences which made no sense whatsoever. This was the first of several "experiments" he conducted to see if teachers and editors actually read the work submitted to them. Marshall conducted another such experiment when the *Adirondack Enterprise*, a newspaper published near his family's summer camp, ran a series of local gourmets' favorite recipes. Bob submitted a recipe for "broiled eggs," which called for the eggs to be first hardboiled, then sliced and broiled. He signed the submission, "Mrs. Rob M." A few days later the recipe was published.[4]

Such pranks foreshadowed the highly developed sense of humor with which the adult Bob Marshall entertained scores of people. But for the most part, his career at the Ethical Culture School was unexceptional. His academic work was satisfactory but not as good as might be expected of a bright boy from a family in which books and ideas were of utmost importance. "Bob did a great deal of reading outside of school," his younger brother George recalled, "and it was just assumed that we would go to school and get through it, and then on to college." But both Bob and George tended to be average students because they were "interested in many other things."[5]

When school was out, Bob and George made their own entertainment. "He and I had a whole series of imaginative games," George recalled, "some involving sports, some involving a kind of Lewis and Clark expedition. I think we must have counted up about twelve or more such games that we had at various times. . . . Bob may not have been too strong as a child, but he was always active in basketball, track, and cross country. And there was baseball, rowing, walking, climbing, and tennis in the summer."[6]

Bob and George were avid sports fans. They hung pictures of their favorite players on the walls and ceilings of their bedrooms and followed the fortunes of their favorite teams. (Bob liked the Pittsburgh Pirates.) Bob knew the names and statistics of the players and teams; he compiled ratings of them and got family members to do the same. His father kept up with him on baseball news for many years and, upon returning from his office in the evening, he would tell Bob and George who won the important games of the day.[7]

At home, the Marshall children were supervised by a series of German governesses, or Frauleins, who were supposed to teach them German; it was the language of their grandparents and one of several that Louis Marshall spoke. But the boys sometimes had other ideas. "I don't think they ever taught us much German," George recalled with amusement, "but I do remember Bob teaching them baseball. . . . They were very nice; they'd play ball with us."[8]

Bob started very early to entertain his father. He wrote humorous poetry, sometimes in German, for Louis. "He was very original," says George, "had a great sense of humor even though he was very shy."[9]

Some of his favorite early subjects were the North American explorers; he composed verses about them even before he could write. He would compose them in his mind at night after going to bed, then recite them to his mother in the morning. Nearly eighty years later, his brother James still remembered one such verse, celebrating the Spanish explorer, De Soto:

> *Desoto was a man quite brave,*
> *He wasn't feared of a little wave.*
> *His death was in a land quite new,*
> *And some of his men died too.*[10]

Another composition, written at the age of eight, celebrated Samuel De Champlain's discovery of the Adirondacks. The opening lines suggest that Bob was already aware of changes to the landscape since the days of his heroes:

> *Where once the Indians used to dwell,*
> *From the steamboat comes a smoky smell.*[11]

Those lines suggest also that he was a young romantic, and that is a major key to his development. The cultural historian Perry Miller notes that in the nineteenth century a doctrine called romanticism "became conventional among landscape painters in Europe, England and America: that of a fundamental opposition of Nature to civilization, with the assumption that all virtue, repose, dignity are on the side of 'Nature' . . . against the ugliness, squalor and confusion of civilization." This exaltation of nature spilled over into other aspects of human expression in the mid-to-late 1800s. For over a century it greatly influenced how people viewed themselves and their place in the world. As an artistic style, romanticism was past its prime by Marshall's boyhood, but its influence reached far into the twentieth century. It was strongly reflected in the conservation movement and in much of the art and literature of the Adirondacks to which Marshall was thoroughly exposed. [12]

It appealed so strongly to Marshall that he built his life around it. From early childhood to his final days, he would consistently exalt nature and disparage civilization. In his best book, *Arctic Village*, he would assert that Eskimos and pioneers living in the Alaskan wilderness were happier than most people living in modern cities. In his most important article, "The Problem of the Wilderness," he would urge wilderness lovers to repulse "the strangling clutch of a mechanistic civilization." His descriptions of natural phenomena would be effusive and laudatory, reflecting not only the viewpoint of the nineteenth century romantics but sometimes their style as well. His descriptions of cities, by contrast, would be full of references to smokestacks, crowding, and chewing gum stuck to the sidewalks.

His childhood interest in exploration was another manifestation of his romanticism. At eleven he caught pneumonia. To keep him "from hopping around," somebody read him a book entitled *Pioneer Boys of the Great Northwest,* an adventure story about two young men and their fathers who happen to join the Lewis and Clark expedition. The book is in little danger of being listed among the classics of American literature. But to a pneumonia-stricken eleven-year-old it was a masterpiece, "a splendid narrative [of] the most thrilling of all American explorations." He lost himself completely in the story and reread it from one to three times a year until he finished high school.[13]

From then on, by his own account, Bob spent many hours "in the heart of New York City, dreaming of Lewis and Clark and their glorious exploration into an unbroken wilderness which embraced three-quarters of a continent." But the more he learned about exploration, the more he realized there was little left to explore. He wished he'd been born a hundred years earlier.[14]

But Bob managed to carve out a life of adventure even though the golden age of American exploration was past. He did this by starting at a young age to explore the Adirondack wilderness from his family's camp in the heart of that region.

Their camp complex, which the Marshalls shared with five other families, was on a thickly forested hillside overlooking Lower Saranac Lake, in the heart of the Adirondack region. Everyone called it Knollwood. Since the Marshall family never owned a car, they would travel by rail from New York City to Saranac Lake Village. From there it was a mile and a half ride by rowboat across the lake, or a four-mile surrey ride around the lake, to Knollwood.

The Marshall's cabin sat thirty yards back from shore, well hidden among the tall, virgin hemlocks, birches, and spruces that crowded the water. The walls and ceilings of the cabin were of white pine, the floors of finished fir, the trim and railings of spruce or birch logs to which the bark still clung. The outside was shingled with cedar shakes.

Inside, the bookshelves bulged with works ranging from Plato and Shakespeare to Adirondack lore and contemporary novels. The walls were decorated with an assortment of moose antlers, prize fish mounted on plaques, and the heavily antlered head of an elk sticking out above the living-room fireplace. If the elk could have seen with its glass eyes, it would have looked across the room to a porch facing the lake; but it never would have seen the water, for Louis Marshall would not allow any of the trees blocking the view to be cut.[15]

Bob Marshall was six months old the first time he went to Knollwood. He spent the entire length of each of his boyhood summers there and returned for at least part of every summer until he was twenty-five years old. It was there that his romantic inclinations were reinforced, for his life at Knollwood (representing nature and wilderness) was far more joyful than life in New York City (representing civilization).

For several years, however, the rather civilized game of baseball was Bob's favorite pastime, even at Knollwood. He was a permanent fixture on the narrow ball diamond wedged between the cabins and the tennis court where endless games of "Knollwood League" baseball were played. He kept detailed records of the games. "We won the game 14 to 10," he wrote to his father in August of 1916. "If necessary we could have won by more, as James, who was twirling great ball, only pitched five innings in order that Mr. Arnstein might have a chance. Mr. Neely did some great hitting, and also made a great catch. James caught a fly in the tennis court." More complete descriptions of the games and other news were published in Bob's newspaper, *The Morning Moon.*[16]

"Pop," as Louis was called by his children, occasionally grabbed a glove and joined in. This added a whole new dimension to the contests, as James later recalled:

> He would take a stand among the trees in the outfield, vest flopping, Congress gaiters, ready-made black bow-tie attached to his collarbutton and all, and when a ball came in his direction and with his nearsighted eyes he located it, he would throw it. At seventy he no longer took the field. But nevertheless he would get up to bat and if by chance he "connected" with the ball one of us ran for him. But if he didn't hit it was fun anyway. There was much to laugh at and the "post-mortems" at the supper table were as important to him as they were to his sons and daughter.[17]

When Bob was in graduate school, he wrote a ten-page history of Knollwood baseball, which he titled "The Knollwood League, 1916–1923." He calculated that "a total of over 5,000 delightful afternoons were spent at the ballfield by players and spectators."

At Knollwood, 1919; left to right, George Marshall, Ruth (Putey) Marshall, James Marshall, Irwin Edman (a friend of James M.), Bob Marshall, and Lenore (Mrs. James) Marshall (Photograph courtesy of the Adirondack Museum, Blue Mountain Lake, New York)

And the games, he wrote, "stimulated health, strength, deftness, a democratic spirit and the ideals of sportsmanship."[18]

It was typical of Bob to write such an opus, for his enthusiasm, when running high, could not be contained by mere participation. When he was involved in something, he had to write about it, analyze it, and keep statistics on it. Indeed, his lifelong penchant for compiling statistics was so strong as to seem compulsive.

One of the biggest days at Knollwood was the Fourth of July. The family would begin with a reading from the Bible. Then, as

James recalled, "Pop" would lead his wife and four children on a parade, "each carrying a flag and none carrying the same notes as we sang loudly all the patriotic songs we knew."[19]

But even ordinary days were great fun. After breakfast, there would be an hour or two for Bible study, followed by tennis or swimming. Afternoons—if there wasn't a ball game going—were devoted to long walks or to rows on Lower Saranac Lake, activities in which Bob took exceptional delight. Then, in the evenings, Pop would sit out on the porch and read aloud from the works of James Fenimore Cooper (one of the great romantics), Charles Dickens, or William Thackeray. Clad in his usual shirtsleeves and suspenders, swatting insects constantly, he would deliver his dramatic renditions. The youngsters cheered wildly when a hero triumphed or a villain got his due. Sometimes it was so exciting that the younger children could not sleep afterward.[20]

It was fun also to walk in the woods near the cabin. "I was privileged," Bob later mused, "to explore the mighty tract bounded by the Forest Home Road, the Knollwood Road, Lower Saranac Lake, and Fish Creek—an immense expanse, about three-quarters of a mile by three-eights of a mile, in which one could, with diligence, occasionally get beyond the sounds of civilization. This almost trailless area was a real wilderness to me, as exciting in a different way as the unexplored continent which I had missed by my tardy birth."[21]

Often he was up before breakfast, tramping around while the woods were still fresh and soaked with dew. He got to know every ridge and game trail, every brook and boulder, in the immediate vicinity of the camp. In true explorer fashion, he gave names to them all: Found Knife Pass, Squashed Berry Valley, Hidden Heaven Rock.[22]

He also began going out at night, and in the process overcame a childhood phobia that might have hampered his career. "He was afraid of the dark," James Marshall remembered, "and made himself, when young, walk in the woods at Knollwood at night without a light. He told me once that he felt that this helped him to be alone in the forest."[23]

Thus his penchant for hiking was established early. And the study of plants and trees was a natural outgrowth of both his ardor for walking and his father's interest in botany. Every year Pop had the children inventorying the flora around Knollwood, looking for new species, learning how to identify them, and recording the date that each flower made its first appearance. When Pop was away, as he often was, Bob sent him detailed reports about the plants and trees he'd seen on his excursions.[24]

Louis also taught his children that conservation work was very important. In 1915, when Bob was fourteen, Louis was again a delegate to yet another state constitutional convention. At this convention, he made an impassioned speech against an amendment that would have allowed timber harvesting in the Adirondack and Catskill Forest Preserves. "It is as certain as anything on earth can be," he said, "that if we in any way relax the limitations which we are now seeking to place on the Adirondacks, our waterways are doomed and our agricultural lands are doomed."[25]

The amendment was defeated, and Louis Marshall learned a lesson which he passed along to his children. "I remember Father telling me a number of times," Bob later wrote, "about the great pressure which was brought by commercial interests to keep Article VII, Section 7 [the "Forever Wild" clause] from being put in the 1894 constitution and to get it out of the 1915 constitution. I know that all over the country whenever an area with commercial values is set aside primarily for primitive recreational enjoyment that there are commercial interests which fight such reservation tooth and nail."[26]

Bob Marshall's childhood, then, was both happy and instructive. There was, however, one tragedy: When he was fifteen, his mother died of cancer. Her death, in George's words, "pulled the rug out from under" both him and Bob. Traumatic as it was, it had a liberating effect on Bob, for she had been an extremely protective mother.[27]

Surprisingly little has been written or recorded about Florence

Lowenstein Marshall. She was, in a sense, invisible behind the enormous personality of her husband. Even her sons have much less to say about her than about Louis Marshall. We do know, as mentioned, that she was strongly interested in some Jewish welfare organizations and in the education of young Jewish women. We know from a statement by James Marshall that she—not Louis—usually disciplined the children when they needed it. We know from George Marshall that she was extremely "reserved." And we know that Bob considered her overprotective.[28]

When Florence Marshall died, Bob's older sister Ruth—nicknamed Putey—became a surrogate mother. Bob thought Putey offered many advantages over his real one, as he explained to a friend twenty years later, following Putey's death, also of cancer:

> [Putey] grew up under the terrible inhibitions which came from being the daughter of a prominent citizen of the Victorian age. . . .
>
> After Mother died when Putey was 18 and I was 15, [Putey] became a sort of second mother, only she was much better than the original one because she was more tactful and understanding and was in the same class of human beings rather than in the parent class. But she helped me through innumerable difficulties which a child gets into between 15 and 21—everything from bandaging my foot when I ran a pike pole through it (Mother would have sent for a doctor instead of doing the whole job herself) to helping me get over my abnormal fear of girls.[29]

Though the subject is Putey, the statement tells a great deal about how Bob viewed his mother. He obviously resented her "Victorian" inhibitions and general approach to child rearing. Through her reserve and protectiveness she had reinforced his shyness and made it more difficult to overcome. Even worse, she had tried to discourage him from pursuing the adventure that he so very much craved.

By the time of his mother's death, another important figure had entered Bob's life, a man who assumed something of a parental role also, but who most definitely was not overprotective. Herb Clark, whom Paul Schaefer had met with Bob atop Mount Marcy, was a veteran Adirondack guide with many talents. He was of average height, wiry as the fishing rods he handled so adroitly, and endowed with angular features that further accentuated his leanness. As a child he had known poverty and hunger, but those never stunted the development of his keen wit and masterful ability to spin yarns.

In his younger days Clark had been well known around Miller's old hotel on Lower Saranac and in various other social establishments between Vermont and Saranac Village. After working a variety of jobs in several places, he eventually made his home around the Saranacs, where he spent five summers rowing a freight boat twenty-four miles each morning and guiding in the afternoon. He became a master rower of Adirondack guideboats; in 1890, he finished second in an all-Adirondack rowing race held on Lower Saranac Lake.[30]

In the late nineteenth century it was customary in the Adirondacks for the more affluent camp owners to hire family guides, who would take family members and guests hunting or fishing, educate the children in various outdoor pursuits, and sometimes do odd jobs around the camp. The Marshalls' first guide, Ed Cagle, had resigned two years before Herb's rowing victory in order to open a livery stable. Herb was known as a hard worker, so the Marshalls hired him. He immediately hit it off with the children, especially Bob, who later wrote of him:

> I cannot speak authoritatively of what Herb meant to the others, although I have strong suspicions. I do know positively that to me Herb has been not only the greatest teacher that I have ever had, but also the most kindly and considerate friend a person could even dream about, a constantly refreshing and stimulating companion with whom to discuss both passing events and the more permanent philosophical relationships, and to top it all, the happy possessor of the keenest sense of humor I have known.[31]

Herb took the youngsters for walks, regaled them with stories, sang them old religious camp songs and French-Canadian ballads, and taught them to use a map and compass. Of course they could not always be certain whether what he told them was true, but it was great fun trying to sift out the facts from his amusing fiction. Bob recalled several of Herb's whoppers in a biographical sketch of his favorite guide written for the Adirondack Mountain Club in 1933:

> For my brothers and myself, Herb would make up the most amazing fables. A rock on Lower Saranac with a peculiar dent was where Captain Kidd had bumped his head. The Ausable River below the present Olympic ski jump was where the Monitor and Merrimac had fought their famous battle, and an old lady who came limping along as he told us this tale was used as a circumstantial evidence, for her shinbone had been taken off by a stray shell at the time of this great conflict. There were those great heroes of our youth: Sliny Slott, a sort of reverse Paul Bunyan, who did everything inconceivably poorer than you could imagine it could be done; Jacob Whistletricker, a man with many marvelous drugs; Joe McGinnis, who got the fantod, a disease in which one shrinks to the size of a baseball; Susie Soothingsyrup, a gay young lass of many virtues; and of course the Grandfather pickerel, which we would someday catch, with gold teeth and spectacles.[32]

Like most Adirondack guides, Herb was more hunter and angler than mountaineer, but on August 15, 1915, he took Bob and George to climb their first mountain. They chose Mount Ampersand, a 3,352-foot peak that dominated the view across Lower Saranac Lake from their camp. Though not especially high, it was quite steep and offered a fine view of the Saranac region and the higher ranges to the east. Bob was then fifteen years old, George was twelve, and Herb was forty-six.

As they climbed, the excited boys kept craning their necks for a glimpse of Round Lake through the trees. At the steepest part of the climb there were some ladders that had been constructed by "the Hermit of Ampersand"—a fire observer whose official name was Walter Channing Rice. The pitch there was so steep that it was dangerous to keep leaning out over the edge in search of vistas. So Herb told his two young alpinists that those were the

Bob Marshall, Herb Clark, and George Marshall (Photograph from Peaks and People of the Adirondacks, *by Russell M. L. Carson. Doubleday, 1927)*

ladders upon which Lot's wife was turned into a pillar of salt for disobeying the warning never to look back. He thought it quite possible that the same fate might be theirs if they continued to look back for views from the ladders. They got the message and reserved their gaping until they reached the top.

It was worth waiting for. They could see Round Lake, all right, but also a host of others, including Big Ampersand Pond, where Ralph Waldo Emerson, Louis Agassiz, and other intellectuals had conducted their famous "philosophers' camp" in the 1860s. To the north were the Saranacs and dozens of other blue ponds; and, most intriguing of all, to the east, an ocean of blue green rippling ridges rose high above Ampersand, looking nearly as untrammeled as the entire region must have appeared to Champlain when he explored it in 1609.[33]

Even then Bob's appreciation for natural beauty was keen, and he was already starting to make written descriptions of his hikes. Of one taken that summer with a group of people, he observed:

> On the walk, the talkers admired the obvious things, but we admired the real beauty of the woods, not just a steep precipice, a big rock, or a glimpse of the lake. We admired the fine trees, beautiful flowers, lights and shades among the trees, and the hundreds of other things which make the woods so superior to the city.[34]

Bob's remarks show youthful arrogance. Yet any smug feelings about his superior aesthetic tastes would not last for long. They would be replaced by an almost desperate hope that enough people would come to share his appreciation for wild places to help save a few of them.

Bob's thirst for adventure grew even stronger the day he discovered the writings of Verplanck Colvin, who had devoted thirty-five years in the latter 1800s to surveying, and mapping the Adirondack region. (His expeditions were famous for the hardships they demanded of his crews. He once confided rather ruefully to his journal that his men "could not be persuaded to proceed further, exhibiting their torn clothes and soleless gaping boots as evidence of their inability.") In his later years Colvin became involved in the fight to preserve the Adirondack wilderness; he had, in fact, testified before Louis Marshall and the other delegates to the New York State Constitutional Convention of 1894, urging them to adopt the "Forever Wild" clause.[35]

Four dusty volumes of Colvin's multi-volume *Report of the Topo-*

graphical Survey of the Adirondack Wilderness were buried at the bottom of the bookshelf in the Marshalls' cabin at Knollwood. Despite the ominous title, the report was written in a flowery nineteenth-century style that would appeal to a young romantic. One day during his early teen years, Bob picked it up and was immediately enthralled. Here were vivid accounts of wilderness explorations nearly as hair-raising as those of Lewis and Clark. According to Colvin, the remote sections of the Adirondacks were

> filled with the most rugged mountains, where unnamed waterfalls pour in snowy tresses from the dark overhanging cliffs. . . . and here the panther has his den among the rocks, and rears his savage kittens undisturbed save by the growl of bear or screech of lynx, or the hoarse croak of raven taking its share of the carcass of slain deer.[36]

The howling wilderness described by Colvin was right outside his back door. Moreover, Colvin was not some hazy figure from a history book, but a contemporary of his own father. Bob shared his discovery with George. "We decided to penetrate those mountains," George later wrote, "which previously had been accepted as a scenic backdrop along the skyline across the lake, and see what lay beyond."[37]

With Herb as their guide, Bob and George began to expand their operations. By the summer of 1917 they had climbed four mountains and taken several overnight camping trips. From the beginning, Bob kept detailed records of these excursions. A letter he wrote that summer to his father reveals both his proclivity for recording details and the extreme delight that he found in these trips:

> . . . We had a good time on our camping trip. The weather except from 12:30 to 9:30 A.M. Thursday was in the pink of condition. We did the same as in the other 8 camping trips we have taken, each of which brought a letter of description, and therefore I will not write you the same stuff for the ninth time. However two out of the ordinary things occured [sic]. Firstly, when going to the toilet I by ac-

cident sat on a golden rod which contained a bee and was stung. Herb said it served me right disturbing him, and pointed out that if anyone did that on him when he was working he would do just the same. Secondly, we climbed Stoney Creek Mountain. It is easy climbing, although about as high as Ampersand because Herb took us up a good way, where the slope is gradual and there are only big trees set well apart. The view from the top is well worth the climb.* While you can not see so much owing to the thick covering of timber on the top, the views you get are very pretty.

Rating the four mountains in the Adirondacks by me for *niceness of view and all around pleasure in view and climb* I would rate as follows:

N.O.V.	A.A.P.I.V.A.C.
Ampersand	Stoney Creek
Baker	Ampersand
Stoney Creek	Bootbay
Bootbay	Baker

... Love from,
Bob

*Quoted from numerous authors[38]

There was always a little fishing, at least by Herb, on these trips, and some of the Knollwood members hunted deer and bear in the autumn. But Bob chose to do his hunting with a camera, developing an early interest in photography that he pursued avidly throughout his life. Under Herb's tutelage he stalked white-tailed deer for snapshots, though usually in vain. "I have not gotten a picture of a deer yet," he reported in August of 1917, "but on Monday morning George and I saw one, and tried for almost half an hour to get in a good position."[39]

By the end of his sixteenth summer, nature study, camping, and mountaineering were edging out baseball as Bob Marshall's consuming interests. Though it may have been the "super-year" for the Knollwood League, it was also the summer during which he told his father, following an exciting camping trip, "I am so disgusted with Knollwood League baseball that I will let James tell you about the games." He continued to play in the Knollwood

31

games for several more years, and retained a spectator's interest in baseball all his life, often spicing up letters to his father with such observations as, "I see that my Pirates are still a game ahead of your Giants." But once his appetite for backcountry exploration was whetted, there was little room in his free time for anything else.[40]

The following summer, 1918, Bob, George, Herb, and a friend named Carl Poser climbed Whiteface Mountain, their first peak over 4,000 feet. The sixth highest and the northernmost of the major Adirondack peaks, Whiteface was once described as "the most graceful of all Adirondack peaks." It is less graceful today than it was in 1918, though some would say it has been improved. Among its "improvements" are an auto road to the top, a television tower, a stone hut housing meteorological instruments, a restaurant just below the peak, and numerous ski lifts and trails. But when Bob and his three companions climbed it in 1918, it was just graceful Whiteface, 4,872 feet high. From its top they could see the St. Lawrence River and Lake Champlain; and to the south many of the other high Adirondack peaks were visible. Bob later wrote, characteristically, that the views from Whiteface "do not excel the average views from many other mountains. They contain none of that wildness that adds so much to some peaks."[41]

He found the wildness he was looking for later that summer when he, George, and Herb made their first of many excursions into what is known as the "High Peaks" region of the Adirondacks. On that trip they climbed Mounts Marcy and Algonquin, the two highest Adirondack summits, and Iroquis, the seventh highest.[42]

That was it for the summer of 1918. But during that season a sort of spell came over them, a binding enchantment known by those who venture into high, remote, and wild places. The two teenagers and the man of nearly fifty experienced a camaraderie and spirit of adventure that they had never known before, and they found it addicting. "For the next six years," said Bob, "Herb, George and I found Adirondack mountain climbing our greatest joy in life."[43]

With Herb as chief navigator and Bob as trip scribe, they penetrated in subsequent summers the most secluded reaches of the Adirondacks. Most of the high peaks were some distance from Knollwood, so the travels along the waterways, railways, and country roads from Saranac to the base of the peaks became adventures in themselves. First there was a mile-and-a-half row across Lower Saranac Lake, followed by a walk of about the same distance into Saranac Lake Depot. There they would board the train for Lake Placid. The ensuing ride, said George, "was our compromise with mechanical transportation, but even this had its active phase when the cars dashed wildly around sharp curves, throwing packages and pack baskets from the racks, amid much whistling at thirty miles an hour!"[44]

When the train pulled into Lake Placid Station, in the little town of Newman, they would next stop at Mullen's Corner Grocery to chat with Herb's brother John, who also did some guiding. A few last-minute supplies and they were ready to shoulder their packs and head down the long country road toward South Meadows, their jumping off place.[45]

The last permanent settlement along the way was the old Wood farm, which became a frequent stopping place. Mrs. W. K. Wood and her daughter, Hattie, always had a place to sleep, plenty of food, or a little gossip, depending on the expeditioners' schedule. Their dining room table, George remembered, "was always filled to overflowing with breads and cakes and other delicious foods that were crowded so closely together that one could scarcely see the table cloth."[46]

Continuing along the road toward South Meadows, the three would next pass "Calamity Mountain" (actually Van Hoevenberg), so named by Herb because it was the very spot where Joe McGinnis caught the dreaded fantod and shrunk to the size of a baseball. Next came "Alcohol Brook," where—in truth—lumberjacks would "cut" what was left of their pint bottles after a weekend's debauching away from camp.[47]

South Meadows was the end of the line. There the road simply ended and the real wilderness began. "From here," wrote George, "we made our first climb of Tahawus [the Indian name for Mount

Marcy, meaning 'the Cloud Splitter']; circled the MacIntyre Range in a day; explored the wild Wallface-Scott Pond Plateau; packed to Panther Gorge to climb the Gothics Range; walked to the Saranacs by way of Indian Pass, Preston Ponds, Big Ampersand, and Kettle Mt. Pass; and took numerous other trips into the backwoods."[48]

Once that pleasant transition had been made, they were ready to climb mountains. They packed as many ascents as possible into whatever time they had. Typical was their four-day "Gothics Trip" of August, 1920. On the first day of the trip they carried their packs from Lake Placid to Lake Colden, where they camped overnight. The second day they climbed Mount Skylight, a 4,925-foot peak about a mile from Marcy. That night they camped in the spooky ravine called Panther Gorge.

The third day was to be their principal day of climbing. They planned to traverse a long, high ridge known as "the Range," en route climbing several 4,000-footers, including Mount Gothics, whose giant slides and bare rock suggest Gothic architecture. On that morning they awoke to find themselves in a thick fog, but by the time they had eaten breakfast they were pleased to see the fog lifting and swatches of blue breaking through the clouds.[49]

Bob, who kept minute details and statistics, noted that it was 8:23 A.M. when they left camp. They climbed steeply up Haystack Mountain for most of the morning, with Bob noting the scenery, the number of minutes from one landmark to another, and the plant life they saw. When they approached the summit of Haystack, he carefully recorded that the trees had shrunk to insignificant size and the jagged rocks were beautifully decorated with Greenland sandwort and three-toothed cinquefoil. When they reached the peak of Haystack, he was impressed by the wildness of the surroundings. "As we looked around us," he wrote, "we realized that this was one of the few places east of the Rockies where a person could look over miles of territory without seeing civilization."[50]

Next they descended rapidly some 1,900 feet into a saddle where Bob noticed "as fine a cluster of Ladies Tresses as I have ever seen." Herb, then fifty years old, was setting a rapid pace.

They crossed the saddle and climbed another 1,900 feet to the summit of Basin Mountain. There Bob announced that they had made their descent and ascent of 3,800 feet all together in exactly one hour and three minutes.

From Basin, the most impressive sights were the deep valleys emanating from three sides of the mountain. Never prone to understatement, Bob looked into Panther Gorge and declared it the "fiercest of all the wild places among the great mountains, besides which the celebrated canyons of Colorado look tame."[51]

They stayed there fifteen minutes, then descended to climb nearby Saddleback Mountain. By the time they reached Saddleback, clouds were scudding in and blocking the scenery. Bob's reaction, however, was typically upbeat. "The wonderfully wooded Basin," he observed, "probably the finest big stretch of woodland I have ever seen, was visible and, together with the forest slopes of Saddleback and the neighboring mountains, afforded fine enough scenery to make anyone happy, even though all distant objects were obscured."[52]

When they reached the summit of Gothics at 1:02, Bob was ready with vital statistics. They had walked ten miles and 9,200 up-and-down feet from Panther Gorge. The hike had taken four and one-half hours. After gazing at the scenery and going through the customary ritual of identifying all peaks, rivers, and gorges that could be seen from Gothics, they started the long trip back to camp. As they left, Bob noted that the time was 1:42.[53]

About halfway back, Herb spotted a dead tree perhaps twenty feet long which he decided would make good firewood for the evening. He told Bob to carry it back to camp. Bob dutifully dragged the cumbersome thing behind him, even though it caught on trees at every bend in the trail. "I counted 22 other trees on the way back to camp," he wrote, "which would have done just as well for firewood and meant a lot less work for me, but we had good fun joking about me lugging a tree halfway down the mountain."[54]

They returned to camp at 6:04, having been gone nine hours and forty minutes. As they stuffed themselves with "that almost perfect dish of dehydrated beans and potatoes boiled together," they tallied up the final numbers. They had climbed a total of 9,200 feet and descended the same amount. Bob calculated that this was equal to three and a half up-and-down miles, or "a fifth again as high as the climb up Pike's Peak from its base." Total horizontal miles numbered about twenty.

The fire died, darkness fell, the air grew cold. They watched as a million stars appeared through the "piny canopy" overhead. "As we laid our heads down on this wildest bed," Bob reported happily, "it was with the knowledge of having spent the hardest, the wildest, and one of the most enjoyable days of our lives."[55]

4

Pond Seeker
(1920–1924)

◆ ───────────────────────────────── ◆

People cannot live generation after generation in the city without serious retrogression, physical, moral and mental. . . .

Bob Marshall

When that happy summer of 1920 ended, Bob Marshall faced a challenge that, because of his shyness, was more intimidating than any mountain: He was about to leave home to attend the New York State College of Forestry at Syracuse University.* He had long since decided that he wanted to be a forester. As he wrote in a high school essay,

I love the woods and solitude. I like the various forms of scientific work a forester must do. I would hate to spend the greater part of my lifetime in a stuffy office or crowded assembly, or even in a populous city. If I can combine my greatest pleasure with a useful work, then surely I will have great advantage over most business and professional men. [1]

───────────

*Now called the State University of New York College of Environmental Science and Forestry

After graduating from the Ethical Culture School in 1919, Bob spent a year taking liberal-arts courses at Columbia University. Then he was ready for the more technical program in forestry.[2]

His choice of forestry schools—like so many other of his early decisions—was greatly influenced by his father, who was instrumental in the creation and development of the New York State College of Forestry. Louis Marshall had become a trustee of Syracuse University, a private school, in 1910, and had immediately plunged into an already-begun effort to set up a state college of forestry on the Syracuse campus. In July of 1911, after much persuading and politicking, the school was established. The elder Marshall was then elected to be its first President of the Board, and under his aggressive leadership the school grew rapidly. He had bills introduced in the legislature for new buildings and equipment; he used his influence to get budgets approved; and, when necessary, he made personal visits to the governor. Today, a building on the campus is named Marshall Hall in appreciation of his efforts.[3]

The Forestry College in 1920 occupied twelve scruffy acres at the southern edge of the Syracuse campus, near a prominent hill known as Mount Olympus. Its nucleus was Bray Hall, a typically somber, rectangular brick academic building just recently constructed. From the entrance to Bray Hall you looked out over Onondaga Valley, the city of Syracuse, and the bucolic rolling hills to the west. Bob enrolled in the prescribed courses for the freshman year, which included chemistry, French, botany, engineering, forestry I, geology, zoology, and gymnasium.[4]

For a while, however, he was unhappy. Letters to his family, though often humorous, show him discontent with life at Syracuse and the confining academic program. His father, responding with letters of encouragement and support, was a major influence in getting him through this period of adjustment.[5]

If it took Bob a while to warm up to the Forestry College, it also took a while for his classmates to warm up to him. Still bashful, he did not make friends quickly. The first impression of many classmates was of an individual strikingly different from the others at the college. "I had come from a very conservative family on an Atlantic coast island," recalled one classmate many years later. "My family was especially straitlaced about such things as neatly-pressed clothes and short-cropped hair. But here was this guy coming to class in shaggy hair, a rumpled flannel shirt, khaki pants, wool socks, and sneakers. He didn't socialize with anybody at first, didn't care about the 'bull sessions' we'd have in our rooms. He was just very different."[6]

Despite his initial unhappiness and slowness to make friends, Bob got off to a good start academically. One of the first impressions of another classmate, Neil Hosley, was of Bob preparing for a test. "Before the class he would pace back and forth in the rotunda, notes in hand, systematically memorizing what was in them," Hosley recalled. "He always came up with one of the best marks in the class." For that reason, he made better first impressions on his professors than on his peers. Dr. Carl Forsaith, a demanding teacher known for his tough, penetrating questions, long remembered the first quiz that Bob took from him. "He gave the date," Forsaith observed with amusement, "and added a supplement about the date telling me that some event in our history had happened that day. This was followed by about half a page of answers. . . . It was a perfect paper, short because there was no frilling. It was all neat."[7]

As the months went by, the other students came to appreciate Bob's individuality as much as the instructors did. They were amazed at his encyclopedic knowledge of the Adirondacks and American history; and they noticed, as Neil Hosley put it, that Bob was "always doing something no one else would ever think of doing. He was constantly rating things—the Adirondack peaks, his best days with George, and dozens of others." (Among the most interesting of these ratings was the one Bob kept of Civil War generals. After reading everything he could lay his hands on about the great conflict, he ranked its top two hundred military leaders. He then contacted several of the generals, or their sons, who were still living, and asked them to evaluate his rating. His top five, in order, were Thomas, Grant, Sherman, Hancock, and Sheridan.)[8]

Bob Marshall (front row, far left) and fellow members of Alpha Xi Sigma, the New York State College of Forestry honor society, 1924 (Photograph courtesy of the State University of New York, College of Environmental Science and Forestry)

This penchant for rating things led to some amusing moments at the college's weekly convocations. It was common for an outside dignitary to lecture these august assemblies. Word got around that Bob Marshall was rating the quality of each oration and keeping a record of the exact amount of time each speaker took to deliver his message. The college dean, who customarily presided over the proceedings, could send a ripple of snickers through the audience simply by saying, "I see Bob Marshall looking at his watch, so I'll have to be brief."[9]

Another time, some students began to suspect that a certain teacher was grading their papers without giving them the close reading they deserved. Bob, who had dealt with this kind of problem before, told his friends he would find out whether their papers were being read. In a report involving a figure in millions of dollars, Bob computed the amount of macaroni the money would buy instead of expressing the figure in the conventional manner. He also included a detailed estimation of how many times the macaroni sticks, if placed end to end, would circumscribe the globe. The paper came back without comment, thus confirming the students' suspicions.[10]

Another time, Bob learned that a faculty member, Harold Belyea, had spent the previous summer studying yellow birch trees in the Adirondacks. One day Bob strode into Belyea's office carrying a photograph of a lake with a treeless mountain in the background. He told Belyea that the picture had been taken in the area where Belyea had been conducting his yellow birch studies. He wondered if Belyea could identify the lake. Belyea took a guess. Wrong. He took another guess. Wrong again. Belyea finally gave up and Bob told him the truth. It was a picture of a rain puddle on a mountaintop, taken from close-up at ground level.[11]

Bob ran on the Syracuse University freshman track team, which helped get him through his first year. But he looked forward eagerly to summer vacation and climbing once again with George and Herb. Sometime during his freshman year he and George decided they should climb *all* the 4,000-foot Adirondack peaks, of which, according to their maps, there were forty-two. Along with Herb they eagerly pursued this objective during the summer of 1921. On three major excursions that season, they climbed twenty-three peaks, eighteen of which were trailless and seven of which had never been climbed before to anyone's knowledge. On one of these outings, a thirteen-day expedition they called their "mountain trip," they climbed a total of 50,000 feet and walked 300 miles. By the end of the summer they had polished off the remainder of the forty-two High Peaks.[12]

When Bob returned to the forestry college in the fall of 1921, he didn't tell anybody that he had climbed all those peaks during the summer. Consequently, his classmates were astonished when a story appeared in the November 2 *Syracuse Herald* under the headline, "Syracuse Youth Masters Every Adirondack Peak—Robert Marshall Reaches Summit of 42 More Than 4,000 Feet High."

This news earned him some respect, as did his participation as a sophomore in both junior-varsity lacrosse and cross-country. But he was still shy, and few people knew him well. What finally pulled him out of his shell was a program known as Sophomore Summer Camp.[13]

On the first day of June 1922, Bob was among the sixty students, twelve faculty members, and several cooks who converged on a tiny piece of college-owned property in the Adirondacks to begin a three-month intensive study of practical forestry matters. The Sophomore Summer Camp was located on the southeast shore of Cranberry Lake, a region more gently rolling than other parts of the Adirondacks. Its elaborate network of rivers, bogs, and ponds has allowed it to remain largely undeveloped even today. At the time of Bob's summer camp, however, the Cranberry Lake country had recently been heavily logged and then burned, leaving it scarred and littered with slash.

The camp itself was a spartan affair, consisting primarily of an assembly hall, a few boat docks, a mess hall, a well to supply running water, and a crude but functional septic system. The students and faculty lived in square canvas tents, which were lined up in neat rows and given names like Scrime Alley and Fifth Avenue.[14]

The curriculum was a series of week-long courses customarily running Monday through Friday, with an examination at the end. Weekends were usually free. The surrounding woods was their classroom and laboratory. The courses were in wood technology, mycology (the study of fungi), utilization, ecology, pathology, entomology ("the hunt for bugs"), engineering, silviculture, and mensuration (timber cruising and log scaling).[15]

Bob was in his element. He worked hard at his courses and camp chores during the week, but when the weekends arrived he was off with his pack basket to explore new territory. His pet project for that summer was to inventory and rate for beauty all the lakes and ponds in the Cranberry Lake region. Anybody was welcome to come along, but if there were no takers, he went by himself. As usual, Bob kept a detailed record of these forays. The trips, and Bob's observations of them, are worth examining in some detail, for they provide a glimpse of a young man whose sense of humor, sensitivity to wildness, need for exercise, ability to observe detail, appreciation of history, and indignation at needless destruction are all developing rapidly. The unique blend of traits that characterize the mature Bob Marshall are starting to emerge and come together.

The first weekend in camp was rainy, so Bob contented himself on Saturday afternoon with a walk to nearby Curtis Pond. The next day, however, he convinced a friend, Bill Osborne, to accompany him on a long loop hike on which the pair ended up trudging through several miles of timber slash before returning to camp in the dark.[16]

Next weekend the Pond Seeker was off by himself, this time on an overnight trip to Bog River and Graves Peak, southeast of Cranberry Lake. When he climbed Graves Peak, "whose rocky summit had so attracted the early explorers," Bob had mixed reactions to the view. He wrote:

> What a wild view spread before me! Vast areas of low land stretch on all sides, partly covered by virgin forest, but mostly by second growth, and open spaces with only grass and ferns.
> ... There is not a sign of house or road in the entire prospect, except miles away, at Long Lake West. But what is that moving column of smoke over there to the East? A railroad train as sure as I live. It is no use trying to dream of the olden days, for that train has blotted them out.[17]

That night he wrapped himself in a couple of blankets and went to sleep. When it began to rain there was nothing to do but duck his head under the covers and hope the blankets did not soak through. But they did, and the subsequent damp chill had him up and moving again before five o'clock.

Walking as fast as he could through the chaos of rain-soaked stumps, brambles, and limbs left scattered to rot or burn, he surprised a large buck, which stared at him "as if wondering why anyone should want to enter his private slash." Finally, weighted down with the soggy blankets in his pack, and wet as a dish rag himself, he trudged through the last of the slash and reached his destination, the bare summit of Grass Pond Mountain. A sudden hailstorm came up, and he shivered with cold, yet he managed to stay there for an hour, "enjoying for the first time the finest mountain view in the Cranberry region."

Coming down, he enjoyed some of the benefits of the solitary hiker, who makes less commotion than a group. At Grass Pond he watched several deer feeding peacefully along the water's edge, a beaver swimming a few feet in front of him, and two loons making "the bare side of the mountain vibrate with their shrill cry." It was a wonderful spot and he resolved to "return before long."[18]

Two weekends later he did, but this time he brought along five classmates to help him cut a trail to Grass Pond Mountain. The trail cutters spent Friday night in some old cabins on the mountain that Bob had seen there earlier on his first trip. Then on Saturday they whacked out a mile-long trail to the summit. Bob took the lead, picking and marking the route. Neil Hosley followed him with the ax, while the rest came along behind and cleared out the brush. Bob hoped "that future classes will make use of [the trail], and obtain the best view in the region."[19]

They stayed at the cabins again that night. Sunday morning, their trail work completed, they looked forward to sleeping late and cooking a leisurely breakfast before heading back to camp— except for Bob, whose appetite for exploration was never satisfied. There was a spot nearby that he especially wanted to see, a dark, primeval place mentioned by all the early explorers. Bob was up early and, by his own account,

> . . . rowed across Grass Pond and took the trail to Mud Lake. I knew of this sluggish body of water from the accounts of almost all the early writers. They were unanimous in calling it the wildest and gloomiest place in the Adirondacks. So I let my imagination carry me back sixty years to the days when the tread of wolf, moose and panther were of daily occurence, while man was almost unknown in the region. The lake was not particularly beautiful, but with thoughts of the past in mind, the visit was very enjoyable.[20]

The next weekend included Independence Day, which meant two extra days off. Several different groups of students planned trips in the Adirondacks. Three of these were canoe trips, but a fourth—consisting of only six stalwarts—was a hiking trip to Mount Marcy. The promoter and guide of this last expedition was, needless to say, the Pond Seeker.

The six climbers spent the first day and a half en route to Adirondack Lodge, a traditional jumping-off place for hikes up the "Cloud-Splitter." They made it to Marcy's summit the second afternoon, but their guide wasn't quite through for the day. In the little light that remained, he hustled three of them over to Mount Skylight, a maneuver involving a descent of a thousand feet and a climb of another six hundred.

The following day was Monday, and the Pond Seeker awoke with renewed determination to show his friends the High Peaks region. Unfortunately, it was a miserable day, so they settled for a climb up 5,100-foot McIntyre, where they got only an inside look at a giant cloud for their efforts. They beat it back to Adirondack Lodge in a downpour, cooked a hasty lunch, and hurried on to Lake Placid to catch the afternoon train.

Bob had invited them to his family's cabin on Lower Saranac Lake. They trooped into Knollwood later that evening, wetter than muskrats, but were taken in and refurbished by the Marshalls. According to one account, Bob's classmates were astounded when they saw the Casino, boathouses, and hired help at Knollwood, for their Bob had never given them any reason to suppose that he belonged to a wealthy family. They "enjoyed the splendid hospitality of the Marshall family," as Al Cline later wrote, until Tuesday afternoon, when they returned to Cranberry Lake.[21]

Sometime during the first half of the summer, the students decided to construct a twenty-four by thirty-foot cabin, which they named Sanderson Lodge, after the Summer Camp Director, Wilford E. Sanderson. A small delegation who especially enjoyed carpentry did most of the work, but everybody contributed in some way. Most of the work had to be done on weekends, which presented a dilemma for Bob, who used the time to survey ponds. His solution was to postpone several of his hikes until Saturday afternoon, spending the morning helping with the lodge. This sacrifice

Herb Clark and Bob Marshall in camp on Seward Brook in the Adirondacks, 1921
(Photograph from The Living Wilderness; *reproduced courtesy of The Wilderness*
Society)

was viewed by the others as an indication of the entire class's commitment to the lodge. "Why even Marshall," it was observed in
the *Camp Log*, "the champion pond-hound and hill-galloper, who
saw 94 different ponds while in camp, gave up early starts on his
tramps in order to spend Saturday mornings at work!"[22]

The tramps, however, were his first priority and couldn't be delayed too long for anything. Thus on Saturday, July 15, he helped with the lodge after breakfast, but set out right after lunch "with the main objective to find the corner where St. Lawrence, Hamilton and Herkimer counties came together." On this trip he was searching harder than ever for a glimpse of the past. He camped that night in a meadow near a beaver dam, and by the dying fire observed that:

> ... it seemed hardly possible that I was in the crowded Empire State of today. Not a house or a soul was within miles. Probably none had passed or would pass along the trail for days. The gathering darkness blotted out the unpleasant signs of man. The forest outlined against the rising moon, the deer drinking in the rippling brook, the cool wind from the West were all as they had been when the first pioneer trapper spread his blankets in the untrammeled country, termed Couchsagre, the dismal wilderness. [23]

The past was still on his mind the next day when he reached Nick's Pond, which he later decided was the most beautiful in the Cranberry region. It had high, unmarred banks, and when he reached it the sun was just rising above the trees. A deer fed peacefully along the shore. The pond seemed "as wild as when Colvin first placed it on the map" and he "half imagined" that he was back in the days of that great explorer whose work he so well knew and admired.

After more than an hour, he finally tore himself away from Nick's Pond, continuing toward the intersection of the three counties that was his original goal. He reached the spot where the intersection should be, and after an hour's searching found "a mouldering old post" that marked the corner. "Of course," he wrote, "I had to stand in three counties at once, and do equally foolish things, but behind it all there was a keen sense of gratification that I had realized an old ambition." [24]

Another place Bob especially wanted to visit was the "Five Ponds" region, where one of the last sizable stands of virgin timber in the Adirondacks remained. So at 9:30 on Saturday morning, August 12, he and Bill Osborne paddled out of camp in a canoe. Beaching at Cat Mountain Landing, they set out on foot southwestwardly toward the Five Ponds. Upon crossing the Herkimer County line, they entered a virgin spruce-flat forest, the beauty of which Bob felt there was "no use trying to describe." Suffice it to say, he remarked, that they enjoyed every second of the 14.7 minutes it took them to traverse it before arriving at a pristine mountain pond called Big Shallow.

They spent the night at the edge of Big Shallow. Camping in an undisturbed forest made Bob philosophical. There were precious few such places left in the Adirondacks, he noted that evening. You can almost hear his father talking as he decried the lack of foresight that led to such a condition:

> It was pleasant, as we layed down, to reflect that we were in the heart of a tract of virgin timber about 40 miles square, absolutely unmarred by man. And yet, we could not help regretting that there should be so very few of such tracts left, due to the almost criminal lack of foresight of our legislatures of the nineteenth century.[25]

Bob was well known in camp for his lack of finesse with tools, including the canoe paddle. But on the last Saturday of the summer, he set out by himself in a canoe across Cranberry Lake. After beaching at the site of the Forestry College's Ranger School, he crossed a river and headed up a trail toward High Falls. He strode past High Falls (where "a dozen maidens were sporting on the rocks"), finally arriving at a stand of virgin timber. This was what he had come for—to let the cathedral-like atmosphere of a primeval forest stimulate his aesthetic and spiritual sensibilities as nothing else could:

> Only a subdued light filtered through the dense crowns of the dark spruce and hemlock. There was little undergrowth. The old trail underfoot was the last connecting link with the pioneers of a century ago. Its ancient moss-covered logs had borne the hunters and trappers of that distant day when the North Woods were one unbroken stretch of luxuriant forest, where the wolf, the panther, the moose,

and the deer lived and died without once being frightened by that most blood-thirsty of all creatures, termed man.[26]

Continuing, he crossed the Robinson River, up which he was tempted to explore and "let Stem Analysis, and Camp, and civilization take their course without my presence." Taking immense pleasure from the simple, rhythmic act of walking, he kept going till well past sundown.

That night his stomach, he says, was "out of order, as a result of the strain placed on it by some of the concoctions of my fellow cruisers." That the ailment might have been related to the physical strain of the previous twelve hours seems not to have crossed his mind. In any case, after paddling for two hours against a stiff wind and then lugging a pack over twenty miles of difficult terrain, he "just ate a few pieces of bread and butter."

He was not, however, too tired or sick to reflect on the demise of the Adirondack wilderness before going to sleep. He couldn't help but notice that the wood sorrel leaves on which he spread his blankets had never before been disturbed by man. But as he curled up in his blankets for the night,

> . . . it was a sad sound that came to my ears from the treetops above and the brook below, and the wind and the water seemed to unite to blow taps for the millions of acres of primeval forest that had gone, while about at attention stood some of the few surviving veteran acres of the Grand Forest of the Adirondacks.[27]

The next day he drifted still farther from camp before making his way back along railroad beds and country lanes. It was 7:51 Sunday evening before he reached his tent at camp. On that day alone he walked thirty-nine miles. Upon his return, he decided that he'd "seen a lot of beautiful scenery, but there wasn't a better part of my trip than the great macaroni supper I cooked myself, to break my diet of 50 hours."[28]

Thus ended Bob's summer explorations. When the results were tabulated, he had visited ninety-four lakes and ponds, walked several hundred miles, and climbed every prominent hill and ridge in the region. His account of these adventures, *Weekend Trips in the Cranberry Lake Region*, is notable for its frequent allusions to a vanishing wilderness but also for its humor. In addition to the trip descriptions, the document included Bob's rating of the beauty of the ponds he visited, the beauty of the views from ten mountains in the area, and the relative enjoyment of each trip he took.

When regular classes resumed in the fall, everybody in the College of Forestry Class of '24 knew who Bob Marshall was. More importantly, Bob himself now had a better grasp of who he was. Enjoying the informality of Summer Camp, studying ecologic principles directly in the woods, being recognized for his exceptional knowledge of Adirondack geography and history—all of these boosted his self-confidence and reaffirmed his commitment to forestry.

In 1922, the same year as Bob's Sophomore Summer Camp, some hikers formed the Adirondack Mountain Club. Bob became a charter member and, to help get it moving, wrote for it a thirty-eight-page booklet called *The High Peaks of the Adirondacks*. The club's first publication, it was a forerunner to the modern-day hiking guides, books which provide detailed trail descriptions of backcountry areas.[29]

In the introduction he acknowledged that many westerners considered mountaineering in the Adirondacks to be "more or less of a joke." He was certain, nevertheless, that climbing in the Adirondacks had certain advantages. For instance, "one who really wants to climb need not be contented with one mountain in a day." He recalled that on their Gothics Trip, "we got four different views, we were not so high up that the whole landscape was a blur, we did not have to bother about extreme cold or thin air, and we did not spend most of our time climbing over barren rocks and snow above timber line, but passed through delightful spruce forests." In addition, he noted, there were still several summits in the Adirondacks on which few people had ever set foot, and where no traces of civilization were to be seen.[30]

The book gave a brief description of each peak and how to get there. The peaks were arranged in order of elevation, with a "view rating" for each. Finally, the "composite view rating" was offered "for what it is worth."[31]

The booklet stimulated interest in Adirondack mountaineering. Russell M. L. Carson, an Adirondack historian and climber, told Bob later that it "obsessed" him with the Adirondacks.[32]

In his last two years at the Forestry College, Marshall blossomed into a class leader. As a junior he was elected to two honorary forest societies and wrote a poem, "Dawn in the Woods," for the college yearbook. In his senior year he became class secretary and an associate editor of the yearbook, for which he wrote "The Perfect Forester," a zany story about the misadventures of one Cadwallader J. Applesauce, the "most perfect specimen" ever produced by the College of Forestry.[33]

But the most important thing Bob wrote while he was at Syracuse was a class paper about wilderness preservation in the Adirondacks. In it he said that the residents of New York needed a wilderness to offset the crowding and commotion of urban conditions. Especially urgent was the preservation of the last vestiges of virgin forest in the state.

He went on to argue that even were forestry practices permitted that did not disrupt the basic ecology of the Adirondacks, the aesthetic and inspirational values would unacceptably be destroyed. The Adirondacks, because of their beauty, ruggedness, and close proximity to a huge urban population, were uniquely suited to non-utilitarian uses. They were most valuable to human health and happiness if large sections were preserved for recreation and inspiration. The need for such places was only going to increase:

> The recreational demands which will be made on the Forest Preserve can not be judged by the present number of tourists and campers. People can not live generation after generation in the city without serious retrogression, physical, moral and mental, and the time will come when the most destitute of the vast city population will be able to get a vacation in the forest.[34]

51

With those words Bob Marshall entered the public debate over wilderness preservation. But, as he was to learn, preservationists were a minority in the forestry field. Forestry, even more then than now, was concerned primarily with the science of managing trees *for harvesting*. Marshall's father, in fact, had long been accused of inconsistency for promoting forestry on one hand through his connection with the college and denying its practice on the other through his efforts to preserve the Adirondacks. This Marshall-as-hypocrite view has been well developed by forestry scholar Roger C. Thompson. In his doctoral dissertation for the New York State College of Forestry, Thompson criticized the "wilderness doctrine" that he felt stymied the proper development of the Adirondacks' resources. Commenting on the roles of both Louis and Robert Marshall in the development of this doctrine, Thompson writes:

> It is not unusual to find a sort of ambivalence contained within one individual. . . .
> Thus, it is not surprising to find one individual responsible to a large degree for the growth of the forestry profession on one hand, and the prime mover behind the force denying its public practice on the other. Nor is it surprising to find his son as a member of the profession and a leader of a movement which tends to divide it today.
> To Louis Marshall, the father, and Robert Marshall, the son, forestry is indebted with mixed emotions.[35]

Thompson's suggestion that Robert Marshall was influenced by his father is certainly valid. But his criticism of their actions rests on an old, limited concept of forestry. Louis and Bob Marshall both espoused a broader definition, one not confined to the use of forests chiefly for lumber production. They recognized commodity production as but one goal of forestry; equally important, in their view, were the protection of watersheds, wildlife habitats, and opportunities for backcountry recreation and inspiration. And the Adirondacks were so perfectly suited to these latter purposes that the best way to "manage" them for maximum human benefit was simply to leave them alone.

If forestry is nothing more than the efficient growing and harvesting of commercial trees, then the forestry profession certainly should view Louis and Robert Marshall with "mixed emotions." But if forestry means more than that, then modern foresters— along with several million people who enjoy wilderness each year as a counterpoint to traffic jams, frenetic schedules, and urban worlds of concrete and glass—may view them more positively.

In any case, by the time Bob Marshall left the New York State College of Forestry in the spring of 1924, he had greatly matured and shown a variety of talents. He finished fourth in a class of fifty-nine students and scored first in the nation on the civil service test for foresters. He had also earned a block S letter for running on the Syracuse University cross-country team that won the Intercollegiate Championship in November 1923. He had become a clever humorist, an excellent student, a persuasive writer, a fair athlete, and a promising forester. Yet none of these Bob Marshalls was more important than the one his classmates had seen at Sophomore Summer Camp—the Pond Seeker. The student who wrote the "Senior Records" for the yearbook was right on the mark when he wrote Bob's:

Here we have the Champion Pond Hound of all time, a lad with a mania for statistics and shinnying mountain peaks, the boy who will go five miles around to find something to wade thru. And the man who is rear chainman for Bob will have to hump or get wet, and probably both.[36]

53

5

Bee Stings
and Broiled Eggs
(1924–1925)

◆ ——————————————————————————— ◆

The eggs were like golf balls. When I tried to cut one it bounced off
into the brush.

Richard McArdle

*We'd come to these thickets of vine maple that'd be crowding out a little
Douglas fir seedling, and Bob Marshall would take an ax and walk up to
the little vine maple and hit it at right angles—and his ax would bound
off. He would about belt his head off but he'd never chop the tree off. I'd
walk right in and put a little tension on the tree and give it a clip with my
little ax and cut it off with a single blow. I would flop those vine maples
over one after another. He'd say, "Now you gotta show me how to do
that." I'd put the ax in his hand and show him how to bend a vine maple
over and get a little tension on it and chop it off with one little chip from
his ax. He wanted to learn, he was a good fellow, really, but he didn't
know how to do it naturally. And it'd tickle him to death if I'd be happy
with him and tell him how to do it. He'd do it then as well as he could. But
you'd die to see him, a forester, hitting at right angles at a round, hard-
wood stick, instead of making an angle slash cut into it.*[1]

That's how Leo A. Isaac, forty-three years later, recalled an incident from the summer of 1924. Bob had been assigned to work for

55

Isaac as a summer "field assistant" at the Wind River Forest Experiment Station near Carson, Washington. Bob had looked into permanent jobs with the Forest Service in Alaska, where he wanted to go. But when that did not work out, he registered for graduate school at Harvard in the fall and took this summer position in the meantime.[2]

The Wind River job was an excellent second choice. It was in the country where Lewis and Clark had tangled with Chinook Indians and braved the Great Rapids of the Columbia, surviving on dog meat, roots, and dried fish before reaching the more congenial tidewater. Bob thoroughly enjoyed it.

According to Isaac, Bob was enthusiastic, happy, and eager to learn. At the same time, he was "a very odd chap." Every day off, said Isaac:

> He'd leave the station and he would walk . . . forty miles or more in a day, up these mountain trails, back over, around, through the hills and back out. And he'd come down at night and he'd say, "I went up here and over there and then I crossed around there to that point (on a map) and I came down through this creek and on home."
>
> I used to look at him in amazement and say, "Either you're just an awful damn liar or you ran half of the way," because I knew he couldn't make it *walking*.
>
> "Well," he said, and laughed a little! "I always run down hill."

This was insane enough from Isaac's perspective, but there was more. If Bob hadn't walked his forty miles that day,

> he'd come out after supper and walk up and down the road until he got his forty miles walked in the day. He was a fanatic, but along with it an awful nice fellow, and a good fellow, a willing fellow. But awfully queer, and you had to have an awful lot of patience to work with him.[3]

Isaac's patience was given a rest in mid-September when Bob was assigned to another job. His new boss was Richard McArdle, future chief of the Forest Service. McArdle was researching

Douglas-fir yield in Washington and Oregon. Before sending him over, Isaac issued McArdle fair warning: Watch out for your tools. The boy "used a thermometer like an ax, and an ax like a thermometer."[4]

McArdle watched his tools and found Bob to be a fascinating character. He was amused, for instance, to learn that Bob was studying the eating habits of Forest Service officials. The officials always ate breakfast at Ranger Skaar's kitchen when visiting the region. One day Bob told McArdle he'd been keeping track of how many pancakes they ate. He showed McArdle his statistics:

Kummel	5.0
Munns	4.3
Hanzlik	3.9
Ames	2.5
Clapp	1.5
Munger	1.2
Eldredge	1.0
Meinecke	.05
Winkenwerder	0.0
Average	2.2

McArdle was also amused that Bob never wore the field clothes assigned to him. Instead, he had several half-worn dress suits that he wanted to wear out. McArdle, several years later, recalled an unfortunate incident resulting from this choice of clothing:

When he stepped on the yellow jackets they swarmed inside his pants legs and stung him rather severely at certain tender parts of his anatomy. I can still hear Bob shrieking "Oh dear, Oh dear..." as he ran around trying to get rid of the jackets. McGinn [another forester on the project] was a gent with a hair trigger temper and when he heard Bob's "cussing," he shouted at Bob "If you have to cuss for God's sake cuss like a man."[5]

Another time, Bob, McArdle, and McGinn were camped along Panther Creek near Wind River, where they were measuring ex-

57

perimental plots. They would work all day but have one crew member go back to camp early to have supper ready when the other two came in. McArdle and McGinn knew Bob was a poor cook; so they tried to keep him away from the kitchen. But Bob kept insisting he do his own share. McArdle finally relented and assigned him to cook supper Friday evening, their last evening at that camp. They had little food left, so McArdle told him to cook whatever they had and save a little for Saturday's breakfast. With those instructions Bob set off to prepare the meal. As McArdle told it . . .

> Bob used every piece of a 6-man mess kit, using a larger kettle when he had no space in the pan he was using. First, he told me that he had sliced our one remaining loaf of bread and toasted each slice laboriously over a big fire. Then he combined the toast with (as near as I could figure) two or three cans of evaporated milk, one or two cans of peas and two cans of salmon and I don't know what other ingredients. When McGinn and I got in Bob had what looked like gallons of what he told us was a salmon souffle. Oh, yes, he had found half a dozen big lemons and because he thought salmon needed a touch of lemon juice he added the juice of all the lemons. He was crouching over a raging fire with the biggest kettle sitting in a bit of water in the biggest frying pan (he said it was a rather makeshift double boiler). Bob thought the "souffle" tasted fine but to McGinn and to me it tasted like lemonade with salmon and peas.[6]

That evening, McGinn told McArdle that he planned to get up early the next morning and beat Bob to the job of preparing breakfast. But before dawn McArdle awoke and noticed light reflecting against the tent flaps. His first thought was that they had failed to put out their fire. But then he realized it was raining. He looked out to see Bob preparing breakfast. According to McArdle, Bob "had used the rest of the flour and had made hotcakes which he was stacking on a nearby log."

McArdle went back to sleep. When he and McGinn woke up a couple of hours later, they found Bob experimenting with the recipe he had once invented for broiled eggs. "He had hard-boiled

Bob Marshall of the Forest Service (Photograph courtesy of the United States Forest Service)

all the rest of our eggs," McArdle said, "shelled them (or maybe he didn't) and was frying the whole eggs in copious grease." Bob told McArdle he wanted to make his broiled eggs the "national dish." McArdle, though, didn't think it would catch on. "The eggs were like golf balls," he said. "I couldn't cut one and when I tried to do it the egg bounced off into the brush."[7]

Such were the impressions Bob Marshall made on the boys out west during his first summer in Lewis and Clark country. They would be hearing from him again. But for now, summer was over and he had other eggs to broil back east. He left McArdle's crew, took a day to climb Oregon's highest peak, Mount Hood (he had earlier climbed Washington's Mount Rainier while there), and headed for the Harvard Forest in Petersham, Massachusetts.[8]

The Harvard Forest is a 2,100-acre tract of rolling hills in north-central Massachusetts. The core of the property was acquired by Harvard University in 1907 to serve three major purposes.

First, it was to be a "model forest," a place where modern forestry techniques would be used to demonstrate how forest products could be generated year after year without depletion of the "forest capital." This was important, for during the first quarter of the twentieth century the notion of "sustained-yield" forestry was dismissed by the majority of industrial lumbermen as theoretical pie in the sky. It was considered far sounder business to move into an area, cut the entire forest as fast as possible, and then move along to the next region. If the result was devastation of hillsides, siltation of streams, hellish slash fires, and a boom-and-bust economic cycle for local communities—well, that was unfortunate but unavoidable. The Harvard Forest did much to change that attitude by demonstrating that sustained yield forestry was both economically feasible and physically possible.[9]

The school's second purpose was research. Experiments were conducted on tree growth, forest ecology, and harvesting techniques.

The third purpose was to provide a place for advanced students to conduct field research and practice forest management—which, of course, was why Bob Marshall was there. The instructional program was limited to a handful of students each year. In the fall of 1924, five students began the one-year course for the Master of Forestry degree. All were graduates of the New York State College of Forestry at Syracuse.[10]

Bob checked in on October 11, 1924, fresh from his eventful summer in the Pacific Northwest. He was assigned to a room in the Forest Headquarters building, a ramshackle old house that had been built by a religious colony many years before and that Frederick Law Olmsted reportedly described as, "so far as he knew, the ugliest house in the world." Bob's roommate was his friend and sometimes hiking companion, Neil Hosley. For Hosley, this was a "never-to-be-forgotten experience." Hosley remembered his roommate's unique way of organizing his belongings:

> Each of us had a flat-topped table perhaps 10' long. Whatever Bob brought in, from backpack to mail, was put either on or under his table. When the accumulation got so great that he couldn't find his postage stamps, he would make a solemn vow to straighten things out that evening. After dinner he would start sorting and organizing things into piles on the floor. The piles were neatly placed on the table. The next day the disorganizing started all over.[11]

Bob settled in and soon was enjoying his year at Harvard Forest. True, it wasn't Lewis and Clark country, or even the Adirondacks. But he was with a small group of good friends; he could relax and be himself. He spent nearly every day in the woods, collecting data or setting up new experiments.

Each student was expected to develop a research project for his master's thesis. Bob met with the forest director, Richard T. Fisher, on October 14, and soon identified his project. A certain cut-over section of the forest had grown back as high-quality softwood. This was unusual because most second growth in that region consisted of lower-grade deciduous trees. Bob decided to study the second-growth softwood stand, and also the history of logging in the region, to see if he could explain the anomaly.[12]

The research was time consuming but not enough to preclude his two favorite pastimes, walking and people watching. The Forest had a large ledger book known as the Forest Log. Bob was assigned to keep it for his class. By the end of the year, he was extensively describing the foibles and habits of himself and his peers.

On October 26 we find the whole crew visiting Amherst in the afternoon, a distance of over twenty miles. Bob walked. He had by then decided that he wanted to take a thirty-mile day-hike in every state in the union. Neil Hosley recalls being in the car that gave Bob a ride back to the Forest after he had presumably chalked up his thirty miles in Massachusetts. After climbing into the car, says Hosley, "Bob recalculated his miles and concluded that he was two miles short, so he said, 'Let me out.' Someone pooh-poohed the idea; so he reached over, turned off the ignition, piled out and followed us in."[13]

The few people at Harvard Forest that year had the pleasure of knowing Bob Marshall at his best. His gift for ridiculous humor was readily apparent. To pay off a bet one day, he slid six hundred feet down a dirt driveway on the seat of his pants, wearing heavy socks on his hands to protect them.

He couldn't get near an automobile without something funny happening. One day the Forest's assistant director, Al Cline (who had also taught at Bob's sophomore summer camp at Cranberry Lake), tried to teach Bob how to drive. Going up a hill, Marshall tried to downshift but slammed the car into reverse, at which point Cline suggested he practice instead "on a disc harrow out by the barn."[14]

Bob gave history lessons to his classmates and instructors whenever he could, often noting in the Forest Log the anniversaries of famous historical events. On April 26 his classmates learned that "General Grant would be 103 years old on Tuesday, had he only lived until now." February 11 was duly noted as the birthday of Daniel Boone and Thomas Jefferson. April 1 was the sixtieth anniversary of the Civil War battle of Five Forks; Bob celebrated it by giving "a blackboard talk on the military strategy of that fight and the ensuing Appomatox campaign."[15]

But Bob was better known as a humorist than a historian. For example, when a small fire broke out, he recorded the school's heroic response in the Forest Log:

At about noon, as the men were coming in from the field, they noticed a big smoke near the lumber pile on the Adams-Fay lot. Terror seized the hearts of all, but only momentarily, for in a jiffy Cline's level head cleared and he ordered Upham, Albright, Powell and the fire extinguishers in the Franklin and set out at a wild pace for the lot. Children and even strong men wept as they watched the cars' mad race through Upham's death valley road. Upham himself pictured his own death, embalming funeral, and even believed his wife was collecting the insurance when the car drew up by the lumberpile, which fortunately was not aflame.

The blaze was located in the chestnut cutting. Elmer Prim and Ed Latham were fighting a game but losing fight against the haulicaust [sic]. Straight as arrows from a Flathead's bow, Cline and Powell made their way to the apex of the fire, and shot a furious dose of extinguisher into the ravaging flame. Meanwhile Upham and Albright threw the full power of their virile manhood into the flanks of the fire, and in about five minutes it was practically out. Four fervent fire fighters and especially three fire extinguishers had converted an uncontrolled conflagration into a dying smudge.[16]

Bob put in long days in the woods and at the desk, but he continued to find time to report on the various goings-on around the Forest. Any ridiculous statement, silly blunder, or romantic development was likely to be published. He didn't spare himself, of course. One day while boring into a tree to extract a cross-section of its rings for his research, he had an accident. Writing in the third person, he recorded the mishap:

Marshall . . . started boring away at high speed, and results appeared most gratifying, until suddenly, while boring one of the biggest trees on the lot, with muscles bulging and hair flying, he was precipitated violently into the butt of the tree. Upon recovering and investigating, he found that . . . he had snapped the hard steel borer in twain. He returned home promptly and spent the afternoon in office work and meditation.[17]

By this time, accidents notwithstanding, Bob's research was yielding results: He was beginning to see why his wood lot, after logging, had grown back in high-quality softwoods rather than deciduous trees. The key was the manner in which it had been cut. The early loggers had used a "selective" cutting method; that is, they had cut only the larger trees and left behind the smaller ones. In so doing, they left behind the basis of a good future stand and also prevented the soil from deteriorating. Moreover, the small hemlocks in particular grew rapidly when the larger competitors were removed.

So the early loggers, Bob concluded, had unknowingly practiced good silviculture. Unfortunately, selective cutting had largely fallen out of use for industrial purposes because it was economically most expedient simply to "skin off" the forests in large sections, leaving behind as slash what could not be used. In the Adirondacks and in the Northwest, Bob had seen what this clearcutting did to the *aesthetics* of a forest; now he was learning that even from a silvicultural perspective, it was a method of dubious long-range economic advantage. There were places, certainly, where clearcutting in proper doses was the appropriate method; but it often was abused. An important aspect of Bob's philosophy of forest management was thus secured: He remained for the rest of his life extremely suspicious of extensive clearcutting and spoke out frequently against it.[18]

Meanwhile, in the course of working on his master's thesis, he also developed a theory about the effect of weather on political history. Part of his thesis involved the analysis of tree rings. He had to consider many factors that might influence the annual growth reflected in the rings. And since one such factor was rainfall, Bob began to collect historical data on annual precipitation.

One day, while examining his data, he began to play a little game of history. Each growth ring represented a certain year, and he found it interesting to look at a ring and consider what important events were happening during that year. Eventually it occurred to him that there were marked periods of very poor growth in his tree rings just prior to the years 1828, 1884, and 1912. These were election years, and they were also the times of the "three great Republican catastrophes, when the right-wing domination of the White House was broken after protracted periods of power."

Intrigued with this potential "biological-political relationship," he began to collect weather data from all over the country. He compiled the figures into elaborate tables which showed the relationship between annual precipitation and national election results, on the theory that rainfall affected crops which affected the economy which affected voter behavior. He reported the results in an amusing 1927 article for *The Nation*, entitled "Precipitation and Presidents." The correlations were impressive, but the style of the author, as he vacillated between the absurd and the perfectly reasonable, was more so. In the following paragraph he explained why he broke his data down by regions:

> We are blessed in the United States with a national baby show and a national beauty contest, a national flag and a national flower, a national game and a national guard, a national song and a national cemetery. Almost everything seems to be national except the weather. That still maintains a complete regional individuality.

He had found that in the Northeast, the relationship between precipitation and presidents was near-perfect between 1825 and 1884. During that period, in six cases out of seven when the previous four years had witnessed below-average rainfall, "a new swarm of political parasites descended on Washington."

But after 1884, Bob found, the folks in the Northeast stopped voting on the basis of how wet they were. From then until 1924, "the seven States which the Bureau of Census designates by the formidable group name of West North Central have proved to be [the] political hygrometers." In that region, "the four wetter-than-normal terms were all followed by a continuation of the party in office, while the drier than normal terms produced five political upheavals."

In summarizing, Bob said he was not out "to set up precipitation as an infallible key to our political history." But on the other hand,

historians have so emphasized the petty actions of puny politicians that it seems worth while stressing one factor which even the largest campaign fund cannot alter. The ancient Roman politicians may have been wise when they chose Jupiter as their highest deity.[19]

Bob received his Master of Forestry degree in the spring of 1925. The happy little community at Harvard Forest broke up in April. Bob's roommate, Neil Hosley, was asked to stay on at the Forest, and he remained on the staff there for thirteen years. For Bob, there was new ground to be covered and a lot of country out west he wanted to see.[20]

First, however, he had some unfinished business in the Adirondacks. His friend Russ Carson had found three more 4,000-foot peaks which Bob, George, and Herb Clark had overlooked in their effort to climb them all. Bob and George, going back to their maps, found still one more of exactly 4,000 feet which neither they nor Carson had noticed before. That made four more peaks that had to be climbed. They finished climbing the last one during the summer of 1925, sometime after Bob left the Harvard Forest. It brought the total of "high peaks" to forty-six.[21]

In the next decade just two people bothered to duplicate their feat of climbing all forty-six 4,000-footers; but two years later eleven more had done it, and a tradition was started. A Forty-Sixers club was formed in 1937, and by 1984 over 2,000 blister-soled hikers had joined the ranks of those who had scaled all forty-six High Peaks. (Measurements since 1925 have shown that four of the forty-six are in fact just a little less than 4,000 feet high; but by then it didn't matter, for the number forty-six had become traditional.) Today, when you meet people in the Adirondacks, you are as likely to be asked if you are a "Forty-sixer" as where you are from.[22]

6

Rocky Mountain Greyhound (1925–1928)

◆ —————————————————————————— ◆

Turn me loose and set me free,
Somewhere in the middle of Montana

Merle Haggard

On this occasion I had driven to the Bitterroot National Forest in Montana at the West Fork Ranger Station. A number of telephone calls were coming in the afternoon I arrived there. Since the day was quiet and there had been no rains, I knew the calls could not be about forest fire or fire danger. I was puzzled as to why these calls were coming in. When my curiosity got the best of me I asked the Forest Ranger what was happening. "Oh," he said, "these telephone calls are coming in from lookouts and other people in the forest who have made a wager on the time which Bob Marshall will be getting in from a 40 mile hike which he started early this morning. He is due here . . . some time around dark.[1]

Thus did Floyd E. Carlson recall a typical Bob Marshall outing, one of dozens taken during the three years Marshall worked at the Northern Rocky Mountain Forest Experiment Station. It was there along the Montana-Idaho border, in still another region where his heroes, Lewis and Clark, had some of their greatest adventures, that Marshall became a legend as a wilderness hiker. But the years Marshall spent there—between June 1925, and August

1928—had other significance, too. They were the years during which he gained his most practical forestry experience, read widely on a variety of serious subjects, began to consider socialistic economic ideas, and committed himself to the cause for which he deserves most to be remembered—wilderness preservation.

They were golden years, and they began appropriately with an unplanned addition to Marshall's list of states in which he took a thirty-mile single-day walk. The train taking him to Missoula, Montana in June 1925, was held up just outside Iowa when a rollicking thunderstorm deposited "a young mountain of rocks" on the railroad track. The passengers were told that the train would be stopped for at least ten hours. So Bob, now age twenty-four, immediately set off on foot across the Hawkeye State.

"I . . . obtained," he wrote home happily, "a more vivid impression of Northern Iowa than I could have gathered from a dozen guidebooks, and furthered a rather foolish, but interesting ambition." After getting in his thirty miles, Marshall climbed back aboard the train, which eventually resumed its westward ramble and took him to Missoula, Montana, arriving in mid-June.[2]

Missoula was the main headquarters for the U.S. Forest Service's Northern Rocky Mountain Forest Experiment Station. The Forest Service had always placed a strong emphasis on research. As early as 1902, "forest investigation" accounted for one-third of the agency's budget; and its traditional emphasis on scientific investigation was often given as an argument for keeping the Forest Service in the Department of Agriculture instead of shifting it to the Department of the Interior. In 1915, Chief Forester Henry S. Graves made research an even higher priority by establishing the Branch of Research and giving it, as he said, "the fullest possible recognition." Graves appointed a highly capable scientist and forester, Earle H. Clapp, to head up the new branch, and he gave Clapp the authority to conduct fundamental long-term studies. The studies were to be conducted through a network of "forest experiment stations," one of the earliest of which was the Northern Rockies station.[3]

When Marshall arrived, he was placed in charge of research relating to forest reproduction after fire, but for the first several months he did little on this. Instead, he helped out with other projects as the need arose. Outstanding among such tasks was fighting one of the worst outbreaks of forest fires ever recorded in the Kaniksu National Forest.[4]

He had been on the job only a month when he was ordered to go to the Mount Watson fire, one of sixty-one different fires that had been started in the Kaniksu by a lightning storm on July 12, 1925. A ten-mile auto ride, an eleven-mile motorboat ride across Priest Lake, and a five-mile walk brought him to the site of the Watson fire-fighting operation. What he found there was a spectacle of nature such as he had never seen before. The sight, he later wrote,

> was one such as must have inspired the ancients when they conjured up the picture of a seething, red-hot Hades. Probably Aetna in eruption, viewed in the blackness of midnight from some neighboring peak, resembled it. Over the entire mountainside hung a lurid, shifting, molten, fiery vapor, like the burning gases of a nebulous planet.... There was nothing solid or tangible about it; it was like some ghostlike picture without form or substance, showing the unconquerable, awful power of Nature.[5]

Marshall quickly made himself useful. He wrote: "I was made timekeeper, chief of commissary, chief of motor transportation, camp boss and general handy man." For the next eleven days he worked eighteen to twenty hours a day carrying out these jobs. No two days were the same. One morning the meat order for the day failed to arrive in camp. There were 109 men working on the fire, and supplies were sent in daily from Priest River, forty-two miles away. But on this day no trucks were available to bring in the supplies.[6]

Marshall decided that this wouldn't do. "The prospect of having 109 weary, hungry men come into camp at night after twelve exhausting hours in the fire line without any of the principal items of a woods meal on hand was appalling." So he "rustled around" and finally saved the day by obtaining a quarter of beef from a nearby

Research staff at the Forest Experiment Station, Priest River, Idaho, 1925: Bob Marshall is second from left; Marshall's boss, Bob Weidman, Experiment Station director, is fourth from right, wearing sweater and tie (Photograph courtesy of The Bancroft Library, University of California, Berkeley)

rancher. Similar crises arose each day that "would have brought gray hairs to one predisposed to them." Marshall enjoyed solving these problems, and he did not consider the work to be trivial. "Considering the seriousness of the fire, and the character of the men fighting it, picked up from the lowest and toughest element in the exceedingly tough town of Spokane, it was quite imperative to keep the fire fighters satisfied."[7]

One of his favorite jobs was to walk around the fire line every afternoon to check on the men. The distance varied from six to twelve miles "over exceedingly rough terrain"; so the walk itself was pleasant. Equally so was the chance to talk with the fire fighters. By the end of the fire, Marshall knew each of the 109 men by name. This, he believed, "pleased the men, who felt there was a real interest taken in them, and that if they were lost or caught by fire, someone would notice it. As a result, it made them easier to manage."[8]

Marshall's interest in these men was typical of his personality, for he was always fascinated by people whose backgrounds were different from his. It also resulted, through his letters, in an unusual portrait of a forgotten group of people. Of the 109 men fighting the Watson fire, Marshall calculated that ninety-seven had been "picked up at a moment's notice" and "were, for the most part, the type of men who could not hold down a permanent job." Their main concern was "to get as much time [in] and do as little work as possible." They had little interest in putting out the fire "except that they might get through with the unpleasant labor as soon as possible." On the surface, little about them was likeable.

> Their conversation was largely filthy and their thoughts were uninspiring. . . . Many of them had criminal records. Some were just off long drunks and others were dope fiends. . . . Some had evidently been half starved. They certainly made up for it, as, for once, they could eat all they wanted without cost. One old fellow averaged a dozen eggs every morning for breakfast, and one morning, the fellows counted him eating 17![9]

But if, collectively, they were an unsavory bunch, individually "there were a number of superior types":

> I used to like to talk with them while checking up on a line. Once I learned their names, they became more confidential and now and then I got on to the tragedy which had reduced them to their present extremity. They were much more appealing alone on the fire line than in the evening around the camp fire, with their smutty talk and grumbling.[10]

The best workers, according to Marshall, were those in their thirties. The younger men were too angry and irresponsible; the older ones, too worn out to perform the strenuous physical labor involved. The men over fifty seemed especially pathetic to Mar-

71

shall. "It was about the saddest sight in the whole fire to me" he wrote,

> to see these old men who had thrown away their health and their money and the best years of their lives, struggling up the mountain each morning, dragging themselves into camp at night, in order to make a few dollars from the only opening in sight. It is easy enough to say that it was all their own fault, . . . but somehow this explanation fell short and something seemed radically wrong.[11]

And Marshall soon concluded that something *was* radically wrong. He became convinced that the human misery he saw on the Mount Watson fire line was largely the result of an exploitive economic system—a system that destroyed lives not only in the slums of Spokane but also in the copper mines of Montana, the sawmills of the Appalachians, the factories of Michigan, the wharves of Baltimore, and many other places where poor people worked for rich people's profits.

Marshall's concern for these underdogs, however, was tempered by the reality of the immediate situation. He could muster little sympathy for the "four hard customers" who quit the fire a day early and tried to extort from him some pay they had not earned. The men, Marshall explained, knew that by quitting early they forfeited their transportation out and their travel time in and out. But they tried to bully Marshall into giving them these benefits. Marshall described the confrontation with his usual lively style:

> They were headed by a hard-boiled, keen-minded young boot-blacker, who argued, lied, threatened to smash up the camp, threatened to have all the higher ups connected with the fire kicked out of the service, and finally offered to fight personally. [A] gigantic miner from Butte vigorously backed him up. There was no one else in camp but the two cooks, Roy Tuttle and a boy who was working under me, so it required considerable tact and firmness to meet the situation successfully, but in the end, the four bums headed out along the road for Priest River, 42 miles away.[12]

Marshall and friends in Idaho, middle to late 1920s (Photograph courtesy of The Bancroft Library, University of California, Berkeley)

The fire that these four "bootblackers" walked out on eventually destroyed 2,000 acres of forest. But finally, at the cost of a thousand man-days of labor, it was suppressed and Marshall resumed his assigned duties as a researcher.[13]

Most of the research at the Northern Rocky Mountain station at that time was concerned with western white pine, an important commercial tree in Montana and northern Idaho. Specifically, six aspects of western-white-pine forestry were being investigated: methods of cutting, reproduction, intermediate cuttings, yield, forestation, and fire. Marshall spent time on projects pertaining to all of these areas. In so doing, he found himself in the fall of 1925 traveling to lumber camps and ranger stations, many of which—to his great delight—were remote. On August 31, he wrote gleefully that he'd been camped for several days "14 miles from the nearest permanent habitation, 41 miles from the closest post office and settlement (population 50), . . . 78 miles from the first pavement, electric lights or doctor, and 125 miles from the nearest real town with a thousand or more inhabitants."[14]

This paradise of solitude was on the north fork of the Clearwater River, well into the 28,000-square-mile region that constituted one of the largest roadless forests then left in the country. Though much of this area had been defaced by fires in 1910 and 1919, Marshall found it "delightfully rugged." In the evenings, after dark, he found it "glorious to stroll up the river and feel the mild breeze from the seldom-visited mountains to the east and look up at the clear, peaceful stars, and forget the century and order of civilization which had elapsed since Lewis and Clark first penetrated the unknown west."[15]

Much of his work on these excursions involved the detailed study of how trees grew back after fire or logging operations. He spent a lot of time on his hands and knees, counting seedlings and carefully recording data that might influence how well they grew: sunlight, soil composition, slope, logging debris, ground cover, and several other variables. It was grueling work, and it made him laugh when he compared it with the romantic visions of forestry that he had entertained as a boy. Instead of lassoing grizzlies and riding gallantly down unknown canyons, he found life "much more filled with keeping the meat at the fire camp from becoming flyblown" and "measuring to the tenth of an inch the diameter of pine trees."[16]

Nevertheless it was enjoyable and also educational. Marshall was especially interested in the working conditions of the people he met at the lumber camps and ranger stations he visited. At Falls Ranger Station, in the Kaniksu, he was struck by the haggard appearance of District Ranger Jim Murray. "There were deep, unnatural circles" under Murray's eyes, Marshall observed, "and he looked to be about a hundred years old, while really only in the forties." Besides his normal duties as district ranger, Murray was fighting three large fires and trying to prevent several smaller ones from becoming major blazes. "If ever a man appeared to need a rest cure, he did," Marshall wrote. "But a man can't do much resting on $1,800 a year and 15 days annual leave, not at least with a sick wife and children."[17]

A few days later, at a lumber camp called Beardmore Camp One, Marshall was impressed by the food. "The camp serves uniformly high class meals nowadays," he wrote. "[T]hey are well cooked, clean, and in limitless quantities. From all accounts this desirable situation is in marked contrast to the situation before the war, when the food was poor, dirty, and mostly fried."

The improvement, he was told, had been effected by pressure from the Industrial Workers of the World, a militant labor union whose work was decidedly unappreciated by most business interests of the time. Marshall, however, clearly sympathized with the union:

> That this tremendous improvement has taken place so suddenly can fairly be attributed to the I.W.W., or Wobblies, as they are universally called here. They also forced a revolution in sleeping quarters and today the dirty wooden bunks of yore have given place to iron cots and clean bedding.[18]

Marshall's sympathy for the Wobblies' cause stemmed in part from his contact with Frank Lacy, secretary of the union's Spokane headquarters. Lacy, a $100-a-month trail foreman, had worked with Marshall on the Mount Watson fire of 1925. According to Marshall, he did the "best work of any man" on the fire. Two years later, however, Lacy was dead of tuberculosis, and Marshall was deeply moved by his misfortune.

"He was really a very fine man," Marshall wrote. "I'd be willing to bet that his 40 days of smoke breathing that summer, not to mention the very fatiguing work, hastened his death."[19]

Thus did Bob Marshall begin mulling over the plight of the American worker. His liberal philosophy was beginning to appear.

When his field season ended in late fall, Marshall settled into his quarters in the government building in Missoula for a winter of mostly office work. He found, however, that meeting federal standards for housekeeping was harder than taking a fifty-mile hike in the Bitterroots. "Housekeeping with five ferocious phases is being pursued diligently," he wrote in November of 1925. "Of the quintet just mentioned, going from best to worst, I would rate them as follows: one, cooking; two, making the bed; three, dish-washing; four, sweeping and dusting, mopping, etc.; five, keeping papers, equipment and clothing where they belong." Indeed it was his failure at managing this fifth ferocious phase that led to his first "official bawling out."

One day his boss, Robert Weidman, dropped in. There were two days' dishes in the sink. The bed was unmade. The floor had gone unswept for three days. And, "in some unknown manner, both living room tables were all littered with papers, books and trinkets lying helter skelter, while about one-and-a-half complete changes of clothing were packed off in various corners of the room." Having no excuse, Marshall took the ensuing lecture "with befitting grace and meekness." After that, he claimed, there was "a big change for the better."[20]

Marshall liked to write amusing descriptions of life in Missoula. "I eat breakfast," he wrote in one letter,

> in a counter hash house, lunch in a cafeteria, and supper in the sec-ond best restaurant in Missoula, in which at least one of my fellow eaters is drunk about one night in three. Which may give you an in-sight into my food.
>
> Down at the office the top of my desk looks like . . . the boiler room in a lumber mill. I read, write, and engage in arithmetic and political and economic discussions with the staunch Calvinist who has the other desk in my room. Which may give you an insight into my work.
>
> A couple of weeks ago, between Christmas and New Year, I took a delightful snowshoe trip back into a country where elk still snort and moose still moo. . . . That, a few books, and one indulgence in taking a semi-homely and semi-dumb stenog to the movies may give you an insight into my recreation.[21]

While staying in Missoula, Marshall made several friends who influenced his thinking on forestry and economics. Howard Flint, forest inspector for the Northern Rockies District, was Marshall's "ideal of what the perfect forester should be." Flint had no formal forestry education, yet, according to Marshall, he had "a broader acquaintanceship with the fundamental sciences underlying forestry than any man in the Northern Rockies."[22]

Marshall became good friends with Flint and also with Flint's wife, Elizabeth, with whom he shared a keen interest in writing. Mrs. Flint, while admiring Marshall's unique intellectual traits and incredible energy, was moved most by his simple boyishness. "It has been such a joy for me to watch him unfold and change," she wrote to Bob's sister in 1930." (Just how she knew Bob's sister is not clear from this letter. Presumably, Bob somehow introduced the two.) Continuing, Mrs. Flint said: "He was so modest and shy and there was about him a—not just loneliness, but a sort of child-like aloneness that he drew out all the mother in me till he seems, as I said before, partly one of mine, too."[23]

This maternal reaction is one that Marshall seems to have elicited in many women. Besides the shyness and loneliness mentioned by Mrs. Flint, there were other qualities that made women want to mother him. His very appearance—that toothy, impish grin and soft, round face—was one. Another was his playfulness. When he got around children he often acted more childlike than they did—he would do somersaults, give endless piggyback rides, and perform all kinds of stunts for their amusement. In this respect he was much like the child who is quiet when he first meets you, but starts cutting up when he begins to feel comfortable. In later years, when Marshall had several girlfriends, this playfulness certainly made him unique and amusing—a fun date.

There's a temptation to analyze this boyish quality in terms of his relationship to his mother. Perhaps her "cotton batting" approach (as Marshall later referred to it) taught him to act boyish around women. It seems like a logical conclusion. But it is only speculation because we really have few details of their relationship.

In Missoula, Marshall also overcame his shyness long enough to make friends with Virginia Boutelle, a young teacher of French and Spanish at the University of Montana. It was easier for Marshall to talk to her because she was already engaged to be married, and thus the possibility of courtship was removed from their relationship. She, Marshall, and "two or three others" went hiking together around Missoula. She remembered Marshall as a man who "enjoyed life" and "lived by his own ideals."[24]

In 1928, Virginia went back to her home town, Seattle, to marry a Dr. Harry Olmsted. Marshall kept in touch with her, though, and in later years looked her up whenever he was in Seattle.

One of Marshall's closest friends in Missoula was an ardent socialist named Gerry Kempff. Kempff was a ranger at the Priest River, Idaho, Experimental Forest, a research facility operated by the Experiment Station. One forester recalled of him that he "had very socialistic ideas and advocated them at every chance." "Gerry's idea of socialism," continued this skeptical observer, "was a Utopian world where everybody shared equally in the wealth produced. I doubt if he could talk to a total stranger longer than 5 minutes without expounding the benefits of socialism as he visualized them."[25]

Bob Marshall was a frequent dinner guest at the Kempffs. His visits were great fun for the Kempff children, whom he amused by giving piggy-back rides, putting potatoes in his coffee, putting peas in their pudding, putting jelly in the milk, blowing out birthday candles, and various other stunts. For more sophisticated recreation, Marshall and Kempff discussed socialism and compiled a ranking of the top 36 foresters in the United States.[26]

Marshall began also to read widely on serious subjects. He reported in January 1926 that the previous twelve months had beaten "all previous years in quantity and quality of reading. 39 books were completed. . . . " These books he rated on the basis of "instruction, entertainment and aesthetic delight." Among the top-ranked were Sinclair Lewis's *Arrowsmith*, Dickens's *Great Expectations*, J. S. Mill's *Liberty*, and Maugham's *Of Human Bondage*.[27]

78

He took this reading seriously, as he later revealed in a letter to Leon Whipple, author of a book on the history of civil liberties. In the letter, Marshall told Whipple what a "great thrill" his book had given him. "I was out in northern Idaho at the time," Marshall explained, "and was spending a ten-day period in walking an average of 30 miles a day hunting up suitable areas to conduct certain experiments in regard to forestry products." He was carrying as little as possible, Marshall went on, and it was raining constantly,

> but one thing that accompanied me throughout most of this journey in the back of my cruiser's jacket was your book. I recall several days reading it during the lunch hour with the water dripping on it from the pine trees and hemlocks which did not form a very adequate shelter. . . . But the whole jaunt had tone added to it by the very exciting accounts of these grand heroes in the cause of civil liberties, as well as the very lucid descriptions of a less pleasant nature but equally graphic. [28]

Marshall generally worked six days a week and took a very long day-hike each Sunday. Stories of his long-distance hikes in the Northern Rockies began to go around, and even now it's hard for many people to believe his feats of walking have not been exaggerated over the years. Yet Marshall kept detailed records of exactly where he went, and his accounts jibe well with eye-witness reports. Thirty-mile day-hikes were routine and forty-milers were nothing unusual.

He went about these hikes very simply, Floyd Carlson recalled. "He went into a Sears Roebuck or Montgomery Ward store, bought a pair of wool socks and a pair of work shoes that he could hike in, a pair of blue jeans, and a blue work shirt. For food he carried a small bag of raisins and a hunk of cheese. And so, going light, with no other equipment, Bob Marshall was on a 40 mile hike." [29]

On Yom Kippur, September 1925, however, Marshall took an unusually short hike. Yom Kippur, the Day of Atonement on the Jewish calendar, is a time for quiet reflection. So Marshall went out that morning to be alone and to think. The sky was the color of

Marshall leads Missoula Mountaineers on a ski outing (Photograph courtesy Virginia Olmsted)

cold steel as he climbed a hill near Honeysuckle Ranger Station in the Coeur d'Alene National Forest, Idaho. From the hill he looked out over a river valley, on the opposite side of which stood a hillside of virgin timber, "looking very somber, for there were no hardwoods to give it bright color."[30]

For three hours he sat on a rock contemplating the scene, getting up at intervals to walk a short ways down the trail. When the day was over he compared this method of reflection with the manner in which he would have observed Yom Kippur back in New

80

York. Here in the woods, he found, "there was no wandering of thoughts to the chance of the Pirates in the World Series, or the next Sunday's walk, nor even to the less frivolous subjects of pine reproduction or the political situation." On the other hand, he was "forced to confess"

> that in Temple . . . it has in the past been impossible to banish such thoughts from my mind and that, at best, fasting, hard seats and dull sermons are not conducive to deep thought. Therefore, I feel that my celebration of Yom Kippur, though unorthodox, was very profitable.[31]

The woods, in other words, were Marshall's temple. A pristine mountain wilderness or a virgin pine forest did more for him spiritually than any work of human architecture. This explains much about his motivation to preserve wilderness. He simply hated to see something debased which to him held so much spiritual value.

A few months later, in February 1926, Marshall went on what proved to be one of his most uncomfortable hikes in the Northern Rockies. It was not long miles or physical hardships that caused his discomfort, but the presence of several young women. He had been asked by a Mr. Shumaker, a public relations man for the Forest Service's Northern Rockies District and secretary of the Montana Mountaineers, to go along with the club on one of its Sunday hikes. The party was to meet at a certain bridge in Missoula. As Marshall approached the bridge, he says,

> I smelled a rat. A short distance ahead walked five females, all dressed up in hiking costumes. I shot by them at a five mile [per hour] pace and proceeded toward the bridge, hoping to meet Shumaker there and receive a little encouragement, but not a man was in sight, but three more ladies.[32]

Summoning his courage, Marshall was able to make enough conversation with the ladies to confirm that they were indeed the Mountaineers. He crossed the river with them, but was further dismayed to find on the other side "two more of the knickerbockered sex," making a total of ten. Marshall described his uneasiness and eventual rescue as follows:

> I began to feel like a janitor in a girls' seminary. Still no sign of Shumaker. The ladies were both friendly and talkative. I kept up a mechanical conversation while my mind and eyes were occupied with the horizon in the hopes of seeing the lost leader. Just as I had about given up hope, he appeared, swinging over the bridge, and I began to appreciate what Thomas must have felt at Chickamauga when Granger's Corps marched up with colors flying.[33]

Marshall had overcome his shyness in the almost exclusively male world of foresters and lumberjacks. But in mixed company he obviously still carried a great deal of the bashfulness of his youth.

Another hike of this period is noteworthy for the reflections it evoked about the vanishing wilderness and for the description it inspired of a night spent with a mountain family. It happened that in 1926 Washington's Birthday fell on a Monday. Consequently, Marshall had a two-day vacation. So on Sunday morning, he borrowed a pair of snowshoes and took off from Missoula for the Continental Divide, seven miles distant.

As he crossed the Divide, he observed that "up here, the same trees were still standing that had shaded Lewis and Clark on their journey." He found it easy, as the deep blanket of snow enforced the feeling of solitude, to imagine once again that great expedition that fired his imagination for so many years. "Indeed," he wrote, "I do not believe the adventure of [the Lewis and Clark] expedition ever seemed so vivid to me as it did when I stood in the center of Lolo Pass, with a young blizzard howling and a snow-buried trail leading down into the greatest forest wilderness still left in this country."[34]

Yet even the great Selway Wilderness was already ticketed for mechanical intrusion, and the knowledge of this made the experience bittersweet:

> In a few years, the road from Lolo Hot Springs will push through this country and cut the last great wilderness in two. I am certainly

glad I had the chance of standing at its edge in mid-winter before this wilderness is ruined forever by a highway.[35]

It was after dark that evening when he arrived at the mountain cabins of the Erikson family. Though they had never met before, the Eriksons treated Marshall "like a long lost brother." After a couple of hours of talking, he was assigned to sleep in a cabin with "old Gus" Erikson. Old Gus believed in sleeping warmly. So, "after carefully considering all possible means of ventilation, with a roaring fire in the stove," Marshall flung off all his bedcovers. The heat, however, was the least of his troubles:

I had just about gotten myself adjusted to the extremely rugged topography of my bed, when the bed bugs burst out in full strength. ... [Dozing] was out of the question until midnight and the fire had died down and the vermin became more sluggish. I had just about fallen to sleep about 2 AM when a cat crawled over me. I hurled him halfway across the room, but he was game and came back immediately. It was about three when I taught him proper manners. After a few minutes of further adjustment, with still noticeable attacks of my bed fellows, I entered the land of Nod once more, only to be ... awakened by the loud sneeze of Gus's pet dog close by my ear. I drove him off, too, and wrapped myself around the miniature Mt. Marcy in the middle of my bed, [and] fell asleep until, about an hour later, the alarm went off.[36]

Marshall's hiking and other activities were curtailed by an acute ulcer in the summer of 1926. He was sent home to New York for treatment and recuperation, missed four months of work, and lost thirty-five pounds. The time off and inactivity, gave him a chance to reflect on his future plans. He wrote his boss, Robert Weidman, that he might take a leave of absence from the Forest Service to pursue his doctoral degree. This would be a good time to do so because for the next year he had to stay on a very restricted diet—which would be hard to do while traipsing around the Northern Rockies and staying at lumber camps. On the other hand, he had only been with the Forest Service a year. During that time he had felt pretty useless because he was still learning many technical aspects of the work. Did Weidman think it would be a breach of faith for him to leave now?[37]

Weidman's reply tells a lot about how Marshall was viewed by the foresters there: They saw him as a hard worker with good potential who needed seasoning. Weidman offered to assign Marshall to field work centered around the Priest River branch station. Marshall could then avail himself of Mrs. Kempff's cooking, which, said Weidman, would prevent him from "yielding to the gastronomic allurements of juicy beefsteaks and other foods on the usual bachelor's camp menu."[38]

Weidman then urged Marshall to return for at least another year because he needed more experience. Specifically, said Weidman,

> Although you are strong on the essential qualities desirable in a novice either in research or administration, . . . you are very weak in the mechanics of field work and field living. You are awkward with the tools and equipment that are necessary to a forester's work in the woods, and you lack orderliness in certain aspects of field work. . . . To overcome these weaknesses you need nothing more than field and office experience in an organization such as the Forest Service.[39]

So Marshall postponed his studies and returned to the Rockies in September of 1926. "I am now entirely well," he wrote to a friend shortly after returning, "and good for 35 miles a day, or at any rate I took the 35 mile walk from Wallace [Idaho] to Thompson Falls [Montana] last Saturday without any ill effects."[40]

Throughout 1927 and into 1928, Marshall continued to work hard, write a lot of letters, read a lot of books, and visit the major wilderness areas in the region. On various occasions he trekked through (among others) the Flathead River country in what is now the Bob Marshall Wilderness of Montana, the Mission Mountains and Cabinet Mountains of Montana, and the area now called the Selway-Bitterroot Wilderness in Idaho. It was in this last wilderness that he had the most exciting adventure of his life so far.

The Selway region is classic Northern Rockies backcountry,

home of elk and deer, black bears, mountain goats, and a remnant population of grizzly bears. The scenery is spectacular, and Marshall, whose writing was sometimes unpolished but always vivid, described it well. Referring to the climb from Elk Summit to Grave Peak, he wrote:

> The trail passes turquoise tarns set in granite and beargrass, from which streams cascade with a freshness only found at seldom visited sources. . . .
>
> In the sweeping panorama, which stretches 15 miles to the serrated wall of the Bitterroots and 75 miles in every other direction, the dominant impression is of immense wilderness. Needlelike peaks rising unscalably into the sky, spacious plateaus suddenly dropping into gloomy gorges, wooded basins meeting on irregular fronts with snagstrewn burns, deep blue ponds and bright parks alleviating the harshness of granite, goats moving with poise and dignity along ledges impending over air—all these are as unaltered as in the ages before even savages had ventured to this igneous upthrust.[41]

Enchanted by this scene, Marshall strolled along on a bright September day in 1927. Near a notch in the mountains called Friday's Pass he looked up to see a pair of grizzly cubs feeding on the hillside above him. He was less afraid of these cubs than he would have been of two female hikers. He stood watching them until he suddenly heard a crashing noise behind him. He wheeled around and saw a large adult grizzly lumbering toward him.

Marshall raced for a nearby whitebark pine and began to climb. About ten feet up, he trusted his weight to a dead branch. With a sharp crack the branch snapped and down came Marshall. "While gravity was doing its worst," he later wrote,

> I recollected the testimony of old hunters that bears will not molest people who feign death. It seemed a slim chance, but not half as slim as wading into that mass of ferocity with bare fists. So I landed and lay. It seemed as if I reposed for aeons. About the dawn of the Cenozoic Era I heard strange rumblings above me, and concluded

85

that another geological upheaval was in progress. I opened my eyes and looked up the hillside just in time to see three bears disappearing over the ridgetop.

It was a terrible blow to my self-esteem.[42]

Back in Missoula following this adventure, Marshall sent a telegram home which stirred up no small amount of interest. "SAFE IN MISSOULA AFTER TEN GLORIOUS DAYS IN SELWAY WILDERNESS," said the wire. ". . . LETTER GIVING DETAILS OF BEING TREED BY GRIZZLY MAY EVENTUALLY FOLLOW STOP HAPPY NEW YEAR."[43]

A few days later Marshall received a letter from his brother James, whose sense of humor was also keen. "Your grizzly telegram," said James, "has considerably aroused this part of the country, including a recital by father of the number of times he has told you to carry a gun, and not to go alone, and to wear rubbers when it rains."[44]

But regardless of his father's admonitions, being treed by a grizzly was a milestone for Bob Marshall. It was an experience that he shared with few people of the 1920s, and more with explorers like Lewis and Clark. He was at last getting a taste of high adventure and true wilderness. And he liked it.

While Bob was in the Northern Rockies, his father kept him informed on various threats to the Adirondack wilderness. In one of his letters, dated November 7, 1927, Louis made a statement which in effect was an appeal to Bob to keep fighting for wilderness after Louis was gone. Referring to a conversation with a would-be developer of the Adirondacks., Louis told Bob:

> I said half jocularly in the course of my argument that I would continue the fight as long as I lived, and if I did not succeed in finishing it I would put a clause in my will in which I would ask my children to continue the fight. I am quite sure that they would do so whether I asked it or not.[45]

Also that fall, an amendment was proposed to the New York

State Constitution to allow a road to be built up Whiteface Mountain in the Adirondacks. Bob received copies of his father's letters to newspapers arguing vehemently against the proposal. "Let us preserve some of the simple things," Louis argued. "Let us know that there is somewhere in our State a region which is not commercialized and citified, and to which those may repair who yearn for a restoration of their shattered nerves amid the vast silences of the eternal mountains and the primeval forests."[46]

But the road was approved anyway, and what bothered Bob Marshall was that no organization seemed to exist to fight such proposals with detailed, factual arguments. He was especially disappointed at the failure of the Association for the Protection of the Adirondacks to mount an effective campaign. The association had long used watershed protection as its primary argument for preserving the Adirondack forest. Bob felt it was time to argue on different grounds: The beauty of the Adirondack forest was reason enough to preserve it. Referring to the APA's secretary, Marshall asked a friend,

> What the hell is the matter with that old fossil [Dr. E. H.] Hall? Last spring, in the annual report of the Association, he made what seemed to me exceedingly feeble remarks about the devastation of the private lumber companies, which Reckwagel answered very effectively. Hall didn't have a single basis of fact. All he was doing was to repeat the 30 year old cry of devastation. Maybe he's right, but if so he doesn't know, and you don't and I don't. . . . Why doesn't the Association do a little simple research; make a study of the recent cuttings of the important lumber companies; and publish a scientific report on devastation in the Adirondacks, rather than to keep up its baseless threnodies. If it finds there really isn't any devastation, then it can concentrate on what is really the vital issue anyway, the destruction of aesthetic values.[47]

Marshall kicked off 1928 with a New Year's hike in Yellowstone National Park. He then sent his friends and relatives a kind of formal announcement of the event. It said:

87

Mr. Robert Marshall takes pleasure in
announcing that he walked 30
or more miles in one
day for the
100th
time on Sunday,
January 1, 1928 in Yellowstone
National Park

r.s.v.p.

g.(od) d.(amn)

s.(oon)[48]

In the meantime a controversy was brewing in the Adirondacks
over naming a peak after him and his brother George. In a recently
published book their friend Russ Carson had referred to a 4,404-
foot peak in the Dix Range as "Mt. Marshall" because, Carson
said,

> They made the first recorded ascent of this peak, and their many
> valuable contributions to the cause of mountaineering in the Adiron-
> dacks have given them top rank among both past and present ama-
> teur climbers in the region.[49]

Bob and George had mixed feelings about being thus honored,
but they certainly were happy to see that Carson had also named a
previously unnamed peak "Herbert" in honor of Herb Clark. Carson also proposed four other new names for peaks, including one in
honor of the then still living Adirondack explorer, Mills Blake.

Soon after Carson's book appeared, an attorney and Adirondack
Mountain Club member named Theodore Van Wyck Anthony em-
barked upon a vigorous campaign to repudiate the six new geographic names proposed by Carson. When a New York State Conservation Commission map entitled *The Trails to Marcy* appeared
with all of Carson's new names on it, Anthony successfully petitioned the agency to retract the names on the grounds that they
had not been approved by the State's Commission on Geographic
Names. He then personally paid for 1,800 new maps to be issued

by the Conservation Commission, "with all six objectionable names omitted." The following year, 1929, he was able to get a state law passed which prohibited the naming of any natural object after a living person.[50]

Anthony claimed that his opposition to the six new names was based mainly on this principle. Many people agreed with him and so supported his efforts to have the names removed. But there were some, including Louis Marshall, who thought his primary concern was to make sure no mountain was named after a Jew. In a letter concerning the matter to the Association for the Protection of the Adirondacks Louis Marshall typically came right to the point:

> While I entirely appreciate the desirability of orderly procedure in respect to the naming of geographic localities, I am sure that the Committee in reaching a conclusion . . . will not be oblivious to the fact that the present movement is the result of the bitter anti-Semitic bias of the person who is responsible for the outburst. I refer to Mr. Anthony of Newburg . . . [51]

Was Louis Marshall being defensive, or was Anthony really carrying out a personal vendetta? Some letters written earlier in his campaign suggest that Anthony's primary concern was indeed with the naming of Mount Marshall. One of his first actions after the release of Carson's book was to circulate a letter to selected Adirondack Mountain Club members in which he criticized only the naming of Mount Marshall after "two of Mr. Carson's intimate personal friends, *now living and members of the Adirondack Mountain Club*" (his emphasis).[52]

But why didn't Anthony mention Herb Clark and Mills Blake in this first letter? Carson had also named mountains after them, and they too were still living. Anthony's only initial reference to them was a vague statement that "Mr. Carson's other changes will be temporarily ignored" or "considered when brought up."

Apparently anticipating that he might be accused of anti-Semitism, Anthony closed with this rather strange disclaimer:

> This letter will doubtless cause some of my enemies in the Club to accuse me of religious prejudice, because forsooth Robert and

George Marshall are Hebrews, sons of Louis Marshall, a member of the great New York City law firm of Guggenheimer, Untermyer & Marshall, a prominent member of the Club, and, as quite generally believed, the presiding genius of its invisible Sanhedrin. You may also suspect religious prejudice. If so I am sorry, as I have none. Neither have I any personal animus, as, when Chairman of the Club's committees on Maps and Outings, I appointed George Marshall a member of those committees, had him as an over-night guest at my home and know him to be an agreeable guest and able co-worker. I do, however, admit a pro-Gentile leaning on all points in controversy and if that be religious preference "make the most of it."[53]

The disclaimer, of course, also made sure each reader knew that the Marshalls were Jews. In a later letter to a Club member who sympathized with Anthony's "big purpose" but questioned the need for the religious reference, Anthony clarified his motive; and it did, unfortunately, smack of personal hatred. He said:

Our friend, Louis Marshall, has effectively disguised his race by assuming his present name. I believe I am entitled to pull off the disguise. If his name was Marshallowitski, or Guggenheimer, or Untermyer it would speak for itself. He is trying to "get away" with his "100% Americanism" by disguising his race under the most honored name in American jurisprudence.[54]

The image of Louis Marshall "disguising" his Judaism is, of course, laughable, since he spent his whole life publicly defending it. But such statements as these were sadly common in the 1920s. Shortly after World War I a vicious book called *Protocols of the Elders of Zion* was revived by European anti-Semites. It claimed to reveal a sinister conspiracy by Jewish capitalists and communists to dominate the world. In America, auto-maker Henry Ford, a hero to millions, swallowed the whole story and vigorously publicized its theme in his newspaper, the *Dearborn Independent*. Louis Marshall spent hundreds of hours publicly repudiating *Protocols* and appealing directly to Ford to stop his attacks.[55]

And what was Bob Marshall's reaction to the mountain-naming

controversy? He despised Anthony's motive, of course, but agreed with his objective. He told Carson:

> Of course both George and I agree with Anthony's thesis, and the mere fact that he resorted to misleading statements doesn't alter this opinion. Neither does his bigoted and unpleasant phraseology. . . . Consequently if anything comes up at the Annual Meeting about the Club disapproving the name Mount Marshall it will have my hearty though unavoidably inarticulate support.[56]

Bob's father kept him updated on this matter, and, despite the bitterness involved, kept a sense of humor about it. One of his letters contained the following anecdote:

> The other day James and I were taking luncheon at the Bankers' Club and Mr. Early stopped at our table and inquired about you and George. James jocularly referred to the fact that Early was growing very stout. He answered that he recognized the fact but did not know what to do about it. I advised that he should walk up and down Mt. Marshall several times a day during the coming summer. He laughed very heartily, because he had been keeping in touch with the discussion with regard to that celebrated mountain. As a matter of fact I am reminded of it almost daily by some of my friends, all of whom, however, seem to be greatly pleased by the outcome of the raid.[57]

Despite Anthony's successful campaign to keep "that celebrated mountain" from being officially named Marshall, many Adirondack Mountain Club members continued to call it that. After Bob's death in 1939, the Forty-sixers of Troy petitioned the State to have a peak officially named after him. There followed some thirty more years of misunderstandings, record searching, and petitioning. Finally, in 1972, the U.S. Board of Geographic Names officially applied the name of Marshall to a 4,360-foot peak in the MacIntyre Range. "Named for Robert Marshall," said the Board's Decision List, a "conservationist who made the first recorded ascent of this mountain."

There was, however, one final irony. The peak that was finally named Marshall was the one Carson had named Herbert, after Herb Clark, in 1927. Some hikers had continued to call it that. But in order to get a peak named after Bob Marshall, the Forty-sixers were forced to deny the same honor to one of Bob's best friends and greatest teachers.[58]

Bob Marshall somehow found time to do a lot of writing during his three years in the West. Besides taking a course in creative writing at the University of Montana and writing detailed letters home, he cranked out between 1925 and 1928 seven articles that were published in journals, magazines, or newsletters. Three of these were rather technical pieces relating to his research on tree growth and precipitation cycles. At the opposite extreme was a zany parody of modern sociological inquiry, entitled "Contribution to the Life History of the Northwestern Lumberjack."

Published by the magazine *Social Forces* in 1929, the lumberjack article was based on detailed records of loggers' eating habits, table manners, and use of profanity that Marshall compiled while visiting lumber camps. For example, Marshall reported that he clocked between 300 and 400 loggers in nine Idaho camps during 144 meals. "Not only the first bolter and the last Fletcherizer were clocked," he assured his readers, "but also the average man, say the twentieth fellow to leave the table out of forty." The "average woodchopper," he found, "spends just 35 minutes a day in food assimilation." Moreover, he continued, "there is in each camp a fastest man or group of men who waste but 21 minutes diurnally in the mad dash for sustenance."

He was equally precise in quantifying the table manners of his subjects. "As regards bread spearing," for example, "33 percent of the diners commonly depended upon their forks to harpoon the staff of life."

Turning next to the lumberjacks' conversations, he provided a rank-ordered list of the loggers' favorite topics. These were compiled while acting as a "silent listener, watch in hand, to 1800 minutes of confabulation." Topping the list, at twenty-three percent of talking-time, was the category of "pornographic stories, experiences, and theories," which more than doubled the second-place category, "personal adventures in which narrator is hero."

Finally, Marshall analyzed the lumberjacks' highly acclaimed use of profanity, which was important, he said, because "it is the virility of [the lumberjack's] adjectives and interjections which differentiates his oral activities from those of ordinary mortals." Among the findings:

> ... it transpired that an average of 136 words, unmentionable at church sociables, were enunciated every hour by the hardy hewers of wood. ... [P]rofane words were overwhelmingly in the majority, for they constituted 96 of the 136 maledictions. Of the remaining 40 ... , 31 were of sexual import and 9 were excretory in nature. Unfortunately various heritages from Anthony Comstock's activities make it impossible to mention individually these profanations and obscenities.[59]

The lumberjack article, which first appeared in the Forest Service's Northern District newsletter, was roundly enjoyed by foresters and many others. It was typical Marshall humor—totally absurd yet based on a certain genius for observing human foibles.

Less famous at the time, but at least as important, was a short piece Marshall wrote for the Forest Service's national newsletter, the *Service Bulletin,* on wilderness preservation. Throughout the 1920s, wilderness had become an increasingly controversial issue in the Forest Service. To understand the controversy, we must backtrack briefly to 1924. That year, a young forester in the Southwest, Aldo Leopold (who later would become one of the most important environmentalists of the twentieth century) convinced his regional boss to forbid building a road across the Gila wilderness in the Gila National Forest of New Mexico.[60]

The Gila became the prototype for wilderness reservations in the national forests. Within the next year, five more areas were declared "roadless" by district foresters* in western national

---

*District Foresters are now called, more accurately, "Regional Foresters."

forests: the area now within Grand Teton National Park; the Two Ocean Pass country, now the Teton Wilderness; the Absaroka Forest, now the North Absaroka Wilderness; the Middle Fork of the Salmon River country in central Idaho; and parts of the Clearwater country in Montana, now in the Bob Marshall Wilderness.[61]

The following year, 1926, Chief Forester William B. Greeley gave wilderness an official boost when he wrote all the western district foresters, asking them not to plan roads into areas "adapted to wilderness forms of use." He also gave them guidelines for size, economic uses, and recreational uses of "wilderness areas."[62]

There were two political motives behind this rather sudden move by the Forest Service to preserve wilderness. One was a burgeoning public interest in outdoor recreation, reflected in the increased activism of outdoor groups such as the Isaac Walton League, the Sierra Club, The Mountaineers, and the Appalachian Mountain Club. In 1924, President Coolidge responded to this growing interest by appointing a National Conference on Outdoor Recreation to examine the need for recreational lands and make recommendations for federal policies. After working on this for five years, a conference subcommittee recommended in 1928 that twenty-one Forest Service areas, totalling twelve million acres, be set aside as wilderness.[63]

The second motive of Forest Service officials to preserve wilderness was their desire to prevent the National Park Service from gaining jurisdiction over several tracts of their lands. Since its establishment in 1916, the National Park Service had expanded rapidly under the aggressive leadership of its first director, Stephen Mather. Throughout the 1920s and '30s, a great many Forest Service areas were proposed as further additions to Mather's park system. These included tracts in the Olympic Mountains and North Cascades of Washington, the White Mountains of New Hampshire, the boundary waters of northern Minnesota, and the High Sierra of California. Also, proposed additions to existing national parks—including Yellowstone, Crater Lake, Yosemite, Rocky Mountain, Grand Canyon, and Carlsbad Caverns—would have transferred even more land from the Forest Service to the Park Service.

In retaliation, Forest Service officials were just beginning to promote the national forests as a kind of blue-collar alternative to the
national parks. The forests, they began saying, were places for the
ordinary guy who could not afford the hotels and souvenir shops of
the national parks. There were few developments in the national
forests, but there were also few rules and few crowds. You could
bring your family, have a picnic, gather wood for your campfire
(but be careful with it), hike in the mountains—or take a genuine
wilderness trip into some of the ruggedest country on the continent. Marshall, in fact, would later co-author an attractive book
for the Forest Service promoting these very uses.[64]

A great many foresters, however, resisted this entire approach,
especially the idea of wilderness. Though many enjoyed outdoor
pursuits like hunting and fishing, few thought of themselves as
providers of recreation or preservers of beauty. Instead, they took
pride in their silvicultural training and their ability to produce per-
petual supplies of lumber while maintaining relatively healthy
forests.[65]

Thus a forester named Manly Thompson wrote an article for the
Service Bulletin of May 14, 1928, arguing against wilderness. His
main point was that since only one-half of one percent of the population were wilderness users, it was bad policy to set aside large
areas for so few people to use.

Marshall, who had been having friendly arguments with foresters in Missoula about wilderness, wrote a rebuttal to Manly's article titled "Wilderness as a Minority Right." In this piece, which
appeared in the August 27, 1928, *Service Bulletin*, Marshall began
by questioning Thompson's figure of 0.5 percent while granting
that the precise figure was not the main issue. "The real question," he wrote, "is whether this minority, whatever its numerical
strength, is entitled to enjoy the life which it craves."

Democracies, he went on, are based on the idea that the will of
the majority should govern; consequently, there is a tendency to
ignore the rights of minorities. But the outstanding champions of
democracy—Voltaire, Mill, Paine, Jefferson—all recognized this
danger and all made strong pleas for the protection of minority
prerogatives. Moreover, in the United States at least, not only are

minority rights protected, but minority *interests* are often catered to at public expense. "Thus public funds maintain museums, art galleries, universities, swimming pools, and the patent office."

He then explained why wilderness is such a potent symbol to the minority who use it. "A small share of the American people," he wrote,

> have an overpowering longing to retire periodically from the encompassing clutch of a mechanistic civilization. To them the enjoyment of solitude, complete independence, and the beauty of undefiled panoramas is absolutely essential to happiness. In the wilderness they enjoy the most worthwhile or perhaps the only worthwhile part of life.

An impressive list of great American thinkers have felt this longing, Marshall observed. People such as Jefferson, Thoreau, Melville, Henry Adams, and William James all took inspiration from wilderness. And such "men of action" as Washington, Jackson, Lee, Grant, Sherman, Sheridan, Cleveland, and Roosevelt viewed the wilderness as "a fundamental part of their life."

Finally, Marshall concluded, it was a wilderness lover who wrote that people are "endowed by their creator" with such inalienable rights as "life, liberty and the pursuit of happiness." And for certain people, "the full enjoyment of these rights is possible only in the wilderness."[66]

The article stirred up no exceptional interest at the time. Yet it is possibly the most articulate answer ever given to those who continue to charge that wilderness preservation is "elitist." Marshall probably got the basic idea from Aldo Leopold, who had written in 1921 that foresters had a duty "to meet the needs and desires of the minority" who like to use wilderness. Marshall took Leopold's statement and bolstered it with examples from his own wide reading in American history and political thought.

The article reflects the maturation of Marshall's thinking on wilderness since he first came to the Rockies. His arguments up to then had been enthusiastic and heartfelt, but based mostly on his romantic belief that nature was superior to civilization. This article still showed plenty of romanticism, but it was far more sophisticated and persuasive. Marshall was learning how to use arguments that would have wide appeal and also how to apply theoretical principles like "the pursuit of happiness" to tangible issues like public land use. In future years he would become even more skillful at putting ideas into action.

By April 1928, a year and a half had quickly passed since Marshall had recovered from his illness. He wanted now to return to school. "I have decided on Johns Hopkins for the coming winter," he wrote home on April 14. "I will study under Livingston, who is the outstanding plant physiologist in the country, but will also take work in the Physics and Chemistry Departments."[67]

7

Baltimore Liberal (1928–1930)

◆ ──────────────────────────────── ◆

... if you called me a son of a bitch I might feel badly but not entirely overwhelmed; but when you call me Mr. Marshall, it just makes me feel so thoroughly miserable I want to knock my head against the side of a house.

Bob Marshall

"I have been working about 18 hours a day in this miserable town where there are no mountains within miles and where you have to see the sunset across sidewalks spotted with chewing gum and gasoline and across the tops of endless brick houses, every one of which looks just like every other one."[1]

Thus Bob Marshall described his life in Baltimore, Maryland, where he was attending Johns Hopkins University. But despite his distaste for the urban environment, he was enjoying himself immensely. After moving into a room near campus in September 1928, he promptly threw himself into a whirlwind of activity. In the next two years he would earn his Ph.D. in plant physiology, pursue a busy social life, explore an unmapped wilderness in Alaska, publish half a dozen articles, and make a concerted attempt, along with a handful of colleagues, to change the course of his nation's forest policy.

99

Marshall's mentor at Johns Hopkins, Dr. Burton E. Livingston, was a competent scientist who had established the university's department of plant physiology in 1909. Livingston did a lot of research on how climatic factors and soil conditions affect plant growth. Under his direction, Marshall soon had a project of his own underway. It was a series of experiments to see how evergreen seedlings react to the drying out of their soil. The general procedure was simple enough: He planted conifer seeds in sand beds, watered each one regularly for twenty-four days after it emerged from the soil, then stopped watering and watched what happened. It was tedious work, though, because many factors—such as air temperature and soil composition—had to be tightly controlled while variables like water content of the seedlings had to be carefully measured. During peak work periods, Marshall got out of bed between three and five in the morning and worked until eleven at night. During slack periods, his days were almost as busy with other activities.[2]

Sometime after arriving in Baltimore, Marshall's social life changed radically. As he told his old friends Gerry and Lily Kempff,

> Of course, working such long hours it is necessary, for psychological reasons, to indulge in quite a bit of social activity, and I have been having a very good time in this respect. . . .
>
> I have seen a show every week or two, several concerts, dance most every week and go to one big evening dance at the University every month, and of course, since I am accompanied each time by some more or less pleasant and comely maiden, time does not hang too heavily.[3]

Obviously, something important had happened to Marshall since the time in Missoula when he couldn't bring himself even to talk to a few women hikers. The change is so abrupt and complete that it's one of the great puzzles of his life. Some of it occurred because he had gained a lot of self-confidence while working in the Rockies. And he was, of course, extremely eligible—wealthy, well educated, full of energy, full of humor, physically fit, and not bad looking when he dressed up. So it wasn't hard for him to find a date for dinner (he never ate at home anyway) and a show afterward. But well into his twenties he had never even seemed *interested* in women. Now suddenly he was dating several at once. We cannot account for the change, but whatever its cause, the old, shy Bob Marshall was gone. In his place was a fellow who loved to dance, socialize, and entertain comely maidens.

Unfortunately, Marshall's papers tell virtually nothing about who his new girlfriends were. Only one is specifically mentioned in the letters for this time period. This is a Dr. Lynch (no first name is mentioned, but apparently she represented the professional class of comely maidens) who insisted, to Marshall's chagrin, on calling him "Mr. Marshall." Bob told a friend that he planned to tell her:

> ... if you called me a son of a bitch I might feel badly but not entirely overwhelmed; but when you call me Mr. Marshall, it just makes me feel so thoroughly miserable I want to knock my head against the side of a house. My name is Bob, always has been Bob, always will be Bob, and unless you want to be very cruel I hope you will use that title.[4]

While at Hopkins, Marshall began donating to such organizations as the League for Industrial Democracy, whose stated objective was "education for a new social order based on production for use and not for profit." He also became "one of about three people who more or less ran" the Johns Hopkins Liberal Club.[5] In retrospect, it seems inevitable that Bob would become a social activist. His father's concern for civil liberties and for progressive environmental controls was extremely influential. So were Bob's contacts with outcasts and laborers in the Northwest who, he felt, were victims of an unfair economic and social system. It was a time, moreover, when leading intellectuals such as John Dewey, Charles A. Beard, and Thorstein Veblen were, in the words of Arthur

Schlesinger, Jr., "reorganizing the liberal mind and reconstructing the liberal tradition."[6]

Marshall, who took pride in the currency of his thinking, was well aware of the writings of at least one, and perhaps all, of these men. Marshall listed John Dewey as one of his three "idols of apotheosis" among philosophers, the other two being Thoreau and Thomas Paine. In his 1929 book, *Individualism Old and New*, Dewey advocated what he called "democratic collectivism," a socialistic economic system arrived at through the participative process rather than through coercion, as in the Soviet Union. The scientific method, rational planning, and public participation would be key tools in bringing this about.[7]

Many of the same principles—collectivism, public participation, national planning, and the application of science—were prominent in Marshall's own liberal vision. Anxious to apply this vision to the real world (another Dewey tenet), Marshall turned to a national problem on which he was an expert—the deforestation of the country. For several decades, various alarms had been sounded about the rate at which American forest lands were being destroyed by fire and imprudent lumbering practices. Within the forestry profession there was an ongoing controversy about the best way to solve the problem. One side saw the solution in strict federal regulation of the timber industry—in effect forcing lumbermen to practice forestry in a way that would reduce fire hazards and ensure an ongoing supply of wood. The other side, more sympathetic to the industry, urged what it called a cooperative approach—developing joint fire-management programs between industry and government, for instance, or using tax incentives to encourage better forestry on private lands.[8]

The "cooperate with industry" faction appeared to have won in 1924 with the passage of the Clarke-McNary Act. This measure provided for an extensive fire-management system between the federal, state, and private sectors, and, by reducing certain economic risks, encouraged landowners to use less destructive cutting methods.[9]

The act had been hailed by many as a great landmark in forest policy. As Marshall, in his unique way, later put it, "foresters and conservationists rollicked in the happy assurance that... forestry would flourish on every side."[10]

But in 1928, Major George P. Ahern, a veteran forest administrator, privately published a little booklet in which he claimed that forestry, in fact, was flourishing on very few sides, if any. Ahern cited evidence that three disastrous things were still happening in the woods: First, fire damage was increasingly excessive, due in great part to irresponsible lumbering methods. Second, virgin forests were being destroyed at a rate that would eliminate them altogether in twenty to thirty years. Third, private timber companies were still doing nothing to ensure ongoing crops of trees. Eighty-one million acres of potential forest land was now barren of trees, and the nation was losing timber at a rate four times faster than it was growing back.[11]

Inspired by Ahern's book, and following his own liberal inclinations, Marshall jumped eagerly into the controversy. In the space of fifteen months he published two articles and one small book about the issue. "Forest Devastation Must Stop" appeared in *The Nation* in August 1929. "A Proposed Remedy for our Forestry Illness" appeared in the *Journal of Forestry* in March 1930. And in November 1930, his thirty-six page booklet, *The Social Management of American Forests* was published by the League for Industrial Democracy.[12]

In these articles, Marshall asserted that private forest ownership had generally resulted in"the devastation or decimation of the forests' productivity, in deficiently controlled run-off, in disastrous soil erosion and in the ruination of the forest beauty." In contrast the experiment of public ownership had resulted in "a perpetuation of the timber supply..., in the protection of soil erosion and in the preservation of some of the most stupendous outdoor beauty existing anywhere."[13]

Marshall concluded, therefore, that the forests should be nationalized and managed for everyone's benefit instead of depleted for private profit and the pursuit of an "outmoded ideal." But public opinion was "so conservative" that most of the forest lands would be devastated before a large-scale program of public acquisition could be carried out. So, in the interim, strict regulation of private forestry should be adopted.[14]

For several years, Marshall had been trying to repress his urge to explore unmapped wilderness. He told himself that while the days of physical adventure were over, opportunities for mental exploration were greater than ever. "This exploration," he later wrote, "might take the form of scientific discoveries, of original philosophic contributions, of the creation through some artistic medium of a new form of reality."[15]

During the winter of 1928–29, however, as the prospect of an unobligated summer loomed ahead, the old Lewis and Clark syndrome began to surface again. He found himself poring over maps of Alaska, that "Great Land" where a few isolated tracts of unexplored wilderness still remained. He wanted badly to go, yet he had trouble justifying the trip to himself on the grounds of exploration alone. He felt at the time "that exploration should have a social justification," and he did not think that making a rough map of a remote Alaskan region would add much to anybody's happiness but his own. And so, as he later said, "I pretended to myself that the real reason for this expedition was to add to the scientific knowledge of tree growth at northern timber line." He had a general theory that the timberline in the Arctic was moving slowly northward in the wake of the last great glacier. By collecting some data to test this theory, he could justify the trip, even though his primary purpose was simply to have an adventure.[16]

After finishing his work at Johns Hopkins that spring, Marshall began the two-week journey by train and steamboat that would finally put him in Fairbanks, Alaska. There, according to his maps, all "railroads and highways ceased."[17]

The area he had picked to explore was a 15,000-square-mile section of northern Alaska's Brooks Range, which divides waters flowing southwest into the Pacific Ocean from streams running northward into the Arctic Ocean. It was a vast mountain wilderness of impassable bogs, steep canyons, U-shaped valleys, razor-sharp crumbling ridges, and somber gray limestone peaks. Grizzly bears and wolverines patrolled the willow-choked streambeds; moose browsed the stunted shrubbery; giant herds of caribou followed ancient migration routes across the tundra.[18]

When Marshall arrived in Fairbanks, he was met at the depot by his partner for the summer, Al Retzlaf. The two had been put in touch with each other during the winter by the Alaska School of Mines, where Retzlaf had been taking a course. An eight-year veteran of Alaska, Retzlaf had hunted and prospected in several parts of the Great Land. He was thirty-two years old, stood just over six feet tall, and had short, sandy-brown hair, which he combed straight back from a slightly receding hairline. His jaw was square and his gaze was icy; but Marshall found him very likeable and was impressed "with his energy, competence, and willingness to do whatever needed to be done." The two explorers, according to Marshall's accounts, got along very well.[19]

In Fairbanks Bob and Al boarded a one-engine seven-passenger Hamilton cabin plane bound for the tiny settlement of Wiseman. While the pilot maneuvered the craft "with great skill and without a good map," Marshall gaped out the window at the braided channels of the Yukon Flats and looked on with amazement when the plane frightened three caribou. The latter, he observed, "galloped wildly around, terrified by the mysterious disturbance of their wild haunts."[20]

Equally amazing was the reception they received upon landing in Wiseman on July 22, 1929. A crowd of about twenty people greeted them with warm smiles and hardy handshakes, happily briefed them on the people and country they would see, and carried their bags the half-mile from the airstrip to the village.[21]

The settlement was located on the middle fork of the Koyukuk River, just north of the Arctic Circle. It served approximately a hundred people, about half of whom were white prospectors and trappers and half of whom were Eskimos. Many of these people had wandered into the hills on hunting or prospecting trips, but nobody Bob talked to had been up the north fork of the Koyukuk River into the Brooks Range.[22]

Bob Marshall (right) and Al Retzlaf (Photograph courtesy The Bancroft Library, University of California, Berkeley)

In honor of the newcomers' arrival, the citizens held a dance at the Pioneer Hall. Martin Slisco, the stocky roadhouse proprietor who treated Bob and Al "like brothers," lent them each a pair of shoes for the event. Five women (all Eskimo) and about twenty men (mostly white) turned out. For Marshall, it was a magical evening that he never forgot. As he wrote in his posthumous book, *Alaska Wilderness,*

> With the day still bright at midnight despite rain, with the long-yearned-for Arctic actually at hand, with the pleasant Eskimo girls as partners, with the queer old fashioned steps which the prospectors had brought into the country at the start of the century, with friendly strangers smiling and welcoming, and with little Eskimo kids having hopping races with me—that evening seems today a dear, half-remembered dream.[23]

On the morning of July 25, everything was ready. Leading two horses—Brownie and Bronco—Marshall and Retzlaf took the dirt road northwest out of town. After crossing over to the North Fork of the Kuyukuk, they worked their way northward for ten days. They fought mosquitoes most of the way and slogged through long stretches of sedge tussocks—knee-high tufts of cottongrass which are too tipsy to walk over and too thick to walk easily between. On the seventh day out of Wiseman they climbed a high ridge and gazed out over the Brooks Range. About ten miles to the north was an imposing pair of mountains which looked to Marshall like gateways into the Arctic watershed. Exercising the explorer's prerogative, they christened the two "portals" the Gates of the Arctic. The name has become popular, and today the two mountains are part of the 7.95-million-acre Gates of the Arctic National Park and Preserve. (Marshall also named the two individual mountains comprising the Gates; he called the western one Frigid Crags and the eastern one Boreal Mountain.)[24]

They were almost to the Arctic Divide when heavy rains turned them back. On the return trip, they had a scary experience. They were camped on a little island inside the vee formed by the junction of two rivers, the North Fork of the Koyukuk and the Clear

River. It had been raining hard for several days when, at three in the morning, Marshall woke up and looked outside. In the long twilight of arctic summer he could see that the backwater behind the island was no longer a pool but had become a steady current that had risen nearly to their campsite. He got up, moved the cooking gear back from the water, and went back to bed. As he did so, he casually mentioned the situation to Al, who looked for himself, whereupon, Marshall reported, all was immediately "fire and consternation."[25]

Retzlaf began to shout: "Hurry, get up. We've got to get out of here God damn quick. The main river's cutting back of our island. If we're not damn fast we'll be cut off from everything."[26]

Marshall began to get dressed as fast as possible while Retzlaf, already dressed, took off with the horses. In spite of the urgency, part of Marshall remained, as usual, the detached observer. He looked at his watch. It was 3:23.

Al was back a few minutes later, still leading the horses. It was too late, he said, to pack them up. The water was up to his thighs and rising. They had a few minutes left in which to ferry whatever gear they could carry themselves. "Never mind the little things," Retzlaf called as he raced off with his packsack and a box of food. "Just pack up the tent and the bed rolls, but for heaven's sake hurry."[27]

Al was across the channel and back three times before Marshall could finish striking the tent. Al grabbed a box of food for his fourth trip while Bob followed with his partner's bedroll, "which also contained a great many stray items." Now the water was up to their waists, and the current was nearly strong enough to knock them over. One more trip would have to do it. This time Al carried saddles, tarps, and shovels while Marshall ferried the tent and some more bed gear.

Safe on the peninsula, with most of their equipment salvaged, Marshall again checked his watch. 3:54. The evacuation had taken thirty-one minutes. By a little after four A.M. their escape route had become impassable.[28]

That morning, Marshall remained philosophical and, in a sense, even happy. For he wanted more than anything else to know that there were still places where nature held the advantage over humans—and here that surely was the case. Before going back to sleep, he walked once more to the edge of the raging river. "Mankind may be taming nature," he wrote in his journal, "but no man standing on the bank of the North Fork of the Koyukuk at 5 AM on this gray morning would even claim that nature has been conquered."[29]

Indeed, his own problems were far from over. For he and Retzlaf were now trapped inside the vee of the two swollen rivers. They had to cross the Clear River, coming in from the northeast, in order to get on the east side of the North Fork and travel southeast back to Wiseman. To do this, they thought they would have to build a raft and float across—a very dangerous proposition. To Marshall, the religious implication of their predicament was interesting. He had just been reading Joseph Wood Krutch's book, *The Modern Temper*, in which Krutch argued that modern science was cutting people off from traditional religious beliefs. Marshall felt himself to be an example of this, writing in his journal: "If I were born 100 years ago I would no doubt say that all we could do would be to shove [the raft] off and pray, but as it is that solace must be omitted and we will have to trust our lives to nine logs and the torrent of the Koyukuk." Marshall, in other words, no longer considered himself a practicing Jew. He referred to himself in later years as an agnostic.[30]

In any case, he and Al escaped their trap without having to raft either of the wild rivers. Instead, they were able to ford the Clear River at a spot where a new channel was being cut. The old channel was filling in with a wall of rocks and the new one was still fairly shallow. Thus neither channel was as deep or swift as the rest of the river. By walking with the current and using the horses for support, they made it across, though several times the current knocked them over.

Three days later they were back at the Wiseman roadhouse, eating caribou liver in front of the fire and telling everyone about their narrow escape. It was, as Marshall said, "a glorious conclusion to a glorious adventure."[31]

Bob Marshall returned to the East Coast in early September 1929. On September 11, his father died suddenly, in Zurich, Switzerland, while working on the volatile problem of Jewish resettlement in Palestine. The esteem in which Louis Marshall was held was evident in a memorial service held for him in New York later that year. More than 2,500 people attended, including delegates from more than seventy-five legal, civic, religious, and philanthropic organizations.[32]

Bob was, of course, saddened by his father's passing; but as a naturalist he accepted death as a part of an ongoing cycle, and he was quite philosophical about it. In response to a friend's condolence he wrote:

> I tremendously appreciate your letter at the time of Pop's death. Fortunately, I suppose due to the general philosophy I have about life and death, I didn't take his passing as emotionally as you imagine. The significance read into death is of course an individual matter. Between the most glorious conceptions of heaven and the unbearable ideas about hell there is infinite room for divergence. Personally, I do not believe in any hereafter and my guess is that death means oblivion. Yet it is a perfectly inevitable event, and nothing which is inevitable seems tragic.[33]

The key difference between a tragic death and a normal one, Bob continued, was the factor of happiness. This he thought was a "dual factor" involving the individual's personal happiness and the happiness he brought to other people. And in both these respects, his father "lived a remarkably happy life."

Finally, Bob noted that his father had always been active and would have preferred death at seventy-three to an old age of inactivity and deterioration:

> As it was, during the past year of his life, he averaged ten to fourteen hours a day of work, argued two or three cases in the Supreme Court, appeared before both the House and Senate Committees, argued probably six or eight cases before the Court of Appeals in Albany, read at least a hundred non-legal books and any number of law

articles, took part in active fights in behalf of the Indian, Negro, Jew (dozens of them came to him), the right of free speech in New York public schools, and for the preservation of the Adirondack Forest Preserve.... Then he was taken sick... and passed on in three weeks. To me that seemed the ideal way to die, with flags flying and boots on.[34]

Bob greatly admired his father's activism, but in many respects their personalities were quite different. Bob was more athletic and less intellectual; Louis's economic and political views were much more conservative; Bob's sense of humor was far more obvious (though Louis was by no means humorless). But Bob got from his father two qualities which transcended their differences: extraordinary energy and a deep commitment to perceived humanitarian ideals.

On a more tangible level, the elder Marshall left most of his estate, worth several million dollars, to his four children. Thus Bob was now financially independent. He would always work, but would never be dependent on an employer. This was not only a privilege, but an awesome responsibility, and it helps explain why he became more and more of a social activist during his last ten years. He felt it was up to him to speak out for those who were less free than he was to do so.[35]

On Wednesday, October 23, 1929, the price of stocks on Wall Street took a strange dip. By the end of business the following day, the dip had become a crash and the Great Depression was under way. For Bob Marshall the crash confirmed his worst suspicions about capitalism.

The forest situation was a case in point. The millions of acres of denuded forest land reflected the destructiveness of profit-oriented industry; the growing rate of unemployed lumberjacks and mill workers, whose working conditions were disgraceful to begin with, reflected the inherent brutality of a system whose driving force was not compassion but greed. Most depressing of all, to Marshall, was the lethargy of his own profession. At a time when bold action was needed, most foresters seemed committed to little but the status quo.

There were, however, a few colleagues who agreed with Marshall on the need for change. Most important of these was Gifford Pinchot, the father of the U.S. Forest Service. Now in his sixties and governor of Pennsylvania, Pinchot had been out of the Forest Service since 1910. But he still held legendary status as a conservationist. During the halcyon days of Teddy Roosevelt's Progressive Era, he had single-handedly built the Forest Service into a model of governmental efficiency and professional pride. He was the most famous forester the country had ever known, and for a number of years his name and the word "conservation" were virtually interchangeable in the eyes of the general public.[36]

One morning in late January 1930, Marshall received a call from Pinchot, who was starting a drive to stop forest depletion. Could Marshall come over for lunch? Yes, Marshall replied, he would definitely like to come over to Pinchot's for lunch.

Marshall arrived at Pinchot's Washington, D.C. home at the appointed time. He found there several members of forestry's rather thin liberal wing, including Ward Shepard, with whom Marshall had worked in Montana; George P. Ahern, author of *Deforested America;* and Raphael Zon, a brilliant forest scientist with whom Marshall soon became close friends.

Pinchot opened business by saying that he was "thoroughly disgusted" with a "wishy washy" report recently done by the Society of American Foresters on the forest problem. Pinchot was going to counter it by forming a committee of his own. The committee's purpose would be to "get the profession behind some vigorous action" on the problem.

The committee was thus formed, and Marshall and Ward Shepard were assigned to draft a strong statement. This they did at Shepard's home the next Friday night (though they could not get started till Marshall gave several piggyback rides to Shepard's son).[37]

After several more meetings at Pinchot's, the committee had a 1,500-word statement which they then mailed to foresters all

*Raphael Zon (Photograph courtesy of
Norman J. Schmaltz)*

around the country. Titled simply "A Letter to Foresters," the document accused the profession of accepting forest destruction and, by its silence, condoning it. "In every field of activity," said the letter, "failure to meet responsibility is implacably punished by spiritual decay." The forestry profession, by not taking a stand of deforestation, was facing a moral tragedy.

Foresters, it went on, were obligated to take the lead in developing a cure for deforestation. The cure should be sought along two main lines: federal regulation of private lumbering, and "a greatly increased program of public forests." The statement was signed, in alphabetical order, by seven men: Ahern, Marshall, E. N. Munns, Pinchot, Shepard, W. N. Sparhawk, and Zon.[38]

The statement, predictably, got mixed reactions. The Washington, D.C., branch of the Society of American Foresters shortly afterward passed a resolution favoring public regulation of private logging. This move, Marshall observed proudly, was "the most radical action any forestry organization has ever taken." But most conservative foresters merely dismissed it as an overreaction to a problem they felt was not really that severe.[39]

In any event, working on the letter put Marshall in touch with several people—especially Pinchot and Zon—who shared his views and would henceforth play important parts in his life. Marshall took to Pinchot much as he had once taken to Herb Clark. "Governor Pinchot," he told Gerry and Lily Kempff,

> is one of the most amazing men I have ever met. After 35 years of forestry battles, instead of being discouraged and cynical, he is entering this new fight with as much enthusiasm and interest as a boy of 20.

What Marshall liked even more than Pinchot's enthusiam was his liberalism. Marshall observed happily:

> He thinks Hoover, Hughes, Mellon are all terrible, believes in government ownership of natural resources, is strong for civil liberties and really is interested in everything a liberal should be. Of course he is not really radical in very much but one can't want too much from a man of 65. Perhaps anyway it is better to be just liberal and not radical.[40]

As for Zon, Marshall thought he had "the finest mind of any man in the forestry profession" that he had met so far. "He always looks at things in a new way, shakes up set ideas and makes everybody he comes into contact with think more clearly and more honestly."[41]

Bob Marshall's social life kept getting busier, too. There were lunches with liberal friends, parties in Baltimore and Washington, dinners, dancing, and shows with the women he suddenly couldn't see enough of. One evening, at a party, he was introduced to Supreme Court Justice Oliver Wendell Holmes, Jr. Shortly afterward he wrote Holmes a letter saying how happy he'd been to meet him. "There are so many discouragements these days for anyone with liberal tendencies," he wrote, "that to have met the country's greatest liberal is a stimulant out of all relation to what one has any reasonable right to expect."[42]

As for the women, they still went unnamed in his letters, but became so numerous that he began keeping statistics on them. "My statistics indicate," he later observed, "that I went out with twenty-three different girls on fifty-six of my last sixty-four days before getting my Ph.D. If Dr. Livingston had ever guessed this . . . he would have kicked me out of the laboratory."[43]

Thus Marshall approached courtship (once he finally discovered its pleasures) much as he had earlier approached Knollwood baseball, mountain climbing, thirty-mile day-hiking, and the observation of lumberjacks eating pancakes—going all out, throwing himself completely into the thing, putting more energy into it than most people would even consider, and putting big numbers up on his statistical scoreboard. He does not, however, seem to have been motivated, as many womanizers are, by a need for sexual conquest. His highly developed sense of human dignity would not permit him to view women as mere sexual toys; and besides, if he saw twenty-three women in fifty-six days, very few, if any, of the relationships could have reached an intimate level. If sex was his main objective, he would have had to concentrate on fewer women at one time. He simply enjoyed the stimulation of variety.

On the other hand, having always been wary of women, it probably seemed to him a lot safer to have many casual relationships than one intimate and perhaps permanent one. Also, he was extremely busy and had plans for another, more extended trip to Alaska; so there would have been no point in starting a serious relationship.

In February 1930, *The Scientific Monthly* published an article of Marshall's called "The Problem of the Wilderness," in which he expanded on some of the themes developed in his earlier piece, "The Wilderness as a Minority Right." Although the new article had been rejected by four other magazines, it turned out to be his most important. In it he described the physical, mental, and aesthetic values that made wilderness worth preserving; discussed some of the sacrifices that would have to be made if any wilderness was going to be saved; and recommended forming an organization "of spirited people who will fight for the freedom of the wilderness."[44]

One reason for saving wilderness, he argued, was to provide visitors with a chance for adventure, which he feared was being lost in the modern world. In the backcountry, people could still test their physical limitations, be self-sufficient, and even face danger. "Life without the chance for such exertions would be for many persons a dreary game, scarcely bearable in its horrible banality."[45]

Another important reason for saving wilderness was its unique aesthetic qualities. When you looked at a Rembrandt painting or listened to a Beethoven symphony, you remained somewhat detached from it. "But when one looks at and listens to the wilderness he is encompassed by his experience of beauty, lives in the midst of his aesthetic universe."[46]

Today, the article is considered seminal by wilderness historians. It was not the first call to preserve samples of the American wilderness: the painter George Catlin had done that in 1841 and many others had since followed suit. Nor was it the first attempt at a practical definition of wilderness: the eloquent Aldo Leopold had done that in 1921.[47]

But "the Problem of the Wilderness" knitted together various threads of the wilderness debate that until then had hung loosely about. Moreover, it was original in at least two ways. First, its treatment of the aesthetic values of wilderness was unique. Nobody, including Thoreau and Muir, had extolled the aesthetics of wilderness in quite the same way. (It was this unique perspective that later brought about one of Marshall's most famous one-liners. A skeptic asked him just how much wilderness we really need. Marshall replied immediately: "How many Brahms symphonies do we need?")[48]

The second original thought was Marshall's call for the organization "of spirited people" who would "fight for the freedom of the wilderness." Marshall apparently had some such organization in mind when he sent copies of the article to everybody he could think of who might be interested. It caught the attention of at least two people—Benton MacKaye and Harold Anderson—who would later help him form The Wilderness Society.

Marshall also sent a copy to Forest Service chief Robert Stuart, who, as it happened, had recently issued Regulation L-20, which formally established a "Primitive Area" system on national forests. (It had been written by L. F. Kneipp, a Washington official who was then the Forest Service's strongest wilderness advocate.) From a preservationist viewpoint, the new regulation was an important step forward. It was not, however, a radical departure from previous policy; it simply put the chief forester's stamp of approval on areas already designated by district (regional) foresters and politely asked them to consider recommending others. Specific restrictions on lumbering, grazing, road building, and summer cottages were left entirely to individual districts.[49]

Stuart sent Marshall a copy of the new regulation. "By 1931," he said, "a quite comprehensive system of primitive areas will have been established." But, as Marshall's actions over the next decade would demonstrate, he was not satisfied.[50]

In the spring of 1930, Marshall finished his study of seedling conifers and was awarded his Ph.D. from Johns Hopkins. This was a worthwhile achievement, yet it seems secondary to his myriad other activities. He was already looking forward to his next adventure—another trip to Alaska. This time he planned not only to explore the Brooks Range and do some more tree research, but also to make a study of Arctic frontier civilization. His interest in the latter was well explained in a letter he wrote that summer to his former teacher, Al Cline:

> In almost all economic and social discussions of our present civilization the question seems to arise whether we are happier than our preindustrial ancestors. . . . Nobody made any precise study of what our preindustrial ancestors were like, so such comparisons are purely metaphysical. However, here is preserved on the Koyukuk a civilization very closely analogous to the 18th century pioneers of the Eastern U.S. and the 19th century ones of the West. So it leaves a beautiful opportunity for someone to study what might be termed our contemporary ancestors.[51]

Marshall intended to make such a study by spending a winter in Wiseman and putting his well-developed powers of observation to

117

work. "I know I will have a wonderful time of it," he told Cline,

I have an offer for publication of a book on the subject which will finance the journey, I feel before settling down too narrowly that I should broaden myself out by some study of the social sciences, I crave a little adventure before settling down to the staid placidity of middle age, my health has been adjudged perfect, and so, of course, I am going to go.[52]

8

Wiseman Winter
(1930–1931)

◆ ——————————————————————————— ◆

> I like this damn country.
>
> An Alaskan sourdough to Bob Marshall

*Wiseman, Alaska, January, 1931. Martin Slisco's roadhouse, early eve-
ning. Outside it is pitch dark and colder than a meat locker. Inside, three
prospectors, wearing wool shirts and coveralls, are sitting at one end of a
long wooden table. In front of them are several large bowls and serving
dishes, piled high with moose meat, potatoes, carrots, cabbage, bread, butter, cake, blueberries, and custard pudding.*

*The prospectors are engrossed in conversation. Albert Ness, sixty-three
years old, is saying, "the way things are outside today a person's sure
lucky to be living in here where he gets more than he needs to eat. I see they
figure there're ten million people unemployed now—and thirteen percent of
the people own ninety percent of all the wealth of the country."*

*"Yes, and it's a lucky thing that's so," says Vaughn Green, the Deputy
U.S. Marshal. "If it wasn't for John Rockefeller and Andrew Carnegie
and the Guggenheims and men like that piling up wealth you'd be minus
all the good that's come from the Rockefeller Foundation and the Carnegie
Libraries and all this aviation research that the Guggenheims put up the
money to do."*

*Verne Watts, a short, wiry sourdough with a fast wit, speaks up. "If
them Senator bastards would cut out some of their battleships and spend*

119

the money for aviation research, we wouldn't have to finance people like the Guggenheims to give money for it."[1]
The conversation continues, flowing like a stream of consciousness into such topics as the soul's immortality, freedom, the Klu Klux Klan, dancing, and local gossip. The talkers are paying little heed to a round-faced fellow with wavy brown hair and a spindly beard sitting at a nearby table scribbling furiously into a notebook. They don't realize that Bob Marshall is recording their conversation verbatim. They don't know that in a couple of years thousands of people outside are going to be reading about them in a popular book by Marshall called Arctic Village.

Bob Marshall spent twelve and a half months—from late August 1930 to early September 1931—exploring and gathering data for *Arctic Village*. It was one of the happiest and most educational years of his life. Living with Eskimos, he learned to appreciate cultural diversity and to detest racial bigotry even more than he had before. Living with and observing white prospectors, he opened his mind still further to different ways of defining success and looking at the world. And he came to believe that frontier conditions were essential to the happiness of individualists like Albert Ness, Vaughn Green, and Verne Watts.

Marshall started the year off with a four-week expedition into the Brooks Range. Again he went with Al Retzlaf. This time they set up a base camp just below the Arctic Divide, at the junction of Ernie Creek and Grizzly Creek (both named by Marshall). Then they enjoyed what Marshall called "a week of explorer's heaven." Each day was devoted to climbing mountains never before climbed or exploring gorges and valleys never before explored.[2]

On September 5, for example, Marshall climbed a high peak on the Arctic Divide which he named Limestack Mountain for the pile of gray limestone at its summit. Upon reaching the top he spent three and a half hours making map sketches, taking photographs, and "looking in every direction over miles of wilderness in which, aside from Lew [a man they hired to take back their horses after they had reached base camp] and Al, I knew there was not another human being." The total effect was "an enjoyment such as

Downtown Wiseman, Alaska, 1930 (Photograph courtesy The Bancroft Library, University of California, Berkeley)

another person might get listening to Beethoven's Fifth Symphony played by some dreamed-of super-Philadelphia Orchestra."[3]

Nine days later, Marshall had an exciting encounter with a family of grizzlies. He and Al had set up a camp at the junction of Amawk River and the Upper North Fork of the Koyukuk. Then they split up for the afternoon, as they often did. Marshall had gone about two miles up the Amawk and was basking in the knowledge that he was covering ground which probably no human had ever set foot upon. Suddenly he was rudely awakened from his daydream by three furry figures. The following description of his encounter must have made interesting reading to the folks back home:

> ... I looked up and my heart stood still, as the books all say. About 150 feet ahead were three grizzlies! One hundred and fifty feet may seem like a long distance to a catcher trying to throw a man out stealing second, but between three bears and a human being, 11 miles from the closest gun, 106 from the first potential stretcher bearers, and 300 air-line from the nearest hospital, it dropped to the realm of the microscopic. The closest bear was small, probably a two-year old, the second was of medium size, the third appeared about like two elephants and a rhinoceros. Suddenly my heart stood even stiller, for they reared up, one after the other, from little to gigantic, just like so many chorus girls going through some sprout in sequence. [4]

Fortunately, however, the grizzlies did not attack: no sooner had they reared up than they turned and disappeared into the willows.

For Marshall the expedition was a total success. He climbed six previously unscaled peaks. He explored and mapped forty-two miles of previously unvisited river valleys. He made growth observations of six different timber stands, laid out four sample plots to determine tree size and density, and started a new experiment on seedling growth north of timberline. And he saw fifty-eight white sheep, seven grizzly bears, two moose, and one black bear.

For Retzlaf, however, the trip was disappointing, for he found no gold at all. Yet, according to Bob, Al was gracious and very helpful throughout the expedition. When they returned to Wiseman on September 22, Al left for new adventures and Bob settled in for a winter on the Arctic Circle. [5]

Before going into the Brooks Range, Marshall had arranged to rent a sixteen-by-eighteen-foot log cabin from Martin Slisco. For a total of sixty dollars a month, Slisco threw in a year's supply of wood and meals. And while Marshall was off exploring, the road-house proprietor winterized the cabin by shingling it with ripped-up sections of cardboard boxes. "It gives the house a wierd but unique appearance," Bob observed. "[but] with the cabin freshly mudded in addition, new dirt shoveled on the roof and a fine, large heater, I am all set for sixty below."[6]

The cabin's interior was decorated in typical Arctic-frontier fash-ion. A large window on the southern wall permitted a picturesque view of the steep, snow-covered mountains beyond the river. The walls were paneled with canvas, once green but now faded "under the influence of considerable moisture, to a dozen different shades of blue, green, gray and brown, all hodge-podged together." The walls were bare except for a large calendar with a picture of a startled mama bear and two cubs being attacked by hornets while two hunters advance furtively in the background. "The Surprise Party," read the caption beneath the picture.

In the center of the cabin floor stood the all-important stove, which served as heater, kitchen range, and drying room. Directly above the stove was a large rack where Bob hung his wet clothes for drying.

Of his other furnishings, Marshall considered his two bookcases to be the only "highbrow feature" in the apartment. One of the cases consisted of six unfinished boards hammered together to cre-ate four two-foot shelves; it was "devoted to the humanities." The other ("for the sciences") was two egg crates placed next to each other.

The shelves were filled with a sixty-six volume library that ranged widely in titles, from Spengler's *Decline of the West*, through Shakespeare's complete works and Plato's *The Republic*, to Vilhjal-mur Stefansson's *The Friendly Arctic*. His intellectual interests had expanded widely since the days when he was content to reread *Pioneer Boys of the Great Northwest*.

Marshall was determined to keep this new study area orderly. "There is not a trace of the usual chaos of papers, books, maga-zines, gloves, snowshoe straps and the like," he claimed, "but an immaculately clean oilcloth surface whereon I can spread the work

Interior of the Wiseman cabin where Marshall spent the winter of 1930–1931 (Photograph courtesy of The Bancroft Library, University of California, Berkeley)

of the moment without having first to shovel clear a small space on which to set my papers."[7]

By mid-October winter weather had set in. Bob fell into a pleasant routine of interviewing Wisemanites, joining their daily activities, and compiling elaborate statistics on numerous aspects of their behavior. Most days he was up around seven A.M. He ate breakfast either by himself or with Martin Slisco, who would help wake him up by relating "the latest details of his contemporary love affair."[8]

Mornings were usually spent working on his notes, reading, or chatting with visitors. After lunch, he might visit around town or go for a walk.

These walks were especially cherished. As Marshall later recalled, there were many afternoons when "I walked out along the trail, while the far below freezing weather made my nose tingle. The southern sky would be brilliant with sunset colors, the snow all around would change from a strange purple to a dark gray, and diminutive Wiseman when I returned would be twinkling with lights."[9]

From there it was on to the roadhouse for a "loquacious" supper. The sourdoughs would drop in to eat and talk, and when their bellies were full they would turn on Martin Slisco's Victrola and dance with the Eskimo girls. At this point Marshall would often go visit a cabin or igloo* for an evening's conversation with the inhabitants. Finally, the day was ended with a walk back to his cabin: a pleasant stroll through the frigid air, "while the northern lights rolled brilliantly across the heavens." At such moments he felt that life "could not possibly be more splendid."[10]

He was soon well known around the settlement. People dropped in on him, a dozen or so a day, to borrow a copy of *The Strange Death of President Harding*, to listen to the *Hungarian Rhapsody*, or (most often) merely to talk. One by one, little by little, they told him their life stories.

He found them to be an introspective group. Having few diversions, they thought a lot about life and death. They were, as Marshall observed, "actively aware" of their existence.[11]

Such a one was Pat Kellecker, seventy-three years old, blind in

---

*The igloos of the Alaskan Eskimos, unlike those of the Canadian Inuit, were not made of snow. The Alaskan Eskimos built theirs of logs, twigs, and moss.

one eye, fervidly Catholic, and extremely well read. Like most frontiersmen, Pat had strong feelings about freedom. He explained these feelings to Marshall when he dropped by the cabin one cool October day.

"The greatest thing about the Alaskan frontier," said Pat, "is that man here is his own master. I've gone out and worked fifteen hours a day here and it doesn't seem half as long as working ten hours outside. I imagine a man outside that has to work for wages without any interest in his work is more or less in bondage all the time. There's a touch of slavery about it as I see it."[12]

Marshall often played music on his phonograph to help his visitors relax. One day when he had first moved into his cabin, four veteran Koyukukers came to visit. Three of them—Verne Watts, Poss Postlethwaite, and Bob MacIntyre—were old sourdoughs who had been in Alaska since the gold rush of 1898. The fourth, Harry Snowden, was an Eskimo whose ancestors had inhabited the Arctic for centuries.

Marshall welcomed them and cranked up the magical machine. He "didn't want to be highbrow" by starting off with a classical selection, so he placed *Ol' Man River* on the turntable. This was heartily approved by everyone except Harry Snowden. The Eskimo, Marshall observed, "sat through a dozen popular songs with the most complete lack of expression on his face that I can imagine in a human being. His high cheekbones, his protruding lips, his half-closed eyes, his completely immobile countenance might have been a model for some painting of the god of boredom."

But then, with some trepidation, Marshall placed Ravel's *Bolero* on the turntable. Immediately, Harry sprang to life. A broad smile came across his face and he said excitedly, "That's good, Bob." Then a few minutes later, "Gee, that's fine music."

By the end of the recording Harry was sold on the *Bolero*. "Gee," he said, "isn't there a lot of music going on there! Play it again, Bob!"[13]

For the next three weeks Marshall puzzled over Harry's excited response to the *Bolero*. Then, on a dogsled trip into the bush with Bobby Jones, he thought he caught a glimpse of the answer. They stopped for an evening at the abandoned boom town of Coldfoot, once *the* metropolis of the northern Koyukuk, but now empty. (The last resident had committed suicide during the dark days of the previous winter.) That evening at dusk Marshall walked by himself to the confluence of Slate Creek and the Koyukuk. He watched as the pinks, oranges, and purples of the sky, the dark greens of the spruces, and the brown of the mountains all slowly merged into black. As darkness closed in and the stars came out, he became aware of a musical accompaniment to the visual beauty he was enjoying. The wind and the rushing of the Slate Creek waters seemed to be playing a symphony. Sometimes the wind would rise to a great crescendo, and sometimes it would die down so low that only the constant rushing of water could be heard. It reminded him of the *Bolero*, "never the same at any two instants but still exactly the same throughout the whole song."

Then he realized why Harry Snowden and the other Eskimos loved Ravel's composition:

> Because the Bolero is a perfect counterpart of the music they have heard from earliest childhood out in the wilderness of the north. The drums are the rivers rumbling unvaryingly and the rest of the orchestra is the wind howling, the ice cracking, snowslides coming down the mountains, rocks tumbling over one another, the wild animals howling. It represents to the natives all the chaotic music of nature in its wildest moments.[14]

After a night in Coldfoot, Marshall continued by himself down the Koyukuk to Porcupine Creek, where he met Sam and Obran Stanich, who explained some additional benefits of frontier living. The two brothers, recent immigrants from eastern Europe, were cutting timbers for a new prospecting hole. Upon seeing Marshall, they canceled their day's work and took him to their cabin. With great pride, they showed him their new home, their prospecting holes, the cabbages, turnips, and potatoes they were growing in their garden. They laughed easily and often, Marshall observed, and he "soon felt as if they were old friends."[15]

Neither Sam nor Obran could read or write. Both spoke only broken English. They had wandered into Porcupine in 1916, filed a claim there, and worked it ever since. With a lot of diligence they made themselves three or four thousand dollars a year, enough to live on and even put a little away. Marshall was impressed with the dignity these uneducated immigrants had obtained through their frontier existence. He felt they had gained a sense of self-worth that otherwise they might have missed out on:

> ... up here, though they work more laboriously, and go through greater physical hardships than they ever would in industrial civilization, though they lack conveniences which even the most poverty-stricken New York family would have, still they live with every comfort they crave (except women), are not only interested in but actually excited about their work, talk as eagerly of it outside working hours as any scientist might speak of his investigations, get thrills first hand from hunting, difficulties overcome, beautiful nuggets uncovered, people met unexpectedly, and are conscious always of the joy of being their own bosses and guiding their own destinies.[16]

These were the frontier virtues that Marshall would later attempt to preserve by arguing against federal schemes to develop Alaska. He was witnessing a way of life that, while not desired by the majority, was precious to those who chose it. There were few places left, even in the 1930s, where such a life could be lived. Were they not worth preserving?

Most of the sourdoughs thought so. Marshall listened to each of the white adults in the region speak about his life in the Koyukuk. He concluded that fifty-four of them were happy, twelve were unhappy, and nine were ambivalent.[17]

Those who were happy usually listed personal freedom, lack of rules and regulations, and beautiful scenery as the prime reasons for their contentment. Pete Haslem, who left a job driving a trolley car on Coney Island to join the gold rush in 1898, spoke about independence: "Outside you've got your nose to the grindstone all the time," he explained, "and the boss is looking down your neck." Prospecting was a gamble, "but you've always got expectations and that means a lot."[18]

Those who were unhappy usually longed for the creature comforts available Outside. Then, too, there were the mosquitoes and the cold.

"Summertime the mosquitoes are suicide," one crusty prospector told Marshall, "and winter time you're always running risk of losing your hands or feet. If I ever made a stake I'd get out of here quick as I could."[19]

Marshall was also keenly interested in the Eskimos of the region, whose culture was a mix of ancient native customs and newly introduced white men's practices. Their patriarch was a sixty-five-year-old man named Big Jim.

Jim's status derived from his competence at obtaining furs, meat, and other essentials. In the communal Eskimo culture, goods acquired by one individual were considered the property of everyone. Enormously industrious, Jim contributed more caribou hides and moose meat than anyone else. In addition, he had a reputation for wisdom and kindness.

Jim and his wife, Nakuchluk, lived in a clean, spacious cabin that was the center of Eskimo winter activity in Wiseman. Marshall often visited this cabin after supper to chat with the Eskimos and learn about their customs.

Entering Jim's house through a vestibule in the front, he would be greeted warmly by Jim and several others who had settled in for the evening's conversation. At one end of the cabin, the women would be seated on the floor, working patiently, scraping animal skins with instruments made of bone, iron, or obsidian. Some would be smoking pipes, others humming contentedly to themselves.

In the center of the room, facing the women, would be three or four men seated on chairs—Jim Oxadak, Arctic Johnny, Harry Snowden perhaps. If Big Jim happened to be eating some soup, the liquid would be seeping through a hole in the side of his mouth; he had once had two such holes, one on each side, used for inserting ivory ornaments when he danced.*[20]

---

* Marshall's description of Big Jim evoked a humorous letter from Supreme Court Justice Benjamin Cordozo, a friend of the Marshall family, "I have just reached the point in your narrative," Cordozo wrote, "where you have made an evening call at the cabin of Big Jim. I thought perhaps I could put up with him till I found that the soup oozed out of holes on either side of his mouth. Then I abjured him altogether. Let him not come to visit me here in Babylon."[21]

One evening Marshall entered the cabin to find Jim completely engrossed in one of the favorite Eskimo pastimes—recounting a funny story. In this particular case Marshall could not follow the plot, for it was being told in the complicated Eskimo language. But it was obviously funny, for Jim could barely get through it without losing himself in laughter, and the listeners were equally amused. The whole room was reeling with laughter. Jim's wife, Naku-chluk, was in such hysterics that Marshall thought she would choke. He later learned that the story was about an old Eskimo who spilled an enormous pancake on his head while trying to flip it.[22]

Marshall believed that the Koyukukers—both Eskimo and white—were exceptionally intelligent. To prove his point, he gave the Stanford-Binet intelligence test to everybody who was willing and able to take it. Among Eskimos, the adults and older children scored lower than average on the test. This, Marshall thought, was easily explained by cultural differences between them and the people for whom the test was actually designed. The younger Eskimo children—aged three to nine—had received instruction in English and other subjects commonly taught in American schools. They scored exceptionally high. Twenty-two percent of them were in the "Very Superior" class, whereas only seven percent of American children Outside scored that high.[23]

Marshall observed also that the Eskimo language was extremely complex, that many Eskimos picked up English very fast, and that many were remarkably good at reading and making maps. A woman named Ekok, who had no experience with maps, once drew him a detailed picture of the Alatna River from memory, plotting every bend and twist with great accuracy.[24]

The white prospectors, Marshall thought, were also uncommonly bright. Only eight of the seventy-seven white adults had a high school or better education. Yet those willing to take the I.Q. test did far better than average. Eighty-three percent of them knew fifty-five or more words out of one hundred on the vocabulary test, whereas fifty-five was only the *average* among American

adults Outside. Marshall believed this to be the result of "an amazing variety of reading superimposed on vigorous intelligences." He
counted subscriptions to seventy-six different magazines in the
region, most of which were passed around liberally. The Pioneers
of Alaska had a much-used library in Wiseman, and Marshall was
forever loaning his own books to the Wisemanites.[25]

And finally, Marshall thought there was a kind of natural selection at work in the Arctic. "The work of the Koyukuk is so varied,
including as it does for most men the diverse occupations of mining, sledding, boating, hunting, trapping, fishing, gardening and
logging, that unless a man has better than normal ability he will be
swamped under the casual necessities of life."[26]

These observations are persuasive, yet there are several problems with them, some of which Marshall recognized and others he
did not. The Eskimo children's I.Q. tests, for example, could well
have been influenced by Marshall's rapport with them. He admitted this, noting that the tests were never given until the children "had come to make my cabin a regular playground, and had
ridden piggyback hundreds of yards on my shoulders." Also, all of
these children were taught in the same school by the same teacher.
Marshall noted that the children were "without exception enthusiastic about school." So their high I.Q. scores may have been as
much a reflection of their education as their natural intelligence.[27]

Marshall said that he himself was "doubtful of the value of mental tests." And he may have been trying to prove only that Eskimos
should not be dismissed as simple-minded. But he strongly implied that they are *more* intelligent than the average person. He
noted approvingly, for example, in *Arctic Village:* "Both the present
Wiseman teacher and her predecessor agreed that the Eskimo children were on the average brighter than the white children they had
taught Outside." This leads to an intellectual quagmire for anyone
as liberal as Marshall. For if one race is smarter than another, then
logically some races would have to be *slower* than others. And that
is the stuff on which is based the racial prejudice and discrimination which Marshall despised. He never recognized this difficulty
openly.[28]

In regard to the white residents, there was a problem in that thirty-two of the seventy-seven white adults refused to take the test. Marshall did not say whether this was comparable to the proportion of Outsiders who might also be expected to refuse or in some way avoid the test. But certainly many who refused were afraid (or in fact *knew*) that they would do poorly on it.[29]

Of those who did take the test, there is no question that several were well read. But further conclusions about the interaction between their environment and their intelligence, however interesting, are speculative at best. Even a scientist works from a personal point of view, and Marshall's was romantic.

The Wisemanites loved to dance. Special dancing celebrations were held on Independence Day, Christmas, Election Day, and other holidays. Prospectors began drifting into town as much as a week prior to one of these holidays, huddling together in conversation, comparing notes on their respective claims. So animated were these discussions that they reminded Marshall of scientists discussing their research. "Only I think," he reported, "perhaps there was more genuine interest and the person who was being told about another's work was not so eager to inject at any cost a recital of his own accomplishments."[30]

The dances themselves were held either at the roadhouse or the Pioneer Hall. The women and men usually sat on opposite sides of the room, while the children frolicked around the entire floor.

The women, mostly Eskimos, came dressed in their best cotton-print dresses, cotton stockings, and beaded moccasins. They were outnumbered two to one by the men, who dressed less formally.[31]

The dances often lasted till breakfast-time the following morning. There were eleven major dances held while Marshall was in Wiseman, and he calculated their average length at ten hours and fifty-five minutes. For the outnumbered women, this meant eleven hours of nonstop dancing. When Marshall witnessed his first major dance, held on Election Day 1930, he thought the continuous dancing of the women was "one of the greatest marvels of stamina I had ever witnessed." But, he explained, "I was inexperienced then and thought ten hours constituted a long dance."[32]

The men got off easier. Since there were twice as many of them, they could sit out about half of the dances, thereby pacing themselves for the long evening.

Once the dances got underway, the participants were caught up in a magical world that seemed to create its own energy. Marshall described this atmosphere well in *Arctic Village:*

> There was something pleasantly exotic in watching the dancers glide along the smooth, spruce floor with their whole preoccupation in having an exuberant time. The unpretentious dresses of the women, and the prevalent flannel shirts and overalls of the men fitted ideally with the simple good humor which pervaded the entire hall. Three out of every four people were smiling broadly as they moved rhythmically past, and loud chuckles and giggles frequently rose above the music of the phonograph. They did not dance for social prestige, for show, for duty. They danced because it was the greatest joy in the world at that precise moment. "I could dance if I didn't have any leg at all," said Ashuwaruk with a wrenched ankle. "I could dance if I was dying."[33]

Marshall himself took great pleasure in these dances. Not graceful, he nevertheless danced away many an Arctic night in the secure, uncritical company of his Koyukuk friends. When he finally left the Arctic, he brought home a love for dancing that lasted the rest of his life.

In Wiseman, Marshall's favorite dance partner was Ekok, the Eskimo woman who once had drawn him a detailed map of the Alatna River. Marshall, by his own admission, had a crush on her. In *Arctic Village,* he briefly told her life story:

As a child, Ekok had been extremely beautiful; she could have had her pick of men in the Koyukuk. Through an unfortunate chain of events, however, she wound up married to a man she did not really love. But she persevered, stayed with her husband and gave birth to five healthy children.

During her sixth pregnancy she ran into trouble. Her husband had by then acquired from the whites a taste for whiskey and gambling. As a result, he failed to provide her with much to eat, and her sixth child, a girl, was sickly from birth. Ekok carried on without complaining; but during the spring of 1930, shortly after Marshall's arrival for his full year in the Arctic, she was forced to send the toddler out to a hospital in Tanana. The day the baby left on the plane, Ekok was heartbroken.

That evening the townspeople held a dance to cheer her up. Marshall asked her to dance. "Sure!" she said. "It's no use sitting here hating myself." But she cried on his shoulder throughout the waltz, knowing that she would never see her daughter again.[34]

"I have never known anyone of any race so capable of adjusting to cruel necessities and yet so sensitive to fine values," Marshall wrote of her in *Alaska Wilderness*. Another time, he enclosed her picture in a letter to a friend and described her as "the remarkably intelligent, amazingly beautiful Eskimo girl with whom, of course, I fell violently in love. Isn't she swell and do you blame me?"[35]

But then, as usual, he turned to other topics and never explained what kind of relationship he had with Ekok. We know only that he greatly admired her and considered her a fine friend.

During the spring and summer of 1930, Marshall took two exploring trips with a trapper named Ernie Johnson. According to Marshall, Johnson was the premier woodsman in the Koyukuk, a man who spent almost all of his time alone in the bush. He had high cheekbones, a round face, and short brown hair. Born in Sweden fifty years before, he had drifted into the Koyukuk during the gold rush of the early 1900s. He stayed there, he said, "because I like it out here among these ruggedy mountains better than anything else in the world." Marshall enjoyed his company very much.[36]

Their first expedition was a twenty-six day dogsledding trip on which they followed the Clear River to its source near the Arctic Divide. The trip had been stimulated by an argument as to whether the Clear River actually "headed against" the divide. Ernie thought it did and Bob thought it didn't.

Most of the days on this trip were cold and crystal clear, creating a visual effect that Marshall found stunning. It was a world, he noted, "of three pure, unblended colors... —the base of fresh, white snow, the dark, green spruce trees set upon it, and the clear blue sky as a covering."[37]

They camped in temperatures as cold as thirty below. The usual procedure was for Ernie to begin stamping down an area in the snow large enough to place their nine-foot by nine-foot canvas tent, plus a little room left over to walk around in. Then he would pitch the tent while Marshall cut down a green spruce. The tree was then cut into blocks to support the stove, while the spruce boughs were spread around to cover the snow inside the otherwise floorless tent.

The stove would have been filled that morning with kindling so that as soon as it was placed on the blocks and the stovepipe attached, a fire could be started. To cook, snow had to be melted, for there is very little free-flowing water in the Arctic in winter.

Next the dogs had to be cared for. Spruce bough beds had to be cut for them; they had to be unharnessed and leashed to trees; they had to be fed. Finally, there was supper to be cooked, dishes to be washed, and snowshoes to be repaired. And, "most tedious of all" for Marshall, was the nightly task of "crawling head-first in my sleeping bag to change my panchromatic films in total darkness."[38]

For many people these procedures, complicated by the subzero temperatures, would be a lot like self-torture. But to Bob and Ernie they were a small price to pay. Marshall called the evenings "very pleasant."

After a supper expertly prepared by Ernie of boiled sheep steak, vegetables, macaroni, and fruit, they would crawl into their sleeping bags for a few minutes of philosophizing before going to sleep. Outside Alaska, the depression was on, so they talked a lot about economics. Marshall defended socialism and Ernie disagreed. Marshall regarded this as "fortunate" because it led to "stimulating arguments on that subject where otherwise we could only have had tedious agreement."[39]

By March 15 they were near the source of the Clear River. They

Marshall and Nutirwik (Harry Snowden) in the Brooks Range (Photograph courtesy of The Bancroft Library, University of California, Berkeley)

climbed to the head of a tributary and agreed that Ernie had been right, for they seemed to be standing on the divide. For Marshall, this was a special thrill:

> I do not know what may be the supreme exultation of which a person is capable, but it came for me that moment I crossed the skyline and gazed over into the winter-buried mystery of the Arctic, where

136

great, barren peaks rose into the deep blue of the northern sky, where valleys, devoid even of willows, lead far into unknown canyons.[40]

But later that year, on another trip, Marshall learned that he and Ernie had made a mistake; they had not been standing on the Arctic Divide, but on the pass between the Clear and Hammond rivers. The Arctic Divide is farther north. (Thus Marshall turned out to have won their little argument.) In honor of their error, Bob named the pass and the creek flowing eastward from it Kinnorutin, Kobuk for "you are crazy." The knowledge of their mistake, however, never diminished the memory of that day for Marshall. Several years later he wrote to Ernie, "In many ways the greatest one day I have ever spent was the day we snowshoed up to the very head of Clear River and looked down over the top into the Hammond River watershed. The thrill of that look into unknown country and the thrill of being the first people ever reaching the head of a great river, are things that stand out forever in a person's memory."[41]

Marshall's second expedition with Ernie Johnson was a seven-week voyage that spanned most of July and August 1931. On this trip they explored the Alatna and John rivers, two major tributaries of the Koyukuk that lie to the west of Marshall's earlier explorations. This time they reached the Arctic Divide, where they spent two days climbing peaks, taking photographs, and surveying the terrain. Although their instruments were relatively crude, the work was exciting. "Some day," Marshall wrote, "when it is accurately mapped by transit or airplane, a number of our creeks and mountains no doubt will be several miles off. But no man by high-powered instruments and machines can ever get the thrill which we got with our pocket compass and our field glasses as we made the first rough map of an unknown empire."[42]

Another day, while exploring a stream they had named Loon Creek, they came to an especially beautiful mountain lake. Marshall's description of it reflects the great thrill he got from wilderness exploration:

137

Nothing I had ever seen, Yosemite or the Grand Canyon or Mount McKinley rising from Susitna, had given me such a sense of immensity as this virgin lake lying in a great cleft in the surface of the earth with mountain slopes and waterfalls tumbling from beyond the limits of visibility. We walked up the right shore among bare rocks intermingled with meadows of bright lichen, while large flocks of ducks bobbed peacefully and unmindful of us on the water of the lake, and four loons were singing that rich, wild music which they have added to the beautiful melodies of earth. No sight or sound or smell or feeling even remotely hinted of men or their creations. It seemed as if time had dropped away a million years and we were back in a primordial world.[43]

A week later they were in Bettles, the little Koyukuk community downriver from Wiseman. The town was crowded with prospectors coming in from their claims to get their winter supplies before freeze-up. All together there were eighteen people in town—almost a mob by Koyukuk standards.

Marshall was especially glad to see Ekok, his Eskimo lady friend, who had just come down the river after taking care of his scientific instruments for six weeks in Wiseman. They enjoyed several nights of dancing in Bettles. On the last evening, Marshall reported, "we just kept on and on, with everyone getting more energetic as the dance progressed. The evening ended at four in the morning on a final dance with Ekok to the tune of *My Blue Heaven*."[44]

Next day Bob and Ernie were off for Wiseman. It was August 22 and autumn was in the air. The cottonwoods and willows lining the Koyukuk were already bright gold. As they moved up the river in Ernie's homemade motorboat, it occured to Marshall that he would soon be leaving the Arctic. While in Bettles he had read more about the great economic depression that was beseiging the industrialized countries of the world. It appeared that in many places the misery had reached unprecedented proportions. Yet out there in the Arctic wilderness, beyond what most people considered to be the civilized world, he had seen "no unemployment, no starvation, no slums, no crowding, and no warfare." It was not going to be easy to leave, and Marshall showed his reluctance the following evening.[45]

It was eight P.M. and they were just two hours from Wiseman. There was plenty of light remaining; they could make it easily. But Marshall announced he did not want to go in. They had been out for forty-nine nights, and he wanted to make it an even fifty.

This was fine with Ernie, who pulled the boat over to a gravel bar. They pitched their camp under a clump of spruces above the riverbank. They ate a lamb stew. The air grew cold. They moved up close to the fire. A semi-darkness enveloped them, dark enough that a few stars twinkled overhead.

"We didn't say very much sitting there," Bob wrote,

> You don't when it is your last camp with a companion who has shared the most perfect summer of a lifetime. We just sat, with a feeling warmer than the crackling fire, exulting in the sharp-edged pattern which the mountain walls cut against the northern sky; listening to the peaceful turmoil of the arctic river with its infinite variations in rhythm and tone; smelling the luxuriance of arctic valleys; feeling the wholesome cleanliness of arctic breezes blowing on cheeks and hair.[46]

Marshall left the Arctic a few days later. On his way home he had a strange experience in Seattle. While eating breakfast in a restaurant, he read in the newspaper that Dr. Harry Olmsted, husband of Virginia (Boutelle) Olmsted, his old friend from Missoula, had just died of polio. He had visited the Olmsteds on his way to Alaska just a little over a year before. He contacted Virginia to offer condolences, and in the next few years grew closer to her than before. She would later provide insight into Marshall's behavior and health at the time of his own death.[47]

9

Writer and Socialist (1931–1933)

◆ ———————————————————————— ◆

> I am all for Pinchot now, and shall certainly support him on the basis
> of his forestry and his niece.
>
> Bob Marshall to Raphael Zon

Bob Marshall returned to the East Coast in late September 1931. He was now thirty years old. He rented a twelve-by-sixteen-foot room on the top floor of an apartment building in Baltimore and went to work on his book about the Koyukuk people. The book, however, was not nearly enough to keep him busy. He soon resumed his attempts to shake up American forestry.[1]

Marshall was concerned that no forestry publication was addressing the issue of deforestation. To prove his point, he analyzed all the articles for 1930 and 1931 that appeared in *American Forests*, the magazine of the American Forestry Association. Of 351 articles, he interpreted only twenty-seven, or eight percent, as "discussing forestry and forest conservation problems." The majority, in Marshall's view, were general outdoor articles more appropriate to other magazines. He reported these findings in a letter to the AFA's president, George D. Pratt. His figures, Marshall said, showed how generally remiss the AFA was in addressing serious forestry problems—in particular, the forest-devastation problem and the need to regulate private lumbermen.[2]

Pratt, of course, responded by defending his organization. The magazine had for many years discussed "the old controversy of federal regulation of the lumbermen." But, Pratt continued, "under present economic conditions which are threatening the very life of the forest industry, it seems to me a much more constructive course to help the industry get on its feet and into a position where forestry can be demanded and widely practiced."[3]

Pratt's response probably reflected the general consensus among foresters at the time. But if Marshall got no satisfaction from Pratt's reply, he at least got encouragement from his friend Gifford Pinchot. He sent Pinchot a copy of the letter to Pratt. The Governor, who always had a flair for the dramatic, came back with the following:

> Your letter to Pratt is a masterpiece. Any time you get ready to resign [from the AFA] let me resign with you at the same time, and let's get a few others to join with us, and you write a statement of the reasons for giving to the press. I think nothing could be better than that and I am with you until the cows come home.[4]

Neither of them resigned, however.

Bob pursued a variety of other activities in the spring and summer of 1932. In April he accepted an invitation to serve on a committee to dedicate a memorial to his father at the forestry college in Syracuse. In May he spoke to the Washington section of the Society of American Foresters on "the 'Wilderness of the Koyukuk' and 'the Wilderness at Home.' " "It will give me a chance to re-emphasize the wilderness idea again," he said. "During the past few years, it seems most of the outdoor people have come around to see it, but still almost nothing has been done to preserve large vestiges of the primitive."[5]

He found time also to enjoy the wilderness himself. In July 1932 he took the hike in the Adirondacks on which he broke the single-day peak-bagging record. There had developed an avid but friendly competition in, as one hiker called it, "the making of ex-

peditious Adirondack expeditions." Bob thought it was great fun
as long as it didn't get too organized. A few months after breaking
the record (and by which time his own had in turn been broken) he
was invited to a conference to establish rules for the sport. He
replied that he would like to meet some of the other hikers, but
couldn't make it. Then he said:

> As for making standards for record climbing, I'm afraid that that is a
> rather futile pastime, because record climbing loses its significance
> as soon as it ceases to be merely an exhilaration thoroughly paying
> for itself, regardless of records established, and becomes just an ef-
> fort for records.[6]

But if the record was secondary, why was it more fun for Marshall to climb fourteen peaks in a hurry than one peak leisurely?
Frank Graham, Jr., in his history of the Adirondack Park, found
"something a little disturbing in all this bustling from one mountain peak to another.... Pull up a pumpkin and sit down for a
while, one wants to say to Marshall." And several foresters, according to James P. Gilligan, thought Marshall "had tremendous inner
conflicts of personality" and that his long hikes and other activities
"represented efforts to establish and prove himself."[7]

There's no question that Marshall drove himself hard. But judg-
ing from his papers and from interviews with people who knew
him well, he was no more or less neurotic than the rest of us. A better explanation may be found in some recent discoveries in exercise physiology and humanistic psychology. It must be remembered that Marshall had enormous energy. Besides being a scientist, naturalist, and romantic, he was an athlete. He played all
kinds of sports throughout his childhood; he ran track and cross-
country in college. His long-distance hikes—on which he alterna-
ted between fast walking and running—were perfect examples of
what is now called aerobic exercise. In aerobics, your heart and
lungs work harder than normal for an extended period of time, but
never hard enough to make you totally out of breath (as you would
if you sprinted all-out). There is strong evidence that some aerobic

exercisers experience a "runner's high." This is a mildly euphoric feeling in which, during the course of a long run, swim, or fast walk, exercisers feel extremely relaxed and yet very attuned to their surroundings.[8]

There is evidence, furthermore, that a pleasing environment is especially conducive to this euphoria. The psychologist Abraham Maslow (along with others) believed that many people have "peak experiences." These experiences, Maslow wrote, are "something like mystic experiences, moments of great awe, moments of the most intense happiness or even rapture, ecstasy or bliss." They occur, Maslow said, in a variety of situations, including "moments of fusion with nature (in a forest, on a seashore, mountains, etc.)" and "from certain athletic experiences." A great number of Marshall's outdoor descriptions reflect exactly this kind of ecstasy and awe. It seems likely, if not provable, that the combination of aerobic exercise and a pristine environment frequently gave Marshall some kind of "peak experience." It put him in a state of mind that he found incomparably pleasurable.[9]

He found such pleasure in late July of the same year, when he went to Maine and climbed Mount Katahdin. He later told Maine governor Percival Baxter that he "remember[ed] vividly the grand spectacle looking northwest from its summit toward what [was then] the largest forest area in the United States without any roads in it."[10]

Earlier that year, Senator Royal Copeland of New York had introduced a resolution in the United States Senate asking the Forest Service for a thorough analysis of the forest situation. The resolution passed, and Earle Clapp, head of the Forest Service's Branch of Research, began mobilizing his resources to produce what would come to be known as the Copeland Report.[11]

Clapp saw the assignment as an opportunity to initiate badly needed reforms in the forest-products industry and make a case for a broader vision of forest management nationwide. He asked Marshall to write the sections on forest recreation. "Unquestionably," he told Marshall, "we ought to paint a broad picture of the part which forests can and should play in the recreation movement in the United States. . . . We shall overlook a wonderful opportunity if we do not go farther than anyone hitherto has attempted to go."[12]

Marshall accepted. Like Clapp, he saw his chance to advocate reforms. In particular, he could plug three of his favorite causes: wilderness preservation, rational planning, and the recognition of recreation as a forest value equal in importance to the manufacture of plywood or the grazing of Herefords. He moved to Washington, D.C., in September 1932, rented a room at 2145 C St., Northwest, and began working on the project.[13]

One of the first things he did was to compile a list of roadless areas remaining in the United States. It consisted of thirty-eight established or potential wilderness areas. The U.S. Forest Service was the primary administrator of twenty of these and had partial ownership of three others. So Marshall sent his data to L. F. Kneipp, the official in charge of the Forest Service's Primitive Area system. Marshall asked Kneipp to designate as "primitive" all the areas on his list that had not been so designated already. Kneipp passed along the request to regional foresters, who responded with the enthusiasm of the stone faces on Easter Island. Most of them felt the Primitive System was just about complete. It had grown steadily to sixty-three areas, totaling 8.4 million acres of federal land. That seemed like enough. Besides, they said, Bob Marshall's recommended areas were either too fire-prone (and thus needed fire-truck trails), too valuable for timber or minerals, too developed already to meet primitive standards, or too heavily grazed by sheep.[14]

Marshall, consequently, found himself badgering individual local foresters to set aside areas. A few months later, for example, he wrote to Meyer Wolff in Missoula: "I do wish that you would hurry up and get that entire country from the Locksaw River to the southern border of Region One [Northern Rockies] set aside as wilderness before some damn fool chamber of commerce or some nonsensical organizer of unemployed demands a useless highway to provide work and a market for hotdogs and gasoline."[15]

Marshall's concern with "useless highways" was not unfounded.

In Pinchot's time there had been 5,000 miles of roads in the national forests; by 1930 there were 42,000 miles, and road-building funds were increasing rapidly.[16]

While working on the Copeland Report, Bob kept in touch with several Alaskan friends. He sent Big Jim a gas lamp and told him that the people in Washington were all very curious about Eskimos. "I tell them all that the Eskimos know how to live better than most white men, but most of them won't believe me."[17]

In October, he learned that Jennie Suckik, a teenage Eskimo girl whose artistic ability he admired, had tuberculosis. He sent Ike Spinks fifty dollars to buy her milk, eggs, cod liver oil, and fruit. Later, when Jennie got worse, he sent $300 to get her into a hospital. She died, however, in January 1933, and Bob was deeply saddened. He felt especially sorry for Jennie's parents, to whom, as he observed, she had been "the single joy in their lives."[18]

Marshall finished his work on the Copeland Report around the end of December 1932. The full report ran to two volumes and 1,677 pages. Marshall wrote three chapters and helped indirectly with several others. He considered it "the best piece of forestry work I have yet done."[19]

His most important chapter was called "The Forest for Recreation." In it he discussed everything from the economics of outdoor recreation to the various reasons why people visit forests. He thought, typically, that a major reason was the pursuit of beauty. In a paragraph fairly dripping with nineteenth century romanticism, he said:

> The joy which [pursuers of beauty] derive from a sunset across some forest lake, from the unfathomable immensity of the panorama off some wilderness summit, from the unmarred splendor of a virgin forest, is not essentially different from what another esthete might derive from the paintings of Rembrandt, from the sculpture of Rodin, from the music of Beethoven, from the drama of Shakespeare, or from the poetry of Keats.[20]

146

He acknowledged, however, that there were many other things people sought in the forest. The important thing was to develop a "rational program" for forest recreation that would provide a balance of opportunities. To secure such a balance, and also to clean up the rather haphazard system of nomenclature then in use for recreational areas, Marshall proposed a system of classifying such areas into seven types.

His first three types—to be called Superlative, Primeval, and Wilderness Areas—were lands that should be kept essentially in their natural condition. Superlative Areas were the few most "unsurpassing and stupendous" natural phenomena—the Yosemites, the Yellowstones, the Grand Canyons. Primeval Areas were to be samples of virgin forests. Wilderness Areas could be any roadless tracts which still retained their basic primitive character and were big enough for somebody to travel in for two weeks "without crossing his own tracks." Marshall proposed that a total of 22.5 million acres be set aside for these three types of areas.

His other four categories—Roadside, Campsite, Residence, and Outing Areas—were parcels on which the natural setting would be manipulated to a far greater degree. Other types of activities, such as timber cutting, might take place on or close to these areas, but in a manner compatible with their recreational uses.[21]

Marshall recommended a combined total of forty-five million acres for these seven types of recreational areas. This represented only nine percent of the 506 million acres of commercial timberland in the United States—a share he thought was reasonable.[22]

The chapter not only reflected Marshall's growing concern about wilderness preservation but established him as a prominent expert in forest recreation generally. Two of his observations were especially insightful. One was that forests often need to be saved as much *from* recreationists as *for* them.

The damage to the forest comes from several sources. Small trees are cut down for fuel and tent poles. Reproduction and underbrush which gets in the way is removed. Trees and the lesser vegetation are killed by abrasion. Gas and oil leaking from cars onto the forest

147

floor seriously injures all forms of plant life. Finally, the mere constant tramping on the forest floor kills the moisture-absorbing ground cover, and packs down the soil so firmly that proper aeration for the roots of the trees becomes impossible.[23]

The other was that forest lands *not* being used for recreation would have to be better managed. For if those lands could not be made to meet, year after year, the nation's demands for wood products, "it is almost certain that the aesthetic and inspirational values will be sacrificed."[24]

The full Copeland Report was published in March 1933. It declared the forest situation "a major national problem" and put most of the blame on the private forest industry. It recommended a massive public forest-land acquisition program and extensive regulation of private timber cutting. Though a comprehensive legislative package to implement its recommendations never passed, the report influenced a great deal of discussion in subsequent years and is considered a landmark in the evolution of American forest policy. Marshall thought it was so important that he personally sent copies to several newsmen, urging them to publicize it.[25]

Meanwhile the Great Depression was getting worse. Over eight million people were unemployed. Banks were failing all over the country. Security, commodity, and farm prices were plunging in a deflationary spiral that seemed out of control. In major cities, people were living in squalid homes built of tin, tarpaper, old cars, and cardboard boxes.[26]

In November 1932, just two months after Marshall arrived in Washington, the American people responded predictably by voting Herbert Hoover out of office and replacing him with Democrat Franklin D. Roosevelt. For the rest of the decade, Roosevelt directed one of the most liberal and active administrations in the country's history. Major programs or reforms were implemented in virtually every sphere of life: housing, banking, employment, labor, public works, farming, social security, utilities, and—not least—the conservation of natural resources. It was called the New

Deal, and Bob Marshall, through his work on the Copeland Report, was part of it right from the start.

The New Deal was a hodgepodge of programs implemented under the general theory that it was better to try *something* than to stand by idle while the country fell apart. There was no clearly defined New Deal ideology. There were, however, several basic beliefs that most New Dealers,—including Marshall—shared. One was that government should own and operate certain natural resources. Another was that large industries needed strict regulation. A third was that workers deserved a better shake than they were then getting. A fourth was that government *should* redistribute wealth through social programs.[27]

Marshall was a strong advocate for all of these positions. But he thought Roosevelt was too timid. As he told a friend shortly after the New Deal began:

> Mr. Roosevelt has not yet shown any understanding of the fact that the only possible way to get us out of this depression under a capitalistic order is for the Government to dump in a tremendous additional purchasing power by a huge public works program, which will not cut wage scales, but if anything raise them.[28]

This, he admitted, would cause inflation, but he saw no better alternative. Then he added, "Of course, I don't believe that any of this in the long run will help and I still feel that the only eventual solution will be Socialism."[29]

In fact, by the winter of 1932–33, Marshall clearly considered himself a socialist. "I wish very sincerely," he told another correspondent, "that Socialism could be put into effect right away and the profit system eliminated." Such statements are revealing of both Marshall and his times. In the 1930s, capitalism was like a drowning man going under for the third time. Many bright and patriotic people thought the best thing to do was to let it drown and find something else. Socialists were common, and the word "socialist" itself had a less negative connotation than it would have in later years. Marshall, of course, characteristically took a strong—and sometimes radical—position.[30]

149

On the other hand, one can't escape feeling that in this case he jumped too quickly for a panacea. His economic arguments, though sincere and articulate, don't ring quite as true as his arguments for wilderness. The latter seem to come from the heart; the former, from a book.

In early January 1933, Marshall returned from a trip to St. Paul, Minnesota, and found a telegram from Governor Pinchot waiting for him. Pinchot had just visited President-elect Roosevelt at FDR's Hyde Park home; FDR had asked him to draw up a statement for national forest policy. Pinchot, "who knew enough to know that he didn't know anything about forestry any more," wanted Marshall to draft the statement for him.[31]

"He limited me to six double-spaced pages," Bob told a friend. "I stressed two things: a huge public acquisition program; and the use of the unemployed in an immense way for protection, fire proofing, improvement cuttings, planting, erosion control, improvements (roads, trails, fire towers, etc.), and recreational developments."[32]

Pinchot at first thought that Marshall dismissed too quickly the option of regulating private timber operations. But Bob "argued him out of regulation with surprising ease" by asserting that the lumber companies were too close to bankruptcy to be influenced by threats of financial penalties. Besides, Marshall argued, if the companies ever did become wealthy again, they would soon control the regulating agency.[33] According to Marshall, Pinchot replied, "I have argued for [regulated private] forestry for thirty years, but I am convinced that you are right—we need something more."[34]

Marshall made several visits to see Pinchot on this matter. His admiration for the retired Chief continued to grow, as he revealed in a letter to Raphael Zon:

> This was really the nicest visit I've ever had with old Gifford. As a matter of fact he still seems remarkably young for his sixty-eight years. I spent the night at their house, and he came bounding up the stairs, two steps at a time, when he got home from an Archeological

Dinner he had to attend to greet me and have me come down to the living room.

Pinchot, moreover, was not adverse to playing the role of matchmaker for a couple of his favorite young single people. As Marshall related it:

> The Pinchots were certainly perfect hosts. They not only provided me with two rooms and a bath (and I had forgotten my pajamas at that), but a most beautiful niece named Rosalyn, and then they had the decency to retire at 9:30, leaving the evening to the beautiful Rosalyn and myself. So, I am all for Pinchot now, and shall certainly support him on the basis of his forestry and his niece.[35]

Marshall and Rosalyn apparently dated several times. About a month after meeting her, Marshall wrote Zon that he had seen his twenty-first movie *(Trouble in Paradise)* "with Gifford Pinchot's beautiful niece Rosalyn and found the niece more exciting than the movie."[36]

Marshall also had an interesting talk with Pinchot one evening about socialism. He was surprised that the Governor had given it considerable thought. Pinchot told Marshall that socialism couldn't be fully implemented with farmers and laborers as unorganized as they were. Marshall thought this was a good point, further evidence of Pinchot's keen insight. "What a splendid service he might do," Marshall concluded, "if during the final two years of public life he would step out completely and fearlessly as a thoroughgoing Socialist."[37]

Pinchot never went that far, but he did submit Marshall's statement on forest policy to Roosevelt in late January. The statement said that private forestry had "failed the world over" and recommended a large-scale program of public forest acquisition. But Roosevelt chose instead to regulate private lumbermen through the pending National Industrial Recovery Act.[38]

In January 1933, Marshall began writing a book that he hoped would popularize the need for forest reform. It became his primary work for a couple of months. His leisure was as unleisurely as ever.

He became active in the Tenants Unemployed League of the District of Columbia, a group to help unemployed people with severe housing problems. He joined a fight against cuts in federal aid to scientific research, and he served as chairman of the Washington branch of the American Civil Liberties Union. In March 1933 he was briefly arrested for participating in a United Front demonstration. Being with the ACLU, he said, "made it easy next day to lead a protest on libertarian grounds agains the action of the police who arrested 38 of the demonstrators and clubbed seven of them so severely that they had to go to the hospital."[39]

He also began to date Georgia Engelhard, a professional portrait painter and leading woman mountaineer. Climbing extensively in the American and Canadian Rockies, she made the first ascent of Helmet Peak in Colorado, and according to a 1934 *American Magazine* article, she held "the Canadian-American Alpine Club record for roping her way up and down 38 peaks in one season." These exploits earned her the dubious distinction of endorsing Camel cigarettes in magazines.[40]

Bob met her through Justice Cordozo, who had been a law partner of her father's. She and Bob took several hikes together in the Adirondacks and the Washington, D.C., area. He kept a chart titled "Walks of Georgia Engelhard & Bob Marshall," which shows that they took fifteen hikes between February and July, 1933. The longest, near Harpers Ferry, West Virginia, was twenty-eight miles on a stormy day.[41]

Engelhard was slender, with reddish brown hair and a happy smile. Marshall enjoyed her company a great deal, but, as usual, he did not tell many details about their relationship. The most he said was this, in a letter to a friend in July 1933:

I have just wound up a delightful affair with another beautiful red-headed girl by two weeks of mountain climbing in which she was fully as good as I. That is over, and we had six swell months out of which we were together at least forty different days visiting back and forth between New York and Washington, and just now together at Saranac Lake.[42]

Georgia Engelhard (Photograph courtesy Georgia Engelhard Cromwell)

Why he had to "wind up" the affair, he doesn't say. In fact, he did not wind it up at all, but continued to see Engelhard as often as possible in the next four years, and grew increasingly fond of her.

Marshall also met some interesting men as he worked the social circuit in Washington. One evening in February 1933, he was entertained at the home of Supreme Court Justice Louis Brandeis. He was not overly impressed with Brandeis. He told Raphael Zon, somewhat arrogantly:

153

[Brandeis gave me] the tritest tirade I've ever heard against forest destruction. . . . He actually quoted "I will lift mine eyes unto the fields" and acted as if he thought it had never been used before in connection with forestry. Isn't it amazing that such a brilliant and great man should be thirty years behind the times on so many subjects?[43]

He was more impressed with Vilhjalmur Stefansson, whom he met a couple of months later. Stefansson was an explorer who once spent a year dogsledding around the Arctic Ocean while the rest of the world assumed he was dead. Marshall had long admired him. "I certainly want to tell you how much I enjoyed that brief meeting with you last week," Marshall told him. "After that long period of hoping and desiring, it measured up to all expectations." [44]

Another important acquaintance was John Collier, executive secretary of the American Indian Defense Association. Collier was a visionary reformer who dedicated most of his life to preserving American Indian cultures. For over a decade he had been fighting the federal government's policy of trying to "assimilate" Indians into white-American culture. In 1928, he had worked with Louis Marshall fighting a water project in the Rio Grande valley which would have stolen water rights from the Rio Grande Pueblo Indians. Working with the elder Marshall, he later said, was "an intellectual lesson to myself, and a moral exaltation."[45]

It is not clear exactly when Collier met Bob Marshall, but they seem to have known each other by January 1933 because by that time Bob had started to write letters in support of Collier's bid to become Commissioner of Indian Affairs in the new administration. Collier, Marshall wrote in one such letter, "has a genuine anthropologist's understanding of the Indians. He is not interested in them for the purpose of converting them to the white man's way of life, but wants to give their own splendid culture a chance to develop to the full." Moreover, Collier had "for eleven years courageously led the fight against the graft, the heartlessness, and the ineptitude of the Indian Bureau." He was "so far ahead of any other possible candidate" that it would be a "great tragedy to the Indians if he were not appointed."[46]

Marshall was not reading too many books these days because, as he said, "there has been too much exciting to read every day in the papers, too much exciting to observe directly in the different levels of society which one encounters." But in May 1933 he sent a short list of books that he had recently read to Lewis Gannett of the New York *Herald Tribune*. They included *Farewell to Reform*, by John Chamberlain ("a most scholarly and convincing argument on the futility of reform as a means of redeeming our economic chaos"); *Ann Vickers*, by Sinclair Lewis ("the same thing... but with a fairly good story thrown in to boot"); *The History of the Russian Revolution*, by Leon Trotsky; *Brave New World*, by Aldous Huxley; and *The Biological Basis of Human Behavior* by H. S. Jennings ("the best layman's book on science which I know [of] by the greatest teacher I've ever had"). When he did read, he read seriously.

The only thing that ever slowed Marshall down was his health, and in late May of 1933 it was "jaundice" (probably hepatitis) that did the trick. He spent several weeks in the hospital at Johns Hopkins, then went to Knollwood until mid-July to finish recuperating. The jaundice, it seems, was "a minor but time-consuming ailment."[48]

While laid up, he finished a few details on his book about the forestry problem. He sent the publisher, Harrison Smith and Robert Haas, a list of thirteen possible titles, ranging from "Public Ownership fo Forests" to "Those Bastards, the Lumbermen."[49]

He was still recovering when the same publisher brought out his book on the Koyukuk, *Arctic Village*. It was a Literary Guild selection for June. Using anecdotes, photographs, direct quotations, and statistics, the book presented an entertaining and revealing view of life in the Koyukuk. All of the characters were colorfully portrayed: Ernie Johnson's pioneering spirit, Ekok's stoic philosophy and intelligence, Big Jim's leadership and religious conversion ("I like God business right away pretty bad," Jim was quoted as saying).[50]

The book sold over 3,500 copies in its first couple of years, a very good showing in the midst of the Depression. Marshall sent every resident of the Koyukuk a personal copy as well as a share of the royalties. By April 1934 these totalled $3,609.00. He kept half for himself and sent personal checks for $18.00 each to one hundred Koyukkers, leaving a little left over "for those children who will come of age in the future."[51]

The Koyukukers were nearly as happy to get these checks as they were interested in reading about themselves in a book. As Victor Neck put it in a thank-you letter to Marshall: "All of us may not agree with you on everything that you wrote about us, but I hope there isn't anybody foolish enough to disagree with you about their checks."[52]

The book was favorably reviewed. An "Arctic Middletown," one reviewer called it; "very interesting" and "valuable," others said. Even H. L. Mencken, the critic's critic, treated it kindly. "Mr. Marshall has written a good book," said Mencken. "His writing is competent, and sometimes, as when he ventures to describe the Koyukuk scenery, it is genuinely eloquent."[53]

Mencken was particularly intrigued with Marshall's reports of the Koyukukers' high I.Q. scores. "The Wisemanites," he wryly observed, "turned out to be on the general level of Harvard professors, members of the General Staff of the Army, and the superior minority of bootleggers, investment bankers, and magazine editors."[54]

Mencken couldn't resist observing also that the Wisemanites had very few do-gooding institutions "to war upon their intelligence, and make it dangerous. They have no politicians. Their police force is rudimentary and impotent. Above all, they are not cursed with theologians." Thus, he noted, "they are freer to be intelligent, and what is more, decent."[55]

And that was Marshall's main point: A society still existed in which people had a great deal of freedom to exercise their intelligence and their personal codes of decency. There was room there for people to move around, to think for themselves, and to work for themselves. But these freedoms existed only as long as frontier conditions prevailed—as long, that is, as the region remained undeveloped.

John Collier (Photograph courtesy the National Archives)

The book, then, strongly reflected Marshall's romantic point of view. He himself was extremely happy in the Arctic, and so he tended to emphasize what a happy place it was. He dedicated the book "to the people of the Koyukuk who have made for themselves the happiest civilization of which I have knowledge." Yet a writer who wanted to argue that the Koyukuk was an *unhappy* place could have found much support in the same book. Marshall noted, for example, that the suicide rate there was "more than seven times that of the United States." He noted also that alcoholism among the Eskimos was already, in 1930, a serious problem.[56]

But the book overall benefitted from Marshall's romanticism. He was excited and enthusiastic about his subject; this showed in the writing and made it fun to read.

On April 21, 1933, the man Marshall had supported, John Collier, was sworn in as Commissioner of Indian Affairs. He soon became known as one of the more eccentric New Dealers, slouching around the office in a geriatric green sweater, his hair often flying in random directions. He sat behind his desk with his legs curled under him like a sleeping deer, smoking a corn-cob pipe which he kept in a drinking glass on his desk. It was rumored that he kept a pet frog in his pocket.[57]

But Collier could get things done, and he implemented major changes in federal Indian policy. One area he wanted to reform was conservation on the reservations. So he appointed Bob Marshall— who shared most of his views—to head up his division of forestry and grazing. The job would start August 1, 1933, and would pay $5600 a year.[58]

10

The Wilderness Society
(1933–1935)

◆ ────────────────────────────────────── ◆

> We want no straddlers, for in the past they have surrendered too much
> good wilderness and primeval which should never have been lost.
>
> Bob Marshall

In November 1934, Bob Marshall, now thirty-three years old, wrote the following to his old Syracuse and Harvard classmate, Neil Hosley:

> The past year has been lots of fun and quite busy with my new job as Director of the Indian Forest Service. There are some 57 different reservations scattered through about a dozen states, where there are either forestry, range or fish and game problems, all of which the Indian Forest Service handles. This makes pleasant variety and lots of fun.

Marshall went on to say that his boss, John Collier, was "the swellest gent" he'd ever worked for. The fellows in the Indian Service were "simply splendid," and while visiting reservations he'd recently squeezed in four thirty-mile walks "with almost unbelievable scenery." So all in all, he concluded, "a person can't be too fastidious."[1]

Marshall's job was indeed well suited to his talents and interests.

He had said in high school that he would hate to spend his life in a stuffy office; this job enabled him to avoid that fate. Traveling six months a year from one reservation to another, he could spend a lot of time outdoors, keep abreast of various wilderness issues, and visit old friends like Raphael Zon in St. Paul and Virginia Olmsted in Seattle. And even when he was stuck in Washington, he enjoyed socializing with his growing number of liberal friends.

The program he was working for—the Indian New Deal—represented a radical shift in American Indian policy. Since the Dawes General Allotment Act of 1887, the Indian Bureau had been trying to get Indians to behave like white Europeans. The Bureau had approached this mission in two basic ways. First, it had divided the reservations into plots of 160 acres or less—called allotments—to be owned by individual Indians. Second, it had outlawed, or in other ways discouraged, many Indian customs, ceremonies, religions, and traditions.[2]

To John Collier and other liberals, assimilation policy was immoral and arrogant. It produced not only extensive poverty, laziness, and alienation, but resulted in huge losses of Indian land. For on most reservations, Indian allottees were persuaded by local whites to either sell or lease their allotments at low prices. Collier, Marshall, and Ward Shepard, in an article for the *Journal of Forestry*, estimated that by 1933 the allotment law and disposal of "surplus" lands had deprived Indians of nearly two-thirds of their reservation property. Moreover, they argued, the system had failed miserably to turn Indians into "self-supporting, independent landowners." "There are today... between eighty thousand and ninety thousand landless Indians, most of whom are paupers or intermittent laborers."[3]

Early in the New Deal, an Indian-reform measure, known as the Indian Reorganization Act, was passed by Congress and signed by FDR. The act directed the Indian Bureau to abandon the allotment system, restored many "surplus" lands to tribal ownership, called for improved resource conservation on the reservations, and provided for a system of limited self-government. The latter was to be accomplished through the formation of incorporated "tribal

160

councils," which would be run under constitutions and bylaws drawn up by the individual tribes, with help from government personnel. Among other purposes, the councils were to prevent any more leasing or selling of Indian land without tribal consent.[4]

Marshall's own responsibilities fell into three categories: forestry, range, and wildlife, each with problems to test his enormous energy and optimism. In the area of forestry his job was to help the tribes consolidate or re-acquire timberlands in and around their reservations and then set up their own logging and mill operations. By teaching the Indians to do their own cutting, mill work, and manufacturing of wood products, he hoped to provide more jobs for reservation Indians.[5]

It was grassland however, that posed the biggest problems. Many reservations were severely overgrazed and their ranges badly deteriorated. In some cases white stockmen had gained control, through long-term leases, of the best grazing lands. In other cases, the Indians destroyed their own lands by overgrazing. The Southern Navajo Agency was an extreme example. An agent there estimated that the Navajos were grazing five times the amount of stock that the range could support.[6]

Wildlife was a problem for several tribes that traditionally depended on game for their livelihoods. In an address to the North American Wildlife Conference, Marshall pointed out that since 1620 the Indians, per capita, had lost nineteen of every twenty acres of land on which they had once hunted and gathered food. And of the land remaining to them, he said, "about half constitutes about the poorest quality land that is left in the United States, of a desert or semidesert type."[7]

One of the first things Marshall did was take a tour of reservations in the summer and fall of 1933. By mid-October, he had visited sixteen reservations between Minnesota and Arizona. Each one, he noted, "had entirely different problems and people and scenery, so it has been very fine." On these visits, he took long inspection hikes, which he felt enabled him to see things more clearly than any other method. As he walked, he talked with as many Indians as he could. "People talk much more freely with me," he later observed, "when I walk up to their houses, dressed in blue jeans and an old cotton shirt, than they ever do when I hop out of an official car in a high-toned uniform. In addition I can get much more accurate and lasting impressions of the forest or range through ten miles of walking than a hundred riding in a car."[8]

As a diversion from solving hard problems, he began keeping a list of interesting names and words encountered on the reservations. His favorite name was "Sits-Down-Spotted-Gets-Up-Striped," reportedly given to an old Sioux woman after she sat down on a hot grill. The longest word was "Muskegmeenanbosko-minnasiganeetibasijigunbadingwaybaquazyshegun"—a Chippewa word meaning "cranberry pie."[9]

While making these tours, Marshall occasionally stayed in hotels, from which he would send out letters and reports. An especially interesting letter, sent on October 21, 1933, from a hotel in Chicago, was in reply to one from a Mardy Murie, congratulating him on *Arctic Village*. Marshall had heard of Mardy and her wildlife biologist husband, Olaus, while he was in the Arctic, for they had come through Bettles and Wiseman in 1924 on a study of caribou. Marshall told Mardy:

> Of course I've heard of you often and your fame still lingers in the Koyukuk as the most beautiful woman who ever came to that region. Jack Hood, Carl Frank, Poss Postlethwaite, and Verne Watts each told me so, and they've seen them all come and go from Dirty Maude to Clara Carpenter. . . . Mr. Murie's fame also lingers in the Koyukuk.[10]

Marshall later met the Muries in Washington, and Bob stayed with them several times in Moose, Wyoming, where Olaus was conducting a landmark study of the Jackson Hole elk herd. Later, Marshall drew them into the Wilderness Society, which Olaus served as president from 1950 to 1957. Both Mardy and Olaus were leading voices for wilderness preservation for many years after Marshall's death.[11]

Around the time Marshall was writing Mardy Murie, his book on forest depletion, titled *The People's Forests*, was published. In it Marshall compared the plight of America's forests to that of a man who has cancer but keeps putting off the painful operation that offers the only real hope of cure. "He continues procrastinating and buying patent medicines which advertise preposterous promises, and all the while his cancer grows worse until it has developed so prodigiously that it is impossible to save him."[12]

Citing data from the Copeland Report and other studies, Marshall alleged that each of the three major forest values—raw materials, soil and water conservation, and recreation—were being destroyed by private timberland owners intent on liquidating their property as fast as possible. It was time to "discard the unsocial view that our woods are the lumbermen's and substitute the broader ideal that every acre of woodland in the country is rightly a part of the people's forests."[13]

Specifically, he recommended that the government acquire some 240 million acres of privately-owned forest. That would bring the total acreage of public woodland to 562 million, or about eighty-four percent of all the forestland in the country.[14]

In the minds of some lumbermen and conservative foresters, the book confirmed Bob Marshall as something of a utopian radical. Other reviewers applauded his courage and skill in addressing the problem head-on, but most fell short of endorsing his plan for nationalization.

Marshall personally urged Franklin Reed, editor of the *Journal of Forestry*, to review the book, even though Reed didn't want to. Reed felt his own views to be so "diametrically at variance" with Marshall's that his review would simply "reek of adverse criticism." But Bob insisted, so Reed wrote an honest review, one calling *The People's Forests* "a dangerous book." He thought it was dangerous because it made nationalization sound so attractive while not closely examining the potential dangers.[15]

In fact *The People's Forests* was not one of Marshall's stronger efforts. The book was readable because he was a good writer, and it made a good case that there was indeed a forest problem. But Marshall's treatment of the solution was too superficial. He asserted, for example, that publicly owned and operated forests would pay for themselves, but he didn't say how. Also, Marshall did not carefully examine less radical solutions, such as cooperative regulation, before dismissing them.

Marshall himself later decided that the book was weak. ("I tried to win my argument too easily.") When it first came out, though, he had such high hopes for it that he personally bought 750 copies and sent 531 of them to senators and congressmen.[16]

Early in 1934, Marshall began dating Georgia Engelhard regularly again. They took two long hikes together in February, including one in what is now the Peaks of Otter Wilderness in the Monongahela National Forest of West Virginia. Their hikes, however, were interrupted when Marshall had to make a fast trip to the West Coast to help settle a timber-sale dispute at the Klamath Indian Agency in Oregon. To save time, he flew between Washington and San Francisco. But upon his return, Comptroller General J. R. McCarl decided Marshall could have saved $27.36 by taking a train and deducted that amount from his travel reimbursement check.[17]

Thus began one of the zaniest duels of memoranda in the history of federal bureaucracies. Marshall countered by explaining that his meeting at the Klamath Agency had saved the tribe $1.15 million, not to mention $73.91 worth of his own time saved by not spending it on a train. It seemed a curious kind of accounting, therefore, to penalize him $27.36.[18]

Had Marshall left it at that, perhaps McCarl would have relented and not have become personally committed to winning his point. But Marshall couldn't resist a few additional observations. "The amount which you are dunning me," he told the comptroller general,

> is not large enough to get excited about, but if you are trying to prevent federal employees from making use of the time-saving which

the airplane makes possible, then I should like to suggest that you take an airplane ride yourself and save enough time to reflect that one cannot perpetually spit in the eye of progress.[19]

If, after taking such a trip, McCarl still preferred the more "ancient and less expensive" mode of travel, that would be fine with Marshall. For walking, he pointed out, was even more ancient and less expensive. "I shall be delighted to walk to the Klamath Reservation in Oregon when next I have to go there."[20]

McCarl came back with less creative but equally determined arguments. Other officials were called into the action and the memos began to pile up. Soon Marshall was carrying them around the country in his briefcase, reading them aloud for the amusement of friends in places like Jackson Hole and Missoula.[21]

Marshall fired his own best shot in a long missive composed over two years later, in which he countered McCarl's implication that his plane travel was enjoyable. "Exactly the contrary is true," Marshall explained,

I left Washington at 5:40 in the evening, cramped into an inadequate seat on a Pennsylvania Airline plane which sounded like a boiler factory at peak production. Alternately I had to keep massaging my right and my left leg, just above the knee, because the cramped position made them fall constantly asleep. . . . At Chicago I had to wait four hours in the airport, where I tried to snatch a little sleep on an inadequate, narrow, and somewhat filthy couch, while vagrant crowds brushed by, loud speakers bellowed out departing planes, and a couple of drunks made the whole room seem like a lumber town saloon when the log drive was finished.

After that, Marshall said, things got worse. Warm air currents turned the plane into "a veritable roller coaster," and from Cheyenne to Salt Lake City he battled a "nauseating sense of seasickness which momentarily threatened to triumph." Shortly before Salt Lake, it did: He lost his breakfast, then last night's dinner, and then he still kept vomiting "as if nature did not want me to forget the technique." He could only conclude that

If there is such a thing as hell on earth, that was it. Were such punishment inflicted by any jury it would be outlawed under the provisions of the Constitution of the United States. Yet that cruel and inhuman punishment I voluntarily underwent because it seemed necessary in order to perform my official duties.[22]

The issue was never officially resolved. Marshall was twice issued checks to cover all his expenses except the contested $27.36. But he sent the first one back and refused to cash the second one, which was found in his papers when he died.[23]

Thus Marshall could be very funny, and he was good at deflating people he considered to be "stuffed shirts," but he sometimes got carried away and hurt people's feelings. Allan Harper, head of the Indian Bureau's Organization Division, once told him in response to an irreverent memo:

Dear Bob:
Every once in a while something or another in your State Papers rouses my primordial instinct of assassination. I usually erupt in free but silent speech, and then tear up the memorandum, breathing umbrage and insult. . . . Yet there remains the untold damage you do yourself by treating other people's work with sarcasm, invective, ridicule, satire, etc., etc. You really ought to have a censor sit at your side with power to write *non expedit* on some of the things you write to our colleagues here in Washington.[24]

In the hierarchy of federal agencies, the Bureau of Indian Affairs is housed within the Department of the Interior. Marshall was fortunate that during the New Deal, the Secretary of the Interior was a wilderness sympathizer named Harold L. Ickes. Few government officials were ever as irascible, as childish, as blunt, as ambitious, and yet as productive and competent as Ickes. Proud of his own grouchiness, Ickes titled his memoir *The Autobiography of a Curmudgeon*. His sputtering tantrums were so well known that FDR called him Donald Duck. He even looked like a curmudgeon—his body was thick, his hair thin, his face jowly and scowly.

*Harold Ickes (Photograph courtesy the
National Archives)*

Yet he was one of the few Interior secretaries to care deeply about conservation and the public interest.[25] He once told a group of Civilian Conservation Corps workers:

> I think we ought to keep as much wilderness area in this country of ours as we can. . . . I do not happen to favor the scarring of a wonderful mountainside just so we can have a skyline drive. It sounds poetical, but it may be an atrocity.[26].

Marshall began in early 1934 to take full advantage of Ickes's wilderness sympathy. He started with two long memos discussing the need to protect thirteen specific areas from intrusion by roads. (As administrator of the Public Works Administration, Ickes had control of an extensive road-building program then going on to provide jobs. This included roads not only on Interior Department lands but also in the national forests.)

"The selection of wilderness areas is a phase of land planning," Marshall told Ickes. "Given the limited area of . . . land in the United States, the question is how much of this area we can afford to set aside for wilderness use."

To answer that question, Marshall proposed a "Wilderness Planning Board"—with no "stuffed shirts"—that would review and recommend areas to Congress for wilderness designation, "just as National Parks are today set aside."[27]

Ickes did not set up the Wilderness Planning Board, but Marshall now had his attention, and this would later prove worthwhile.

Meanwhile, Marshall continued to irritate lumbermen and conservative foresters by raising unpleasant issues. In the spring of 1934, he and several others (essentially the same group who earlier sent out the "Letter to Foresters") sent a petition to the executive council of the Society of American Foresters in which they accused the society's publication, the *Journal of Forestry*, of "no longer represent[ing] the broad social ideals of the founders of the Society." The *Journal*, they said, was okay as an outlet for technical findings, but in the broader, more important field of forest policy, it had lost "the spirit of social leadership which was once a distinguishing characteristic of the profession."

A new editor should be installed, they said, who was independent from the executive director and possessed both high professional standing and strong literary ability.[28]

Marshall followed this up a month later with an article titled "Should the Journal of Forestry Stand for Forestry?" In this piece he examined each of the past thirty-two *Journal* editorials and concluded that "the official publication of the American forestry profession stands brazenly for forest depletion!" He declared that "If such an editorial viewpoint is to continue to come from the official mouthpiece of the Society of American Foresters, then frankly I have no interest in remaining a member of that organization."[29]

There were those, of course, who would have been happy to show him the door. One of these was H. H. Chapman, one of the most contentious personalities in the forestry business. A prolific writer, professor of forestry at Yale, and for several years president of the Society of American Foresters, Chapman seldom met a controversy he didn't like. If Marshall, Zon, and others were afraid of the society being taken over by the timber industry, Chapman was equally afraid of it being dominated by the Forest Service, and he worked with equal vigor to prevent such a disaster.[30]

In a response to Marshall's article, Chapman reminded *Journal* readers that Marshall was, after all, "in favor of a totalitarian program of socialized forestry." Marshall's summary of the editorials, said Chapman, was "not only exaggerated but highly imaginative . . . . How in the face of the published records, such conclusions could be drawn I am not prepared to say." These comments reflected a growing feud between those two strong-headed men. It would become one of the few cases where Marshall developed a personal distaste for an intellectual opponent.[31]

As it turned out, a compromise was reached on the *Journal*'s editorial policy (although Chapman saw it as a victory for his side). In 1935 the editor-in-chief was given more independence from the executive director. A new editor was appointed, Herbert Smith of the Forest Service. But Smith had to sign an agreement that his conduct of the *Journal* would be "independent of Forest Service control."[32]

Marshall squeezed in a twenty-two mile hike with Georgia Engelhard in June 1934. Then he was off again to visit reservations. He had an especially interesting time at the Crow reservation in southeastern Montana. Ranching was the primary industry there, but the grazing situation had serious problems. A few white stockmen had gained control over large sections of range through long-term leases of key lands allotted to individual Indians. Also, grazing boundaries were poorly defined and there were no limits to the amount of stock a rancher could run. The situation was generally chaotic and unacceptable not only to the majority of Indians but also to many white stockmen who could not get a fair chance to lease any of the range.[33]

Emotions were running high when Marshall arrived on June 22 to meet with the Crow Range Committee. He opened the meeting with a few pleasantries, then recalled that his last meeting there had run into the wee hours of the morning. "And if you want to run until one tomorrow morning," he assured the Indians, "I will be ready to be with you until that time."

He then announced that the government wanted the Crows to work out their own grazing policy. He would not tell them what to

169

do, with one exception: "We have to get some system under which it will be possible . . . to control the number of stock that graze your range. That is all we propose to do . . . but I would like to hear a discussion on this matter."[34]

He got discussion all right; it lasted far into the night. The highlight was a speech by a garrulous tribesman, Robert Yellow-tail, who recounted in some detail the history of grazing on the Crow lands and how the Crow had lost control to a handful of whites. The discussion went on and on, with Marshall listening patiently.

After a break for supper, the committee made two important decisions. First, all leasing would be conducted by auction. Second, all new leases would only be for three years.[35]

Marshall stayed there five days altogether, and his report to Collier was jubilant, even for Marshall. "After a year of general turmoil on the Crow reservation," he told the commissioner,

> with pretty nearly riots attending some of the efforts to put the range under control, and Crow politicians booming out deprecations of the Indian Bureau and its officials, it appears as if peace is once more on the verge of being restored and a system of grazing control, satisfactory both to the Crow Indians and to ourselves, may be worked out.

Marshall then described the friendship expressed as the meetings were winding down. There was a feeling "of brotherly love," he reported,

> with old Yellow Brow who last October could not say mean enough things about the Bureau, now rising to remark, in the moonlight which witnessed the end of the out-door conference: "We have had many Commissioners but I think this one means better for the Indians than any one we have ever had". . . . Deer Nose then got up and named me "Ba-tse-ba-tsatsic," which, after considerable discussion among the various interpreters, it was decided meant "Man-with-the-ability-to-bring-all-factions-together."[36]

The Indians were now "enthusiastically behind" the bureau's efforts to control the amount of stock on the range, Marshall said happily. The new policies were approved in July 1934 by the Crow Tribal Council; Collier approved them a month later.[37]

Marshall's handling of this problem illustrates both the strengths and weaknesses he brought to the job. His greatest strength was that he worked well directly with most of the tribes. By several accounts, he was good at winning their trust and confidence. He was also unflaggingly optimistic and enthusiastic. When overly applied, however, this exuberance became his main weakness. He tended to overstate successes, and his enthusiasm for the goals of the Indian New Deal blinded him somewhat to its limitations. The solutions that he worked out to problems were seldom as final and clear-cut as he made them appear.

Such indeed was the case on the Crow reservation, where the large stock operations, whose quasimonopoly was now threatened, reacted angrily. Several of them got together and refused to bid on some 350,000 acres of grassland. Their boycott hurt the Crows economically. Thus Marshall's policy, though constructive, was no panacea for problems that had taken several generations to develop. Grazing controversies continued on the Crow and other reservations long after Marshall had left the Indian Bureau.[38]

Later that summer, Marshall turned his attention to wilderness problems. In August, he was appointed by Secretary Ickes to represent the Interior Department on the President's Quetico-Superior Committee, a group studying the possibilities of an "international wilderness sanctuary" along the border lakes of Minnesota and Ontario. Although Marshall looked forward to working on that committee, he was far more concerned, by the growing controversy over roads in national parks. Under the New Deal's various work programs, the National Park Service suddenly had a lot of money to spend on roads. Marshall and others began to fear that if certain plans were implemented, the wilderness character of several great parks would be ruined.[39]

Much of this controversy was rooted in the 1916 law creating the Park Service. The bill called for scenery and wildlife to be left "unimpaired," but it also said the parks existed for public enjoyment. Director Stephen Mather, who helped write the bill, took this to mean that roads, hotels, restaurants, and concessions were acceptable. He used these conveniences liberally to get people into the parks and promote the Park Service. The result was that for many people, visiting a national park was more like a resort vacation than a wilderness experience. And for those visiting such parks as Yosemite and Yellowstone, it was often more like a carnival, with pretty scenery for the background. To entertain visitors, the Park Service had carved drive-through tunnels in giant Sequoias, dumped soap into geysers to manipulate their eruptions, fed garbage to bears to make them half-tame, and tossed bonfires over cliffs.[40]

Throughout Mather's tenure as Park Service director (1917 to 1928), few people complained about these activities. Ninety percent of the visitors were concentrated in ten percent of the park lands, leaving ample backcountry for those who wanted to escape the crowds. But by the 1930s, as road building in particular was stepped up, wilderness enthusiasts were increasingly disillusioned with the National Park Service. That disillusionment would lead to formation of The Wilderness Society.

There were three specific projects—all in the Appalachians— that especially bothered preservationists in the summer of 1934. The first was a "skyline drive" already being built through the heart of Shenendoah National Park, Virginia. Second was a proposed ridgeline highway bisecting the newly established Great Smoky Mountains National Park. This highway was still being planned, except for a seven-mile section from Newfound Gap to Clingman's Dome (highest point in Tennessee) that was already under construction. Third was a 450-mile "National Parkway" along the Blue Ridge from Shenendoah National Park to Great Smokies National Park. This project had been approved but not yet started.

In the summer of 1934, Ickes sent Marshall south to look over possible routes for the Shenendoah-to-Smokies highway. Several days before leaving, Marshall sent a letter to Benton MacKaye, a friend in Knoxville, saying he'd be there August 11. In 1921, MacKaye had proposed a primitive hiking trail "from one of the

Benton MacKaye, 1934 (Photograph by Harvey Broome; reproduced courtesy The Wilderness Society)

highest mountains in New England to one of the highest in the South." The result was the 2,000-mile Appalachian Trail.[41] MacKaye was, as Marshall once said, "a grand fellow but very eccentric." He was a regional planner by profession, a naturalist and philosopher by preference. Tall and lanky, with hollow cheeks and a nose like a sea hawk, he looked like a caricature of an Appalachian hillbilly—especially when he wore his ragged felt woodsman's hat and let his pipe dangle from the side of his mouth, as he usually did.

The same day that MacKaye received Marshall's letter, he received one also from Harold C. Anderson, an accountant in Washington who was secretary of the Potomac Appalachian Trail Club. In his letter, Anderson proposed a federation of hiking clubs to save what wilderness was left in the East. "By gum," said MacKaye to his friend Harvey Broome, another wilderness lover, "we'll put up to [Marshall] this proposal of Anderson's."[42]

On the afternoon of August 11, MacKaye and Broome sat on a bluff overlooking the Tennessee River and planned the pitch they would make to Marshall.

"There was hope in the air in those days," said Broome six years later, "the TVA was getting well under way and the whole country was in a state of flux. The possibility of starting a wilderness movement did not seem hopeless."[43]

They met Marshall that evening at the Andrew Johnson Hotel in Knoxville. But they were sidetracked when Marshall told them he was there to study the Park Service's road plans. "We almost forgot our organization project in our eagerness to press upon him reasons for a low-level routing," Broome recalled. "The upshot of it was that we did not discuss wilderness organization at all that night, but instead were invited to join Marshall and his party the next day on the survey from Knoxville to Ashville."[44]

So the next morning they set out. MacKaye rode with Marshall's aides, while Broome—who could hardly believe how young Marshall looked—rode with him in "an old roadster." They drove into the heart of the Smokies, picked up the park superintendent at Gatlinburg, and continued toward Clingman's Dome on the highway just being built. It was cluttered, said Broome, "by air drills, steam shovels, etc. engaged in the construction work."[45]

After Marshall and Broome climbed Clingman's Dome, MacKaye joined them in the roadster. In the one-hour drive eastward to Waynesville, North Carolina, they talked hurriedly about a wilderness group. "Bob was enthusiastic," said Broome, "He was ever so." Marshall said he would talk with Anderson when he got back to Washington. But he convinced MacKaye and Broome to go beyond Anderson's proposal for an eastern group, and to make it instead a national organization.[46]

This was a key point. There was at that time no *national* wilderness group. There were national groups such as the National Audubon Society and the Isaac Walton League whose interests included wilderness but mainly focused on wildlife. And there were groups such as John Muir's Sierra Club, which focused on wilderness but, at that time, only on a regional level. If there was going to be a real wilderness *movement*, it had to have some kind of national organization. Marshall seems to have understood this better than most of his contemporaries. It is one of the things that sets him apart from the rest.

When Marshall returned to Washington, he asked Secretary Ickes to veto the skyline drive in Great Smokies National Park. "Today," he said,

it is still possible for the hiker or the equestrian to bury himself to his heart's content in the splendid forest of this uninvaded mountain top. He can still receive the unrivaled thrill of the primitive and the exhilaration of life in the grandest environment a human being can know. If the proposed skyline road from New Found Gap to the south boundary of the park is continued this opportunity will be ruined forever.

To emphasize his point, Marshall described his experience at Clingman's Dome with Broome. As he had done so many times before, he compared nature to civilization, and found civilization lacking:

I climbed Clingman's Dome last Sunday, looking forward to the great joy of undisturbed nature for which this mountain has been famous. Walking along the skyline trail, I heard instead the roar of machines on the newly constructed road just below me and saw the huge scars which this new highway is making on the mountain. Clingman's Dome and the primitive were simply ruined for me.

Returning to where a gigantic, artificial parking place had exterminated the wild mountain meadows in New Found Gap, I saw papers and the remains of lunches littered all over. There were about twenty automobiles parked there, from at least a quarter of which radios were blaring forth the latest jazz as a substitute for the symphony of the primitive.[47]

Ickes responded by asking the Park Service to reconsider the road. But Park Service Director Arno B. Cammerer was, in his own words, "committed to the construction" of it, so discussion continued.[48]

On September 11, Marshall had lunch with Harold Anderson. They agreed it was now important to organize a wilderness group as fast as possible and to present a statement of policy to the federal government. They made a quick list of interested people. For the organizing group, of course, there would be MacKaye, Broome, Anderson, and Marshall. Marshall proposed two others as co-organizers: Aldo Leopold, recognized for preserving the Gila wilderness and defending the wilderness idea, and Ernest Oberholtzer of the Quetico-Superior Committee.[49]

The following month, by an odd coincidence, the American Forestry Association held its annual conference in Knoxville, Tennessee. Marshall was a speaker on the program for Friday evening, October 19th. That afternoon, he went out with Broome and MacKaye on an AFA field trip to a CCC camp near the new Norris Dam, twenty miles north of Knoxville. In the convoy of cars, they rode with Bernard Frank, an associate forester with TVA who shared their concerns, and Frank's wife, Miriam. (Frank, Marshall observed happily, was cynical enough "to see through the stuffed shirts who make speeches for wilderness but refuse to fight.")[50]

As the caravan snaked its way through the hills, Frank's car suddenly pulled off to the side of the road. The riders hopped out and scrambled up a bank while friends in other cars hooted at them as they whisked by. The small group huddled around Marshall, who pulled out a copy of MacKaye's latest statement of wilderness purposes. There they hashed out definitions, organization, objectives, and methods of the group, which they decided to call The Wilderness Society.[51]

That evening, when Marshall gave his talk, he was still fired up about wilderness preservation. Mable Abercrombie, a twenty-two-year-old stenographer who worked with MacKaye at the Tennessee Valley Authority, and who later would become Bob's frequent companion, described the occasion:

176

Well, that night Bob made his speech, and the people—everybody in the American Forestry Association and the TVA and others—turned out to hear this great explorer talk about Alaska. And with a glint in his eye he started *right in* just on wilderness. That's all he talked about was wilderness values and how the foresters should try to preserve the wilderness. . . . And the next day everyone said, "I thought he was gonna talk about *Alaska*."[52]

If some of Marshall's listeners were disappointed, one was furious: Arno B. Cammerer, newly appointed director of the National Park Service. Cammerer did not like the way Marshall used the Smokies "Skyway" as an example of bad planning. The next day, in a speech of his own, Cammerer called Marshall's talk an "improper and ungracious attack" on the Park Service.[53]

The newspapers, of course, got good mileage out of this little Interior Department squabble. Marshall ended up apologizing formally to Secretary Ickes for the episode. Ickes bawled him out, but as Marshall said, he did it "in such a way that I enjoyed the bawling out." It surely would have been worse if Ickes had not despised Cammerer, whom he appointed director against his better judgment. He thought Cammerer was an incompetent bureaucrat and, among other things, didn't like the way he chewed gum.[54]

In any case the incident reflected the growing tension between the Park Service and its critics. Meanwhile, MacKaye had Mable Abercrombie type up the statement that had been worked out during the AFA field trip. It was then sent to six people, along with an invitation to join the Organizing Committee of The Wilderness Society. Four of these accepted: Anderson, Leopold, Oberholtzer, and a former Park Service publicity man, Robert Sterling Yard. (The two who declined were John Collier and John C. Merriam, a paleontologist and president of the Carnegie Institute of Washington.)[55]

Now Marshall was fired up even more than usual. "It will be no longer a case of a few individuals fighting," he declared, "but a well organized and thoroughly earnest mass of wilderness lovers." He did, however, have one concern: "We want no straddlers, for in

177

the past they have surrendered too much good wilderness and primeval which should never have been lost."[56]

A week later Marshall had lunch at the Cosmos Club in Washington with Robert S. Yard, who had dreamed for several years of starting "an organization to preserve the primitive." He was ecstatic to be a Wilderness Society organizer. "The Wilderness Society will attract instant and wide attention," he immediately predicted. Within a week of being asked, Yard was planning operational strategy; he wrote Marshall, brainstorming ways to handle organizational memberships. Anderson, returning to Washington from a trip, found Yard "bubbling over with enthusiasm."[57]

Marshall, meanwhile, became enthusiastic about Mable Abercrombie, whom MacKaye had made sure that he would meet. She was pretty and petite, with long straight hair and—perhaps of more importance to Marshall—a love of hiking and square dancing. They began seeing each other whenever he could get to Knoxville.

"About every couple of months Bob was popping back into town," says Mable. "In fact, he and I used to laugh about whether he could get another trip down to visit the Cherokee Indian Reservation so he could get away from Washington."[58]

He was able to get away the weekend of December 15, 1934. Broome, MacKaye, and Mable picked him up at the train station, whereupon they had a "pow wow" (as MacKaye invariably called any sort of meeting) about The Wilderness Society. Then they went out to a tea room in Knoxville for dinner and square dancing. "Bob loved to square dance," Mable recalled. "I don't know why, he just loved it. He was a real funny square dancer. He just *bounced* around, which was part of his personality."[59]

Marshall's relationship with Mable was casual. He would meet her periodically for a whirlwind day or two of hiking and dancing. Then he would write and tell her what a glorious time he'd had and that he couldn't wait to do it again. But it couldn't be for a while because he was very tied up, usually with wilderness issues. Thus he kept it friendly but not too serious or intimate.

Marshall was, in fact, extremely busy with wilderness problems,

Bob Marshall with Mable Abercrombie (Photograph courtesy Mable Abercrombie Mansfield)

but there is another reason why he did not get too serious with Mable. He still felt strongly about Georgia Engelhard. He was not seeing Georgia as often as he would like, but she was his favorite woman, and if he was ever going to settle down with anyone, he wanted it to be her.[60]

In any case, it is not surprising that the three women with whom

Marshall had his closest relationships—Mable Abercrombie, Virginia Olmsted, and Georgia Engelhard—all seem to have been quite independent themselves. Abercrombie, though young and impressionable, enjoyed her time with Marshall and did not, so far as the records show, pressure him for anything more. Engelhard was busy with her own mountaineering and art work. And Olmsted, though widowed and raising a young child, apparently was not looking for another husband. And, of course, all three of these women enjoyed the outdoors.

In January 1935, Marshall struck up a friendship with Irving Clark of Seattle, a graduate of Yale and the University of Washington Law School. Clark worked with unemployed self-help cooperatives under the Federal Emergency Relief Administration. He was also chairman of the Washington American Civil Liberties Union and active in The Mountaineers, a Seattle-based climbing and conservation group.[61]

Clark wrote Marshall in January 1935, complimenting him on *The People's Forests*. "It was the first time I had ever seen the truth about the timber industry in print," he said. He then asked Marshall if he would write an article supporting a move underway to secure national park status for the rain forest and mountains of Washington's Olympic Peninsula.[62]

Marshall thanked him for the compliment, but declined to write the article because he had not yet visited the Olympics. He was, however, "strong to have the very maximum primitive area" set aside there—by whatever agency was willing to do it.[63]

A short time later, Marshall warned Clark not to expect too much from the Park Service. His letter reflected the still-growing disenchantment that he and others were feeling toward that agency. "I need only point out, Bob said,

> the inexcusable fake Hopi watch tower at the brink of the Grand Canyon, the luxurious developments on the floor of Yosemite Valley which have ruined all primitive effect, the sky line drive in the Great Smokies and the elaborate tunnel system on the highway in

that park through Newfound Gap, the tunnel with windows which is so boasted about in Zion National Park . . . and the general artificiality everywhere.[64]

At about the same time, Marshall met Gardner Jackson, a senior counsel in the Agricultural Administration who perhaps embodied as well as anyone the liberalism of the 1930s. Jackson had played a leading role on the side of the accused in the celebrated Sacco and Vanzetti case.* Jackson's "abundant sympathy, courage, and curiosity," says Arthur Schlesinger, Jr., "kept him in the middle of one,fight after another for the underprivileged."[65]

Jackson and Marshall got along together like bacon and eggs. Jackson drew Marshall into several labor and political issues, while Marshall drew Jackson and his wife Dorothy (usually called Dode), into the wilderness-preservation movement.

In mid-January 1935, Benton MacKaye and Harvey Broome visited Washington, D.C. On Sunday, January 20, in a marbly room at the Cosmos Club, they met with Marshall, Anderson, and Yard to form The Wilderness Society. The formal statement of organization had Marshall's stamp all over it. For example, the first paragraph read:

Primitive America is vanishing with appalling rapidity. Scarcely a month passes in which some highway does not invade an area which since the beginning of time had known only natural modes of travel; or some last remaining virgin timber tract is not shattered by the construction of an irrigation project into an expanding and contracting mud flat; or some quiet glade hitherto disturbed only by birds and insects and wind in the trees, does not bark out the merits of "Crazy Water Crystals" and the mushiness of "Cocktails for Two."[66]

---

* Sacco and Vanzetti were a pair of obscure immigrants who, during the red scare of the early twenties, were executed for murdering a Massachusetts paymaster. Many still believe that their trial was unfair and that they were persecuted for being confessed radicals.

The statement went on to acknowledge that most Americans preferred "mechanically disturbed" nature. The Wilderness Society was "cheerfully willing" to let them have most of outdoor America, "including most of the scenic features in the country which have already been made accessible to motorists." The society merely held that those areas yet remaining roadless should continue to be so unless some compelling reason could be given otherwise.[67]

The organization was not looking for a large membership. "Above all we do not want in our ranks people whose first instinct is to look for compromise." There would be no dues, but members were invited to send contributions. "Already," it said, "we have received one $1,000 anonymous contribution." It was from Marshall.[68]

Everyone agreed that Marshall should be president. Marshall thought he should clear this with Ickes. He wrote the secretary, explaining that an organization had been formed to counteract "the propaganda spread by the American Automobile Association, the various booster organizations, and innumerable chamber of commerces, which seem to find no peace as long as any primitive tract in America remains unopened to mechanization." He wanted to be the group's president, and he didn't think this would conflict "with my loyalties to the [Interior] Department."[69]

Ickes disagreed. He envisioned, with good reason, The Wilderness Society fighting at least two of his outfits, the Park Service and Grazing Office. He suggested instead that Marshall do the work of a president "and let somebody else get the title."[70]

This seemed like "a very sound idea" to Marshall, who now proposed that Aldo Leopold be president. It was Leopold, Marshall told Broome, who "proposed the setting aside of extensive wilderness areas for the first time, to my knowledge. He has been head over heels in the fight ever since and he is entirely outside the government."[71]

Leopold, however, did not want it. "It necessarily involves a lot of lobbying on current departmental actions and bills," he told Marshall, "of which I know nothing whatever and I lack the time and desire to find out."[72]

They finally agreed to postpone appointing a president and simply let Yard, as Secretary, run the operation. It was a good decision. In the next ten years Yard churned out reams of newsletters, memos, letters, magazine articles, and news releases for The Wilderness Society. For the first five of those years, Marshall backed him up with money, information, and policy directions. The two men had a unique, friendly relationship that got a lot of results in those hectic last year's of Marshall's life. That Marshall got along so well with Yard is noteworthy, because this seventy-four-year-old former newspaper man, though productive and well intentioned, had a reputation for being impetuous and impractical.

Bob Yard was a small man, with an oval face, tiny eyes, and silver hair. He sported a carefully groomed mustache and dressed formally even on wilderness trips. Educated at Princeton, he had been a reporter for the New York *Sun* and an editor for the New York *Herald* and *The Century Magazine*. A close friend of former Park Service director Steve Mather, he had worked for several years as Park Service publicity director. When he lost that job (he was a poor administrator), he helped form the National Parks Association, a conservation group focusing on national park policies and standards. He then became one of the Park Service's biggest critics. He felt that after Mather left in 1929, "the tendency [was] increasingly toward park extension at the expense of standards."[73]

The mere mention of national park additions sent Yard into indignant tirades. "It is clear," he once told Marshall, "that the Park Service is out to get every last national park it can, irrespective of standards, and that every one it gets it will build roads into and crowd with speeders. Park-to-park highways, built and owned by the Park Service, are planned to criss-cross the U.S. It is an exceedingly dangerous movement against wilderness."[74]

Yard's obsession with high standards made some people wonder if *any* natural attraction would suit him. "The Matterhorn wouldn't meet his specifications for a new national park," said one observer.[75]

By 1935, Yard had lost his paid position with the National Parks Association, again largely for weak administration. It was fortunate for Yard, however, that Marshall considered him "one of the really outstandingly grand men in the whole history of the fight to preserve the primitive in America," and was willing to pay Yard a salary to run The Wilderness Society. The organization, for the first couple of years, was little more than Yard and Marshall in a two-man campaign, cheered on vigorously by MacKaye, Anderson, and a few others. As MacKaye told Marshall, "Harvey and I sleep better nights knowing you and [Yard] are on the job up at headquarters."[76]

The "headquarters" to which Benton referred was Yard's apartment at 1840 Mintwood Place; it was The Wilderness Society's office several years after Yard died in 1945. As Yard put it, "I grabbed $1440 a year from the Wilderness Society [i.e. from Marshall] and chucked in an office without charging rent. I never asked for a raise until just before Bob died and then only enough to pay some doctors' bills and [buy some] unragged clothes."[77]

In Washington, Marshall's private life was nearly indistinguishable from his public life, since most of his friends were social activists or wilderness preservationists. He usually went to his office about nine A.M. and stayed past five P.M. Then he would go out for dinner, often with a friend, or else to a meeting of some wilderness, civil liberties, or socialist group. He occasionally hosted small parties himself, to which he would invite liberals like Gardner and Dode Jackson.[78]

In late January, Mable Abercrombie came up for a weekend. It was her first trip to Washington. As she remembered it,

I stayed by prearrangement with Lin and Caroline DeCauex, newspaper reporters. When Bob came by taxi to pick me up, Lin interviewed him (while to my "depression-minded" amazement the taxi meter clicked). Afterwards we went to the Shoreham Hotel for a Society of American Foresters dance, but that was not enough dancing for Bob—from there we went to a night club. Cinderella got home about two A.M.[79]

Marshall was in the news those days because he had just been denounced on the floor of the House of Representatives by New

York Congressman Hamilton Fish. On Monday, January 28, Fish had proudly produced photostatic copies of receipts totalling $120 for contributions by Marshall to the Veterans Rank and File Committee, a group, in Fish's words, "dominated by well-known Communists." Fish also pointed out that Marshall was chairman of the Washington branch of the American Civil Liberties Union, "an organization that upholds the Communists in their advocacy of force and violence to overthrow the Government." (Also accused in the same speech was Marshall's good friend Gardner Jackson.)[80]

Marshall was cavalier about the accusations. He told a *New York Times* reporter:

> Because I've been up in the Arctic a good part of the past five years, it may be that the Bill of Rights was repealed without my having heard about it. Even if it were so, it would not affect my contribution, because it was to an agency neither Socialist nor Communist, but anti-Fascist.[81]

Thus began a strange relationship. A few weeks later, Fish came into an appropriations hearing at which Marshall was testifying and made similar charges. Marshall then listed Fish as a character reference on a government personnel form, and later started baiting Fish directly. He wrote him a letter congratulating him on his vote on another matter which they happened to agree on. Then he said:

> I have met you once and enjoyed our meeting immensely. It was the time you appeared before the House Indian Affairs Committee to urge that I be bounced from the Civil Service because I was a strong believer in most of the work of the American Civil Liberties Union. While I obviously... did not agree with your viewpoint on that matter I enjoyed having your opinion and also enjoyed very much this recently expressed viewpoint of yours with which I so thoroughly concur.[82]

When spring arrived, Marshall was still feeding Secretary Ickes a steady diet of memos, flattering him for his appreciation of wilderness and pointing out specific places where his influence could well be applied. In April 1935, Marshall wrote Ickes saying that "the danger to primitive outdoor conditions has never been so great as at the present moment." The threat was from "huge funds" available for work relief, funds which resulted in "all sorts of developments in the forest and on the range." Government efforts to provide jobs were wonderful, and Marshall applauded the general concept. But if not managed "with careful regard for esthetic, non-commercial values," they could easily destroy "the most important feature of the outdoors"—its essential wildness.[83]

Marshall then listed his specific complaints, two of which were major Park Service projects. First was the "skyline drive" in the Smokies, which Park Service director Arno Cammerer was still promoting. Second was a proposed Green Mountain Parkway, a scenic road that would wind along the spruce-covered spine of the Vermont Appalachians. If built as planned, Marshall said, this road would "ruin the primitive value" of a popular hiking path in that area, the Long Trail.[84]

Later that spring, Marshall engaged in another long duel of memoranda, this time with a Park Service planner named Demaray*, over the Green Mountain proposal. Marshall's basic argument was that the road was poorly planned. If built as drawn up, it would spoil the enjoyment of those who preferred to hike. Hikers had already been "dispossessed" in one national park, Shenandoah, by a road that totally ignored their interests. He did not think that should happen again. The project was finally abandoned several years later, partly because of opposition organized by Bob Yard.[85]

By June, Marshall was off visiting reservations, but wilderness was still on his mind. Secretary Ickes had "unofficially approved in a general way" the notion of declaring wilderness on Indian lands. Marshall, consequently, was compiling a list of appropriate areas. Since Indian cultures had evolved in wilderness, it seemed to him very consistent with the Indian New Deal to keep some

---

*Demaray later would become director of the Park Service.

reservation lands roadless. Later, however, some people would disagree.[86]

In June, he took an inspection hike in the Grand Portage reservation, through which the state of Minnesota had requested permission from the Interior Department to build Highway 61. After taking his hike, Marshall sent a long missive to assistant Indian commissioner William Zimmerman urging disapproval of the road. One of his arguments was that it would ruin any hope of a guiding industry for the Indians. If left primitive, tourists who wanted to "get back to a less mechanical age" would come and pay money to Indian resorts or cooperative guide associations. But with a highway "piercing right through the heart," few motorists would bother to stop and "even a 240-pound Miss Kummer would not need a guide."[87]

Marshall developed on several other occasions this argument for wilderness-guiding businesses on reservations. He thought it had great potential and used it as a rationale for keeping reservations wild. It is true that such businesses are far more consistent with Indian heritage than, say, uranium mining. The demand for wilderness travel on Indian lands, however, never developed as Marshall predicted. It would have taken tremendous promotional efforts to lure large numbers of wilderness travelers to reservations.

But Marshall had such a strong, intuitive feeling that wilderness was *good* that he sometimes made weak arguments for it. Two other arguments he made in the same memo to Zimmerman were sounder. One was simply that the road would disrupt the ancient way of life of the Grand Portage Ojibway Indians, which up until then had remained largely intact. The other was that the road was unnecessary. As Marshall pointed out, motorists already had the entire Lake Superior coast from Duluth to Reservation River; they had uncountable scenic vistas and 3.5 million miles of road nationwide. It was unfair "to let them ask for the whole world."[88]

In any case, Marshall was not just worried about Indian lands. Later that month, while still in the Great Lakes region, he saw road construction in national forests that he thought was destructive and unnecessary. The new chief forester, Ferdinand Silcox, was another liberal with whom Marshall had become good friends. He told Silcox what he thought about these new developments: "Minnesota, Wisconsin, and Michigan," he said, "a few generations ago were all vast wilderness with myriad lakes and lake country undefiled by civilization." But now Wisconsin's lake country was "about as artificial as Central Park," while most of Minnesota was "devastated by all manner of roads."[89]

Mid-July found Marshall on the Uncompahgre Ute reservation in eastern Utah, where he spent a lot of time negotiating between Indians, white stockmen, and Grazing Service officials over a complex problem involving range rights and the restoration of certain lands to the Ute tribe. Marshall thought he had a compromise worked out, but Collier, back in Washington, hesitated to approve it. Marshall, who loved to send telegrams, sent a feisty one to Collier. "FOR GODS SAKE," it said in part, "CANT JUDGEMENT MEN IN FIELD BE TRUSTED STEWART PAGE MYSELF IN BETTER POSITION TO DECIDE THIS MATTER AT VERNAL THAN OFFICE WOULD BE IN WASHINGTON IF WE EACH WROTE THOUSAND PAGE REPORT." Collier approved the agreement the next day. But the problem of restoring reservation lands to the Utes was not resolved until 1948.[90]

By August, Marshall was back east, spending three days at Knollwood, climbing eight peaks one day—"old friends" he had previously climbed from three to sixteen times. "Take it all + all," he told Mable, "in spite of the more rugged mountains in a few parts of the west, the Adirondacks are still my favorites, and so the day was glorious."[91]

That done, he headed west again for the second time that summer. On a train in Paradise, Montana, he bumped into one of his adversaries, Park Service director Arno B. Cammerer. Marshall's humor, as already mentioned, was occasionally unkind, and Cammerer took more than his share of abuse from Marshall, Ickes, and others. Marshall told Yard:

Cam was his usual friendly, stupid self. The high peak of our conversation came when he said: "I'm with you fellows ninety per cent.

188

The wilderness is still my bible." In discussing the desirability of keeping curves in roads, Cam said: "Any sensitive person—and of course I consider myself one don't you know—knows that curves are aesthetically desirable."[92]

In September—about the same time that Marshall was chatting with Cammerer—the first issue of The Wilderness Society's magazine came out. Called *The Living Wilderness*, it reviewed the society's platform and contained an article on three Forest Service areas threatened by roads—the Selway-Salmon River area in northern Idaho, and the North Cascades and Olympic Mountains, both in Washington State. Marshall wrote this and several other articles anonymously. As he told Yard, "In the first issue I do not think that any names should be signed to the five Wilderness Articles .... [I]t might result in unnecessary difficulties if I, as a member of the Department of the Interior, wrote the articles about the Department of Agriculture."[93]

Though never large, and published only once a year for the first seven years, *The Living Wilderness* was distinctive. There was no advertising at all. There were pretty photographs of threatened wilderness areas. There was poetry and sometimes exceptionally eloquent prose, starting with Aldo Leopold's essay, "Why the Wilderness Society?" in the first issue. "The Wilderness Society," said Leopold, "is, philosophically, a disclaimer of the biotic arrogance of *homo americanus*. It is one of the focal points of a new attitude—an intelligent humility toward man's place in nature."[94]

With these first issues setting the tone, the magazine continued to stress historical, philosophical and esthetic discussions. It helped establish The Wilderness Society as a culturally sophisticated organization.

In October 1935, Marshall spent his annual leave taking a pack trip in southeast Utah, "where 9 million acres still remain roadless, the largest wilderness remaining in the U.S." Then he was up to the Pacific Northwest, checking in with the Neah Bay Indians, looking up Virginia Olmsted, and visiting his new friend, Irving Clark. Clark was one of the few people he'd met who shared not only his enthusiasm for wilderness, but also his interest in social reform. "I cannot tell you," he told Clark afterwards,

Four of the eight founders of The Wilderness Society: left to right, Bernard Frank, Harvey Broome, Robert Marshall, Benton MacKaye; Great Smoky Mountains National Park, 1936 (Photograph by Mable Abercrombie Mansfield; reproduced courtesy The Wilderness Society)

how much I enjoyed our being together in Seattle. I knew that I was going to like you because of your grand attitude on the outdoors. I did not, however, realize that you were also so thoroughly and courageously immersed in the second of my three major interests, the defense of civil liberties. Also I did not realize... that you would be so swell personally. There are plenty of people who live in wilderness areas who are dull as can be, and scads of civil liberty-ites who are pains in the neck.[95]

By late November Marshall was back in Washington. Most of his spare time for the next month or two would be spent promoting wilderness in various places. For starters, he had a meeting with all the Forest Service regional foresters. He had earlier sent Chief Forester Silcox another memo urging several more primitive area designations. Silcox passed it along to the regions and suggested that Marshall talk to them when they came to Washington for their annual meeting in November. The meeting was held on Wednesday, November 26, 1935. Once again the reception to Marshall's proposals was lukewarm. According to the minutes, twelve specific areas were discussed. Marshall himself summarized the disappointing results. He told L. F. Kneipp:

... in spite of the overwhelming sentiment which seemed to be expressed for a strong wilderness policy in the Forest Service at the General Staff meeting, the batting average for the specific wilderness areas [proposed at the meeting] is as follows:

Approved -	1	8	percent
Questionable -	7	59	percent
Rejected -	4	33	percent
Total	12	100	percent

Marshall, however, was "still hopeful that some of the doubtfuls may be approved, and some of those rejected by the Regional Foresters may be reconsidered." He wasn't giving up.[96]

Another major issue was the proposed national park on Washington's Olympic Peninsula, which set up a classic confrontation between the Park Service and Forest Service. In 1935, the Park Service managed a 300,000-acre block around Mount Olympus as a national monument. Surrounding that was the Olympic National Forest. If the national park were established, the Forest Service would lose several hundred thousand more acres to its competitor.[97]

In the past, preservationists had routinely endorsed the Park Service in such situations. But by 1935 that had changed. Benton MacKaye considered the Park Service a "despoiler of the primeval" and believed The Wilderness Society should be "wary indeed of endorsing its extension anywhere." Bob Yard agreed; he felt the Forest Service offered the best hope for preservationists.[98]

Marshall was more analytical. Examining the record of each agency, he began to see patterns. The Park Service was more guilty of "putting in roads where there was no need for them and in destroying wilderness areas." On the other hand, the Forest Service, with its utilitarian tradition, did a poor job of protecting virgin forests. Therefore, he reasoned, if the problem was keeping roads out of areas with low commercial value, an area was safer with the Forest Service. If the problem was keeping loggers and power companies out of primeval areas, the Park Service was better.[99]

So he thought The Wilderness Society would be foolish to become a lobbyist for either agency. "We need to have each of them preserve wild areas," he told Irving Clark. "Obviously, it will be impossible to get all the wild areas we want to have set aside, set aside as National Parks, even if it were desirable which I do not think it is. Consequently, it will be necessary to play with both organizations."[100]

And this is exactly what Marshall set out to do in the fight over the proposed Olympic National Park. In December of 1935 he wrote two letters, nearly identical, one for the Park Service and one for the Forest Service. The Wilderness Society, said the letters, had "not yet decided definitely" whether to support the Olympic Park bill. Before deciding, it wanted to know "what guarantees" each agency could make "to protect those values in which the Wilderness Society is interested." He listed seven specific questions, such as "How big of an area will you agree to keep free from all cutting of timber whatsoever?"[101]

The letters were sent out, not under Marshall's signature but Yard's. Then they sat back and waited for the agencies' replies.

Meanwhile, Marshall kept busy. One day in December, having a few minutes to spare, he dropped in at the Supreme Court to watch his friend Justice Cordozo at work. A few days later the Justice received the results of a "study" Marshall had conducted while there. Titled, "Statistical Study of the Manual Support to the Heads of Supreme Court Justices in Action," it read as follows:

> The head is generally conceded to be that portion of the body where the major part of most people's thought takes place. The Supreme Court is generally conceded to embrace those citizens of the United States who engage in the weightiest thought. It therefore seems of particular interest to observe evidences which have a bearing on the weight of Supreme Court Justices' heads. As an observable indicator of head weight, I have chosen for study the percentage of times that different Supreme Court Justices support their heads with their hands...

Name of Justice	Number of Times Holding Head	Percentage of Times Holding Head
Hughes	11	73
McReynolds	11	73
Butler	8	53
Van Devanter	6	40
Sutherland	5	33
Roberts	3	20
Stone	3	20
Brandeis	1	13
Cordozo	0	0

> One extraneous feature which may have influenced these figures is the fact that Justice Cordozo slept more than any other Justice. He does not sleep with his head in his hand.[102]

Cordozo's reply was also good. "I feel proud," he said, "of the demonstration that I have the lightest head of all the judges. I repel, however, as a foul slander the charge that I slept upon the bench . . . " Moreover, said the Judge, he had been tricked by Marshall's innocent expression:

> Your smiling physiognomy conveyed no end of the mischief you were up to. Rather proudly and transciently I said to myself, "his scoffing and sardonic soul has been awed and impressed by the vision of the mighty nine. He knows us now for the great and inspired spirits that we are." I shall never put my faith again in the physiognomy of innocence. [103]

As 1935 drew to a close, there was one more development greatly bothering Marshall. The state of New York was using CCC money to build a number of dead-end truck trails in his favorite wilderness, the Adirondacks. The hobblebush and red maple saplings had already been cleared on several abandoned tote roads before conservationists learned of this plan. But they soon found out that the Department of Conservation intended to build 120 miles of truck trails, ninety-seven of which would go through the Forest Preserve. Few things ever provoked Marshall as much as this. Suppose the CCC program continued for several more years, which was likely. Would the State of New York, desperate to spend its share, "put a truck trail up every drainage to eradicate completely every symptom of wilderness?"[104]

Using The Wilderness Society and other organizations, Marshall brought this issue to the attention of conservationists nationwide. *The Living Wilderness*, in its inaugural issue, published articles by Marshall and Raymond Torrey, secretary of the Association for the Protection of the Adirondacks, criticizing the truck-trail program. *American Forests* ran pieces by Marshall and State Conservation Commissioner Lithgow Osborne debating the issue. [105]

The key question was whether the roads were needed to improve fire protection. Marshall, who had had experience with severe fire problems in the West, didn't think so. He argued that existing protection—which had greatly improved since 1900—was quite adequate; all the truck trails combined, he estimated, would improve the state's fire damage record by no more than one-tenth of one percent. He feared, moreover, that new roads might actually *create* fire hazards by bringing in more motorists with their campfires and cigarettes and by creating openings in the forest canopy which let in sunlight and dried out the forest fuel.[106]

Marshall offered the Association for the Protection of the Adirondacks $500 to take the Conservation Commission to court on the truck trails. But the APA's president, Augustus Houghton, never told the rest of the organization's board about his offer.[107]

Meanwhile, others got involved in the issue, and Commissioner Osborne stopped construction temporarily. The state's governor, Herbert Lehman, then appointed a five-person committee to study the issue. Chairing the committee was Augustus Houghton, president of the APA. The comittee approved the truck-trail program, and Houghton signed the majority report. Marshall was furious and he began urging APA board members to replace Houghton as their president.[108]

Ninety-five truck trails were eventually built. Many years later, special wilderness designation in some areas closed them to mechanized use. But "administrative abuse" of the truck trails was an issue with Adirondack preservationists up to the 1970s.[109]

11

Indians and Wilderness (1935–1937)

◆ _____ ◆

I think often of that swell Sunday... when we battled through the
laurel slicks to the summit of Pathloser Mountain. Also the sunset
climb of the Pinnacle. It was all a grand day.

Bob Marshall to Mable Abercrombie

One of the first things Bob Marshall did in 1936 was take a three-
day trip to Knoxville and Atlanta. He called it "the three grandest
days I have spent in the east," and it was typical of his whirlwind
tours. He and Mable spent a day hiking in the Smokies, then took
an evening drive to Atlanta with Bernard Frank for a Society of
American Foresters conference. They went to the conference,
then had supper with Mable's parents, who lived in Atlanta; then
went to a meeting of the Georgia Appalachian Trail Club, where
Marshall showed his Arctic slides; then went square dancing. On
the third day, Mable showed Marshall around Atlanta. Later that
evening, they went to an SAF dinner, which they left early for, as
Marshall said, some "very, very, very scrumptious dancing" at a
night club. Marshall flew out of Atlanta at 4:10 the next morning,
arrived in Washington at 9:30 and went to work.[1]

A variety of little projects occupied him that winter and early
spring. In February he spoke to a wildlife conference on the conservation of Indian resources. In March he urged Ernest Oberholt-

197

zer to call a meeting of the Quetico-Superior Committee, saying that unless they stayed active they'd be forgotten. And in between times he wrote a short article for the *Journal of Forestry* defending The Wilderness Society.[2]

An editorial in the *Journal*, presumably written by the editor-in-chief, Herbert A. Smith, had recently accused The Wilderness Society of making wilderness a "cult." The society's organizers had done so, said Smith, by assuming that wilderness should be saved for its beauty—an assumption they were unqualified to make. "The training necessary for competently weighing questions that concern beauty is training in the field of aesthetics," said Smith. "... Foresters arrogate to themselves too much if they attempt to set themselves up as authorities in such matters."[3]

It's interesting that Smith perceived The Wilderness Society as a foresters' organization. Several of its leaders, of course—Marshall, MacKaye, Leopold, Frank—were indeed foresters. But it was never conceived as a professional foresters' group. In fact, it was organized to give non-professionals more clout in wilderness-policy decisions.

Aldo Leopold, in his beautifully concise way, explained this in a rebuttal to Smith's editorial. "I suspect," he wrote, "there are two categories of judgment which *cannot* be delegated to experts, which every man must judge for himself, and on which intuitive conclusion of the nonexpert is perhaps as likely to be correct as that of the professional. One of these is what is right. The other is what is beautiful."[4]

Marshall also wrote a rebuttal in which he accused Smith of presenting "a totally erroneous conception" of The Wilderness Society. "By way of retribution," he said, "I am looking forward to an early editorial discussing the peril of the wilderness, and the need for vigorous action to save the rapidly dwindling remnant." Such an editorial did not appear. But the strong feelings expressed in these articles indicates what a divisive issue wilderness was in the forestry profession.[5]

In early April, Mable came for a visit. Marshall by this time was renting a room from some liberal friends, the Blaisdells, with whom Mable stayed as a guest. When she left, Marshall sent her a typical letter summarizing the fun they'd had:

> I too have been thinking much and joyfully about your 37½ short hours around Washington. It was a glorious event. I don't know which part I liked best—no individual parts, I guess, but the whole visit . . . from the taxi ride out to Blaisdells to luncheon with wildernessers to the Cherry Blossom walk to the Shoreham dance to the Jackson breakfast to the Trammels walk to the Madrillon dance to the sad farewell. But even that wasn't really so bad because it was the end of such a swell time and the predecessor of another swell time soon to come on Guyot's virgin slopes.[6]

Marshall went on to say, however, that he wouldn't be able to see her again before May 17. The reason was that the Association for the Protection of the Adirondacks was holding a meeting in New York on May 11. They would be voting for a new president. "I have drummed up so much opposition against our present president, Augustus Houghton," Marshall explained, "that I think the bastard can be beaten provided I am there. So I really must be." (Houghton was in fact re-elected at the next meeting, even with Marshall there.)[7]

Also in April, Marshall and Yard heard back from the Park Service and Forest Service regarding their plans for the Olympic Peninsula. The Park Service plan, they decided, was better; it contained fewer roads and called for preservation of certain tracts of big timber that the Forest Service would cut. In early May, therefore, Marshall testified on behalf of The Wilderness Society at a House subcommittee hearing, speaking in favor of the bill to establish Olympic National Park. He emphasized, as always, the aesthetic and spiritual values of a large virgin forest. Only in the Olympic region, he noted, "could one still bury oneself for days in the glory of the most magnificent forests ever created."[8]

The Olympic case was important to the development of The Wilderness Society. Marshall, Yard, and others learned that they could make certain agencies in effect bid for their support. By so doing, they could do the most for wilderness preservation, both on this and future issues.*

Some time in May 1936, Marshall had lunch with Forest Service Chief Ferdinand Silcox, at which Silcox asked Marshall if he might be interested in coming over to the Forest Service to fill a new position, director of recreation and lands. Recreational use of national forests was continuing to grow, and Silcox felt he needed a high-level official to develop progressive policies to meet the growing demand. Marshall said he would send Silcox a summary of his ideas on the subject.

On June 3, he sent the memo. Recreation, he told Silcox, "is fully as important and valid a use of the National Forests as is timber cutting." He believed more people benefited each year from the use of national forests for recreation than for lumber. He believed the Forest Service was making a mistake by stressing timber over recreation, as it was doing in the Olympic Peninsula—for that only reinforced the popular notion "that an area must be made into a National Park in order to safeguard recreational values."[9]

About a week later, Marshall was offered the job. The Forest Service then notified Marshall's Interior boss, Ickes, that this had been done. But, as C. M. Granger of the Forest Service told Marshall, the secretary "took violent exception" to the discussions between Marshall and the Forest Service already held without his consent. "I also have a high regard for the value of Mr. Marshall's services," Ickes told Henry Wallace, the Agriculture Secretary, "and I am very anxious to retain him in the Department of the Interior, if at all possible."[10]

Ickes then talked with Marshall and offered him a better posi-

---

*In *John Muir and His Legacy: The American Conservation Movement*, Stephen Fox says that The Wilderness Society "by an accident of politics... belonged to the Forest Service lobby." It is more accurate to say the society looked increasingly to the Forest Service as being more likely to preserve the greatest amount of wilderness. The society, in fact, would often criticize the Forest Service and, starting with the Olympic Park issue, would not infrequently back the Park Service. It depended on the particular issue. (Fox, *Muir and His Legacy*, p. 212).

tion in Interior. But Marshall was now committed to the Forest Service job. "Recreation has always been my greatest interest in forestry," he said, "and I feel [this] is the most important recreation job in the country. It seems to me more important than that of Chief of the Park Service because the Park Service only administers about sixteen million acres of land, while the Forest Service has control of 188,000,000 acres."[11]

But Ickes refused to approve his transfer, so Marshall stayed in the Indian Bureau.

By then another summer had arrived and Marshall was off once again solving problems on reservations. June 16 found him in northern California, in a car between the Sierra Nevada and Sacramento, trying to scribble a note to Mable. "If you can't read this scrawl," he suggested, "hold the letter toward the sun and spit on it three times and maybe that will eliminate some of the evils from my writing." His tour this time included the Pyramid Lake reservation near Reno, Nevada, where trout were dying and the range was badly overgrazed, and two reservations in Oregon: Klamath and Warm Springs.[12]

Then he went to Missoula, where he met Mable for two days of hiking and visiting old friends. When that was done, Mable went on a horse pack trip with the American Forestry Association into what is now called the Bob Marshall Wilderness, while Marshall went off to the Wind River Range with two Indian Bureau and seven Forest Service officials. Marshall later told Mable:

My six-day trip in the Wind River Mts was glorious. . . . Every one on the expedition was surprisingly wilderness minded and by tactful pressure I managed to get an agreement to set aside 800,000 acres for permanent wilderness: 344,000 in Region 4 [Southern Idaho, Utah, and Nevada], 236,000 in Region 2 [Rocky Mountain], and 220,000 on the Shoshone Reservation. Scenically it is the grandest country I have ever seen.[13]

When Marshall came out of the Wind Rivers he found waiting for him a letter from his sister-in-law, Lenore Marshall (James's

201

Marshall with other Indian Bureau officials, Washington, D.C., 1936 (Photo courtesy The Bancroft Library, University of California, Berkeley)

wife), saying that his sister Putey was extremely ill with cancer. Putey had been treated for cancer three and a half years before, but now it had developed again. On August 1, Marshall received a telegram from his brother James asking him to come east at once. He reached Saranac, New York, where Putey was staying, on August 4. What he found there, he later said, "wasn't Putey, but really some stranger dying under whatever comfort drugs could give." She died on August 4, 1936, at the age of thirty-eight.[14]

It was a sad time for Marshall. His mother's death had been hard because he was only fifteen at the time. His father's death, though sad, had seemed natural because Louis had lived a full life. But Putey's death was tragic, not only because of what she had meant to Bob as his second (and "better") mother, but because she was only middle-aged. Ten days after her death, Marshall wrote a moving letter about her to their mutual friend Russ Carson. In one paragraph he said:

> We climbed dozens of glorious mountains together, rowed and paddled across innumerable lakes and ponds, cut through woods without trail, circled the Fishpond at Knollwood on that primitive forest trail hundreds of times during almost every summer of our lives from the time I was about three until last summer when we spent three last lovely days together in the Adirondacks. On countless evenings with George we rowed among the Islands and explored the deep bays of Saranac Lake while the sky changed from blue to red to black sparkling with stars, and the pine trees faded from detailed, three dimensional living objects to black silhouettes against the red sunset. Those days with Putey were so glorious, so peaceful, that I used to try to think up some sort of life which would keep me permanently at Knollwood and frequently with her.[15]

The same letter also may shed light on the final two years of Marshall's own life. Putey, he noted,

> never even hinted to Billie or the children or Jim or George or myself that anything was wrong. She knew that if we knew, it would cause us a lot of worry and unhappiness which she wanted to avoid. Also she wanted to live out the remainder of her life not as a doomed person but as a live and growing human.[16]

Marshall admired this approach, which he felt to be "typical of her perfect courage." Is it possible that in the same straits, knowing he was fatally ill, he chose to copy her stoic silence?[17]

Marshall turned his attention back to wilderness preservation in the late summer and early fall of 1936. He again urged Ernest Oberholtzer to hold a meeting of the Quetico-Superior Committee, which Oberholtzer did in November. Marshall, meanwhile, hired a friend, Althea Dobbins, to compile an up-to-date inventory of roadless areas in the United States. She came up with a list of forty-eight forested areas over 300,000 acres and twenty-nine desert areas over 500,000 acres.[18]

Among the inventory were thirty-two Forest Service areas. Marshall sent this information to L. F. Kneipp, who passed it along to the regional foresters and asked them again to consider additional primitive designations—the third time such a request was made as a direct result of Marshall's prodding. This time, however, Kneipp also asked the regions not to build roads into these areas until they could be studied further.[19]

And for the third time he got silence. Yet since Marshall's first request almost every region had made some concessions. The Primitive Area system had grown quietly but significantly. By the end of 1936 the Service had sixty-six Primitive Areas, totaling 10.5 million acres, an increase of about two million acres since 1933.[20]

Marshall's conservation efforts on the reservations sometimes conflicted with the goal of Indian self-sufficiency. He tried very hard but was not always successful in working out solutions. Such was the case when an issue arose over some big timber on the Quinault Reservation in northwestern Washington.

The Quinault contained one of the most impressive groves of big West Coast timber—Douglas fir, Sitka spruce, Western hemlock, and red cedar—yet standing. Through this forest ran Highway 101, also called the "Olympic Scenic Highway." To keep it scenic, Marshall wrote a regulation prohibiting the cutting of timber within a quarter mile of the road. But the Indians objected to this, and in November 1936 Marshall came to hear their complaints.

The Indians reminded Marshall that his bureau wanted them to be self-sufficient by harvesting their own timber resources. Many Indians were doing this, but others could not because their land allotments happened to lie near the highway. (The old allotment system, though abandoned, could not be dismantled completely.) The cost of preserving the timber, in other words, was being borne exclusively by a handful of allottees who had arbitrarily been given land that they could not put to commercial use.

Marshall decided they were right. "I confess," he told Collier, "that I had not considered the difficulties of enforcing this [regulation] on a reservation like the Quinault where all the timber is allotted."[21]

He worked out a compromise whereby the scenic strip was reduced from a quarter mile to 200 feet from the road. Allottees would then be allowed to cut *selectively* behind this 200-foot zone. Marshall would, in the meantime, urge Congress to purchase the timber in this quarter-mile strip at market value. He put an Indian forester, Cleveland Jackson, to work immediately cruising the timber to assess its value. Since no funds were available to pay Jackson, Marshall paid him personally; he left the Indian a check for $250 to cover his salary at $175 a month.

"I am tremendously interested in having this preservation take place on that very beautiful portion of the highway which crosses the Quinault Reservation between Quinault Lake and the mouth of the Quinault River," Marshall declared. He met at the first opportunity with a Washington Congressman, Martin Smith, to work out a bill to purchase the scenic strip.[23]

The bill was drafted but never passed. The Indians, meanwhile, decided they did not like Marshall's selective cutting rule. They could not make good money that way, and they were wary of setting a precedent by endorsing the idea. The issue dragged on for many years after Marshall was gone. Today there are no strips of virgin forest along Highway 101 inside the Quinault reservation; just outside the reservation, however, on national forest land, there is a strip that has been preserved.[24]

New Year's Eve 1936, found Marshall upset with Harrison Smith, publisher of *Arctic Village*. The book had sold a total of 3,500 copies, including 170 in the year just past, but Smith had refused to bind some 560 copies that he had on hand. There had been some bookstore requests for it at Christmas time, but the book was unavailable. "I don't know much about the publishing game," Marshall told Smith in a surly letter, "but I do know that ... if every book which sold 170 copies a year went out of print, the publishing business would certainly be extraordinarily unsatisfactory to the public." Smith bound some more copies, but Marshall was not too forgiving. He told the publisher he wished he had done it before Christmas.[25]

The next day—New Year's day—Marshall decided he needed a walk. His list of thirty-mile day-hike states now numbered thirty-four and he thought he might as well make Rhode Island the thirty-fifth. Besides, he noted, "It is nice to know the country, and I wanted to have a mental picture of Rhode Island the next time I heard it mentioned." So he hopped on a train to Providence, then took a bus to Newport, where he looked up a girl he knew named Susan Franklin. Since she wasn't home, he took the bus back to Providence to begin a thirty-two-mile walk. "It was a bleak, cloudy day," he later told Franklin, "which made the country seem very attractive."[26]

Then it was back to wilderness issues. On January 27 he held a fifteen-hour meeting of the New York State members of The Wilderness Society. The Association for the Protection of the Adirondacks had not reformed to his satisfaction, and the Adirondack Mountain Club was less militant than he wished. Consequently, he felt The Wilderness Society needed to be well organized on Adirondack issues. At the January 27 meeting, Marshall appointed several of the most ardent Adirondack preservationists—including John Apperson, Paul Schaefer, George Marshall, and Raymond Torrey—to head committees on pressing issues. Thus was further established the strong relationship between The Wilderness Society and preservationists in the Adirondacks.[27]

Meanwhile, National Park Service Director Arno Cammerer was still making plans for a skyline drive in Great Smoky Mountains National Park. Marshall again appealed to Secretary Ickes, and this time Ickes told Cammerer, in effect, not to proceed without Marshall's approval. "In view of the interest of Mr. Robert Marshall [in the Smokies crest road]," Ickes wrote to Cammerer, "I will want you to discuss with him the proposed route before it is submitted to me for approval."[28]

Ickes also promised Marshall that no surveys would be done "without your prior knowledge and consent." And since Marshall was not about to lend his consent to the project, no proposal was ever formally presented to Ickes. There is today still no "skyline drive" along the crest of the Smokies in the southwest half of the park, as there almost certainly would have been had it not been for Marshall's objections and Ickes's sympathy for wilderness.[29]

A few weeks later, Ickes demonstrated that sympathy again, when the state of Minnesota's request to build a highway through the Grand Portage reservation was considered at an informal hearing in his office. Marshall was on hand to record—with great delight—the secretary's comments. After hearing arguments from both sides, Ickes addressed his remarks to the would-be roadbuilders. No doubt he scowled and blustered a bit before telling them:

> We are making a great mistake in this generation. We are just repeating the same mistake in a different form that our forefathers have made. Instead of keeping areas... which will add to the wealth, health, comfort and well-being of the people, if we see anything that looks attractive we want to open up speedways through it so the people can enjoy the scenery at 60 miles an hour. Don't let us kid ourselves. You want a road and naturally you use the most plausible and persuasive arguments you can bring to bear.[30]

After the meeting, John Bernard, one of the road promoters, said to Marshall, "Do you call that an impartial hearing? Why, I knew the minute Secretary Ickes opened his mouth that we were beaten."[31]

In fact, Bernard was not beaten; he was only delayed. In 1942, Congress authorized Minnesota to condemn Indian lands for the road, and Highway 61 still runs through the reservation, bisecting the once wild and still rugged terrain east of Grand Portage.[32]

Marshall was getting a strong urge to return to Alaska. When he last had left the Arctic in September 1932, he had intended to return the following summer. Those plans had now been delayed long enough. In March 1937, he wrote Ernie Johnson about an expedition to climb Mount Doonerak and explore the North Slope of

207

the Brooks Range. He asked Johnson to hire two other sourdoughs, Jesse Allen and Ken Harvey, for the team. "I would pay
$200 apiece for the month's work," he told Johnson. "I realize that
if a man had to break up his whole summer he would be worth
more than that but [I] thought from the standpoint of the combination of the fun of exploration plus the fact that there might be slack
time at that period of the summer, that the fellows might feel like
coming along for that amount."[33]

Shortly after posting the letter, he heard that Secretary Ickes had
finally decided to approve his transfer to the Forest Service. He
would have to postpone his trip till 1938. He wrote Jesse Allen
over a year in advance, asking him to cache some supplies in the
mountains. "I feel so certain," he said, "that I will take the trip in
1938 that I am ready to get the supplies in there now."[34]

On April 13, 1937, Ickes officially approved Marshall's transfer
to the Forest Service. The transfer would take effect about a
month later.[35]

Meanwhile, The Wilderness Society was experiencing some
growing pains. There were now 576 members, a good amount for
an organization not seeking large numbers. Yard, however, was
worried; he thought the group was too informal. And so it may
have been. It was, in fact, unincorporated, had no president, and
was without any bylaws. "I'm afraid I'm making a reputation for
formality which I don't altogether deserve," Yard said. "[But] nobody will follow a casual bunch because they won't take them
seriously, and nobody will give a dollar to one not properly organized." For a man with a reputation for impractical idealism this was
exceptionally pragmatic thinking. Yard's experience was proving
useful.[36]

Persuaded by Yard's appeal, Marshall sent out a proposed set of
bylaws and a list of thirteen people to serve on a governing council.
The bylaws became official and the society was incorporated on
April 29, 1937.[37]

Marshall's influence was reflected in the five new members
of the governing council, all of whom were close acquaintances.

They included his brother George, who was active in Adirondack issues; Olaus Murie, then studying elk in Jackson Hole; Irving Clark of Seattle; L. A. Barrett, a California forester whom Marshall described as "conspicuous in opposing the majority of his organization in their desire to break up wilderness areas"; and Dorothy Jackson, wife of Marshall's liberal friend, Gardner Jackson. One reason for having Jackson was that, according to Marshall, "we feel it desirable for at least one woman to be a member of our council." She had already been active, lobbying in Congress against developments in Rocky Mountain National Park and working against a proposed highway along the Potomac River near Washington, D.C.[38]

Marshall was still The Wilderness Society's chief source of financial support. He was giving—and would continue to give— from $2,000 to $3,700 a year to the society, which amount paid Yard's salary ("You ought to have as much as a government stenographer," Marshall told him. "It is all I can afford now.") and provided expenses for annual trips by Yard and his wife into wilderness areas, so that he would know the issues firsthand. But since the society obviously needed more than one source of revenue, it began, after April 1937, to assess annual membership dues of one dollar, adding $700 a year to the budget by 1939.[39]

Before leaving the Indian Bureau, Marshall completed a job which later proved to be controversial. By 1937 he had a list of sixteen areas totalling 4.8 million acres on thirteen reservations that he thought should be preserved. He then wrote a proposed executive order declaring each of the sixteen areas either "roadless" or "wild," depending on its size. Collier signed the order on October 25, 1937 (after Marshall was gone); Ickes approved it two days later.[40]

Anyone who knew Marshall would have recognized his stamp on the executive order. It began by decrying the "unprecedented acceleration" of mechanization in the country. It then explained why Indians in particular might benefit from roadless areas. "Almost everywhere they go," said the order, "the Indians encounter the

209

competition and disturbances of the white race." If large areas were set aside, the Indians would always have a place to "escape from constant contact with white men."

The order next addressed the New Deal emphasis on helping Indians earn their own livelihood. It mentioned the great potential for Indian wilderness-guiding businesses, then noted that reservations had to be kept "in a wild enough condition so that some one visiting them might conceivably need a guide."

Finally, the order held agency superintendents "strictly accountable" for keeping the areas roadless and unsettled. Development could occur only where "the requirements of fire protection, commercial use for the Indians' benefit or actual needs of the Indians" clearly demanded it.[41]

The order was held up briefly while the solicitor's office debated its legality. The tribes were not consulted.[42]

The immediate reaction of the Indians to the roadless policy has not been well documented. John Collier in his memoir, *From Every Zenith*, says that no tribe complained for twenty years. Marshall believed that most Indians liked the policy. As he told Collier two years later,

> From what you and Bill Zimmerman have told me about the reception of the Indian wilderness areas, that policy has also met with widespread approval. From what some of the Sioux, whose reservations have been entirely raided by white men, have told me, the lack of land inaccessible to white men is a great loss, or at least to the older members of the tribe. From the enthusiasm with which many of the Crows greeted Robert Yellow Tail's suggestion to introduce grizzly bears in the Big Horn Canyon for the partial purpose of scaring out white intruders, I believe the Crows must feel the same way.[43]

Marshall, however, was probably hearing what he wanted to hear. Whether the Indians favoring wilderness were a strong majority is not known, and probably will never be known. What is known is that in later years the Indians felt increasing pressure to develop these roadless areas. In 1957 the Navaho tribe petitioned the Interior Department to re-examine the roadless policy. The

Marshall (middle) with two Indian friends in the Southwest, ca. 1935 (Photograph courtesy The Bancroft Library, University of California, Berkeley)

Navahos wanted to develop uranium and copper deposits on their land and were also anxious to get a share of the benefits from the proposed Glen Canyon Dam on the Colorado River. Federal Indian policy had by then reversed itself; the government was trying

211

to "terminate" its relationship with as many tribes as possible. The department decided that roadless areas interfered with this termination policy and so abolished them on all but two reservations.[44]

We can now see that Marshall made two mistakes in dealing with this issue. One, as already mentioned, was in being overly optimistic about the prospects for establishing Indian wilderness-guiding businesses. The second was in failing, with Collier, to consult the Indians before pushing through the roadless order. That failure made it easier for the Interior Department later to reverse the order. It also left Collier and Marshall wide open to the criticism that they imposed their will on the Indians.[45]

The whole question of Indian wilderness is filled with irony. On the one hand, how can any Indian cultures be saved without saving some of the wilderness on which those cultures were based? On the other hand, having lost, as Marshall noted, nineteen of every twenty acres they once had, and having been given some of "the poorest quality land yet remaining in the U.S." on which to live, how can the tribes afford not to exploit every economic advantage they have? The American people in general can afford much more easily than Indians to set aside wilderness.

The Indian New Deal in general has received mixed reviews from historians, and a lot of analysis is still going on. One of the major problems was that the Indians themselves, after half a century of being told they should "assimilate," were deeply divided on whether to accept Collier's program. As Kenneth Philp points out, forty percent of the Indians who cast ballots voted not to organize themselves under the Indian Reorganization Act. Only thirty-six percent of the tribes wrote constitutions and just twenty-eight percent drafted business charters. By 1953, most of the principles of the Indian New Deal were abandoned. This occurred, says Philp, "because tribal organization, land acquisition, and federal credit programs under the Indian Reorganization Act had, for the most part, proven unsuccessful. New Deal reformers, like others before them, had made the mistake of imposing their image of what was desirable upon all Indians." Others have argued that Collier's program only made certain tribes more dependent on white institutions.[46]

Yet there were many benefits. Conservation practices were improved on many reservations. Medical care was increased and modernized. Graft within the Indian Service was greatly reduced. Personnel standards were upgraded and more Indians were employed in the service. Historian Lawrence Kelly, while noting the shortcomings of the Indian New Deal, also points out its symbolic importance:

> The Indian New Deal marked a turning point in the nation's attitude toward the American Indian. It resulted in the toleration, if not the actual encouragement, of Indian culture and civilization. It ushered in a more humane administration of federal policy than ever before in U.S. history, and it brought new hope to thousands of Indians, who, a generation later, began to realize the potential for Indian self-determination which it preserved.[47]

As for Marshall, his difficulties reflected those of the program as a whole. His efforts to improve forestry were often fought bitterly by white lumbermen and enterprising Indians. His ambitious plans for setting up sawmill operations on reservations were thwarted by Congress, which never allocated funds for the program. But Marshall, characteristically, was an optimist right to the end. Nowhere in his voluminous papers is there the slightest hint of discouragement. "Yes," he said when he left, "I really have enjoyed it tremendously. . . . I will miss alike the devotion of the Indian Service employees and the marvelous humor of the Indians, and many other things which made the Indian Service job such a constant delight."[48]

12

Back to the Forest Service (1937–1938)

◆ ──────────────────────────── ◆

By this time . . . Marshall . . . had become some kind of holy guru to the wilderness people.

Richard McArdle

When Bob Marshall returned to the Forest Service in May 1937, the recreation business was booming. Between 1933 and 1939, over 2,000 campgrounds, plus many hiking trails, swimming areas, and ski facilities were built in the national forests. Recreational visits during the same period went from 14.3 million a year to 34.8 million, an increase of 144 percent.[1]

Yet Forest Service recreation had no clear philosophy or direction, which put the agency at a disadvantage in its ongoing struggle with the Park Service for recreational turf. So Marshall found himself in the middle of a major push to clarify the Forest Service's role in recreation.

Marshall hoped to put his liberal stamp on many of the Service's new recreational policies: He wanted, for example, to subsidize the transportation of low-income citizens to public forests; to build and operate camps "where groups representing the underprivileged could enjoy the outdoors for a nominal amount"; to change agency practices that he felt discriminated against blacks, Jews, and other minorities; and to acquire more recreational forest land near urban centers. And, of course, he wanted to preserve as much wilderness as possible.[2]

Outside the Forest Service, he continued to socialize with prominent liberals. One Sunday in May, at a luncheon hosted by Gifford Pinchot, Marshall was introduced to John L. Lewis, the labor leader. He was intrigued with Lewis, whom he saw again at Pinchot's the following evening, and also the evening after that at a "stag party." Marshall asked Lewis a lot of questions about labor strategy and the spread of fascism, about which Marshall was especially worried. He recorded his impressions of Lewis in a little paper he called "Three Consecutive Days." He liked the labor leader's "very simple and straight to the point method of expression. In all of the three days I did not hear him say a single stupid thing. Nor did he even once get off into a streak of rhetoric or bombast." When Lewis talked, Marshall noticed, "it appears he has really thought aobut the things he is saying. You never get the impression that anything he says is just a spur of the moment notion to keep up the conversation."[3]

It was typical of Marshall to write out his impressions of famous people he met. He did the same thing with Albert Einstein once when Einstein visited the Marshalls at Knollwood for dinner. Marshall was especially impressed with Einstein's appreciation of natural beauty, his "fine" sense of humor, and his belief that scientists should interpret their discoveries in readable prose to the general public.[4]

Marshall continued also to support The Wilderness Society, and this got him into a couple of good arguments in the spring of 1937. One of his opponents was H. H. Chapman, the Yale forestry professor with whom he had earlier skirmished over public forest ownership. Marshall often argued over issues just for the fun of it, much as another man might enjoy a friendly game of tennis. He usually emphasized that he did not take personally the differences of opinion between himself and his opponent. But this argument with Chapman became personal and it brought out the worst in both men.

The original issue was a plan by the U.S. Reclamation Service to build a tunnel under the Continental Divide in Colorado. The "Rocky Mountain Tunnel" would carry water from the Colorado River drainage into the drier Platte River valley to irrigate sugar beet fields. Some twelve miles of the tunnel would go under Rocky Mountain National Park. Grand Lake at the western edge of the park would become a storage reservoir, possibly altering its natural appearance. Many conservation groups—including The Wilderness Society, National Parks Association, American Forestry Association, and the American Planning and Civic Association—opposed the project.[5]

In April 1937, however, Marshall was surprised to see a statement issued by Chapman saying that the Society of American Foresters favored the tunnel. He sent Chapman a curt letter asking two questions. First, what members of the SAF had authorized him to commit the society to the tunnel? Second, had any SAF members opposed to the tunnel been consulted?[6]

Chapman wrote back but did not answer Marshall's questions. Instead, he simply asserted that he had done his homework while other organizations had not. "My position," he said, "seems to be slightly different... since I have not confined myself merely to thinking up arguments as to why it should not be built." He also announced that "certain agencies" had tried to "suppress scientific discussion" on the matter.[7]

Marshall's reply shows an uncharacteristic amount of exasperation. "Dear Chapman," he wrote,

> I have received your letters... concerning the Rocky Mountain tunnel. Coming from anyone else I would consider them highly insulting. Coming from you, they are mildly amusing, because Chapman is Chapman, and allowance must be made for the meanderings of a psychopathic mind.[8]

The issue was eventually resolved in favor of the tunnel, which was built; but meanwhile Marshall and Chapman moved their feud into the *Journal of Forestry*. Chapman, in three different articles, criticized The Wilderness Society, which he seems to have especially disliked. Marshall felt compelled to defend it, and did so in two published letters to the editor. One of these was a long and detailed rebuttal in which Marshall referred brusquely to "Chapman" (not "Dr. Chapman" or "Professor Chapman"—just "Chapman") thirteen times. By then, their feud had sunk to the level of adolescents who could not break away without slipping in their parting shots. Chapman was in a huff because Marshall had disagreed with him in print without warning him personally. Marshall replied that Chapman had done the same to him. Marshall finally signed off for good with one of his least original arguments. "If what I have done is undemocratic in principle," he said, "then you certainly started it."[9]

Around the same time, Marshall was having a much different kind of argument with his fellow Wilderness Society directors. Bob Yard, who was politically much more conservative than Marshall, worried that Marshall would bring too many "radicals" into the group. He did not trust Irving Clark and was none too elated when Marshall enlisted Catherine Bauer, a prominent New Deal housing expert. Bauer, after receiving information from Marshall, sent The Wilderness Society five dollars and a three-page discourse on what the society should be doing for the common laborer. She noted that wilderness appreciation had a reputation for being "snobbish," but she thought that could be remedied. She thought a great many—"even a majority"—of people would enjoy the wilderness if given a chance to experience it. She thought, moreover, "that factory workers, who experience our machine civilization in its rawest and most extreme form," were the ones who could benefit most from wilderness. Finally, she offered a pragmatic reason for introducing more blue-collar workers to the backcountry: they could broaden the political base of the preservationists.[10]

Marshall liked Bauer's idea, which fit well with his own liberal outlook, but he could never sell this idea to Yard or to the Council.[11] After he died, the society turned to other priorities. In 1940, Yard published in *The Living Wilderness* a letter from Olaus Murie which seemed to put the issue to rest. Titled "Wilderness is for Those Who Appreciate," it argued against Marshall's ideas (one of the few cases where Marshall and Murie disagreed). Murie feared that if too many people were brought into the backcountry without really understanding its subtle values, "there would be an insistent and effective demand for more and more facilities, and we would find ourselves losing our wilderness."[12]

The dilemma continues to plague the wilderness movement today. To escape charges of "elitism," preservationists have cultivated broad public support for wilderness. The price of their success, however, has been that heavily visited wilderness areas have lost an important part of their wildness—solitude. Bob Marshall—though he cherished its wildness—would have erred on the side of more people. He did not want, he once said, "to give lower income groups any aids to travel within the wilderness once they reach its edge." What he did want was to give them a chance to enjoy what he considered the greatest experience in the world.[13]

When Marshall agreed to return to the Forest Service, it was under the condition that he would spend several months each year in the field, just as he had done in the Indian Bureau. The job, he believed, could not be done "in the office on the basis of what was decided 10 years ago." He admitted that part of his motivation was selfish. As he once told Silcox, "Sure it's true that the most stimulating, most ecstatic experiences I've known have come among the forests and mountains. That's why I took up forestry."[14]

By midsummer of 1937, Marshall had packed up his high-topped sneakers, his blue jeans, and his denim shirt for a tour of the western national forests. He quickly developed the habit on such trips of inspecting every large roadless area that he could. Upon return, he would draw a boundary in blue pencil on a small-scale national-forest map, proposing a new wilderness or expansion of an existing one. Since he was usually in a hurry, his proposed boundaries were often rough estimates. This caused problems many years later for his former boss, Richard McArdle, the man he had amused in the summer of 1924 by cooking broiled eggs and analyzing pancake consumption of Forest Service bigwigs. McArdle became Forest Service Chief in 1952 and held the job for ten years, by which time the public demand for wilderness had increased. In response, the Forest Service was following up on some of Marshall's old proposals. "Unfortunately," said McArdle, "[Marshall] had little surveying sense and the maps he brought back left a good deal to be desired in accurately describing boundaries of the areas he wanted designated as wilderness."[15]

McArdle recalled that Marshall once personally showed him some of these maps. "If I had known that I would later be sitting in Silcox's chair, I would have paid more attention to Marshall's free, wide, and handsome boundary indications. You see, in order to set aside these areas... even tentatively... the areas had to be described more accurately than Marshall had done."

In re-drawing Marshall's maps, McArdle sometimes had to make changes. But, he said:

> If even a small acreage was eliminated, the wilderness folks protested loud and long over every small adjustment of these tentatively recorded boundaries. I used to get pretty fed up with their shrill and hysterical protests. Whenever I'd try to explain why the boundaries as recorded originally were not intended to be final, the response was "No such thing; the way they are recorded is the way Marshall drew them and wanted them to be." By this time, you see, Marshall—or his memory—had become some sort of holy guru to the wilderness people.[16]

He was not yet a holy guru when, in August of 1937, he took a pack trip in the High Sierra with Joel Hildebrand, then president of the Sierra Club. They met fifty-three people on the trail one day, which Marshall decided was "too heavy concentration for the wilderness but not too heavy use." He asked Hildebrand to form a committee to study ways in which the Forest Service could "get the use spread out," reduce the impact of pack stock on the vegetation of the Sierra, and otherwise better manage the Sierra high country. Thus Marshall became one of the first Forest Service officials to concern himself with a problem that has since become severe in many wilderness areas—how to manage them in a way that encourages human use while maintaining wild conditions. Marshall's extensive experience as a wilderness user, his strong sensitivity to aesthetics, and his ecological training combined to make him extremely sensitive to this problem.[17]

(Hildebrand later gave him a detailed report that included proposals for new trails, improvements to existing ones, suggestions for improving the "deplorable" condition of campsites, ways to minimize human impact, methods of making wilderness trips easier for poor people, and proposed additions to the primitive area.)[18]

When he left the Sierra, Marshall worked his way northeastward, arriving in Ely, Minnesota, on August 28 for a five-day canoe trip into the Quetico-Superior country with a Wilderness Society member named Sigurd Olson. About the same age as Marshall, Olson was a science teacher at Ely Junior College. He was slender and strong, wore his light hair in a crew-cut, and preferred khaki work shirts and pants. In the summer he guided trips into the boundary waters, taking great pride in his outdoor skill. His masters thesis was an ecological study of timber wolves. Already an ardent preservationist, he would later write some of the most eloquent prose ever written about the North American wilderness.[19] He was intensely devoted to the border lakes wilderness.

Olson had met Marshall the summer before he knew that Bob "liked his country in big chunks [and] had the stamina to go with it." So, Olson later recalled, "I mapped out a route that would really cover distance and give him a cross section of the best the border country had to offer."[20]

Olson himself was fascinated by the French "voyageurs," who, in the eighteenth and nineteenth centuries, when the continent was fresh, had traveled through the border lake country in their quest for furs. One evening at the campfire he told Marshall of a voyageur named Jean Le Boliere, who had carried five ninety-pound bundles of fur across a nine-mile portage. The next day, Olson and Marshall came to a difficult portage themselves, and Olson was amused to watch Marshall attack it:

Bob Marshall (left) and Sigurd Olson on a 1937 canoe trip in the Quetico-Superior country of northern Minnesota and southern Ontario (Photograph courtesy The Wilderness Society)

[Bob] had gotten to the point where he liked the feel of the tump line across his head and actually relished buckling down to the weight of a pack....

I know he was thinking of the great Jean as he made the portage that morning. Once I watched him wade up to his knees in a mucky stretch of bog and then climb out over a rocky, boulder strewn hill. And Bob never wore anything but tennis shoes that whole trip. Even with my boots the rocks sometimes hurt my feet, but not a word did he say.[21]

On the fifth day, as they paddled homeward across glistening Lac La Croix, a Forest Service motor boat came roaring at them. The driver stopped and asked if Bob Marshall was in their party. When Marshall introduced himself, the driver told him the motorboat was at his disposal; he could take it wherever he wished. Olson enjoyed what happened next. Marshall, he wrote,

> looked at me and grinned. "No thanks," he told the driver. "We've still got some exploring to do with the canoe. . . . "
> The driver looked puzzled, started the motor, and swung down the lake. A hundred yards away, he hesitated and stopped, then gunned the motor and swept off in a cloud of spray.[22]

Their canoe trip ended the next day. A truck gave them a ride from Moose River back to Ely. There Olson said goodbye to Marshall and never saw him again.[23]

When Marshall left Minnesota, he headed west again. September 7 found him at the Canyon Hotel in Yellowstone National Park preparing for a five-day trip into the North Absaroka Primitive Area. That evening, however, he was more concerned with the South Fork (of the Flathead) Primitive Area in northwestern Montana—part of the future Bob Marshall Wilderness.

The South Fork Primitive Area had been established in 1931. Some previously built plane landing strips in the area were then closed except for Forest Service administrative use. But in July 1937, Regional Forester Evan Kelley had proposed flying in hunters to help reduce the elk herd. The elk population had exploded throughout the 1920s, following widespread fires that, by opening up the forest to sunlight, had resulted in large areas of forage. By the mid-thirties there were too many elk for the food supply. After one especially hard winter, five hundred elk carcasses had been found in a ten-mile strip along the South Fork.[24]

The proposal to fly in hunters had been referred to Marshall, who had the authority to decide on it. He had then checked with a wilderness-supporting forester in the region named Ellers Koch, who recommended keeping the planes out and trying other methods of reducing the elk herd. So Marshall sent Regional Forester Kelley a hand-written letter from the Canyon Hotel vetoing the use of airplanes in the South Fork country. He was especially worried, he said, about setting a precedent for commercial plane use in primitive areas. "Once you make one exception there is no limit to the other exceptions which will be demanded all over the U.S. on the basis of this one."[25]

Marshall then reviewed the alternative ways to solve the elk problem—opening the game refuge to hunting, lengthening the season, and encouraging more hunters to *pack* into the primitive area. These, he thought, should be tried thoroughly "before risking the highly hazardous precedent of opening the area to airplane hunting."[26]

The strips remained closed, and the elk were thinned in other ways. It's interesting to note that an airstrip just outside the South Fork Primitive Area had a much different history. The Schafer Airstrip on the Middle Fork of the Flathead was used increasingly over the years to fly in hunters, fishermen, and other recreationists. In 1978, Congress established the Great Bear Wilderness from 285,700 acres surrounding this strip. But plane use by then was so well established that it was allowed to continue at 1978 levels.[27]

The morning after writing his letter to Kelley, Marshall went off into the North Absaroka range. Along with him was John Sieker, then supervisor of the Shoshone National Forest. Sieker displayed an exceptional appreciation for wilderness, and so Marshall later hired him as his assistant in Washington. When Marshall died suddenly in November of 1939, Sieker took over his position. For many years afterward, he worked diligently, with little recognition, to precisely define and protect many of the areas Marshall wanted preserved.[28]

Sieker got along well with Marshall despite a wide gap in their political beliefs. "I was a conservative Republican and Marshall was a liberal Roosevelt Democrat," Sieker said, somewhat understating Marshall's position, "but we never had any trouble. . . . He was a nice boss to have. He was a hard worker but very considerate of the people working for him."[29]

When Marshall and Sieker came out of the Absarokas that September of 1937, Marshall suddenly became very ill. He was hospitalized in Cody, Wyoming, but the exact nature of his illness was something of a mystery. A Forest Service newsletter reported that he had severe sunstroke. Marshall, however, insisted this report was "greatly exaggerated." "I had no sunstroke," he later told Meyer Wolff, "but only ptomaine poisoning which knocked me out of my head for 20 hours and gave me convulsions which caused me to bite hell out of my tongue, but otherwise did no damage . . . . " Marshall assured Wolff that after three days in the hospital he was fully recovered. "Since then," he said, "I have taken a 30 and a 40 mile walk in a single day."[30]

Some friends, however, thought Marshall's body was trying to tell him to slow down. Harry Gisborne told Marshall bluntly, "We were all mighty sorry to hear that they had to throw you in the hospital in Cody to save you from yourself. Yea Gods, man, you may be the World's Best Hiker, but you are going to become the World's Worst if you don't stop overdoing it."[31]

But Marshall would not slow down. Bob Yard once told him that he, Yard, stayed healthy by resting whenever he felt any sort of weariness. Marshall said that sounded like a good plan. "But," Yard observed, "his own plan seems to have been defiance of physical weakness. He never rested."[32]

As 1937 drew to a close, Marshall was feeling especially feisty. One of his articles and several of his letters during this time are much less congenial than usual.

Some time that fall he arranged for publication of a long segment in *The Living Wilderness* severely criticizing the National Park Service for building trails that were so wide, so oily, and so easy to walk on they destroyed the wild character of the parks. The segment featured letters received by Marshall and Yard from "three

225

active" society members describing over-elaborate trails in Glacier, Grand Teton, Great Smoky Mountains, and other parks. At least two of the letter writers—"Miss Abercrombie" and "Miss Engelhard"—were girl friends of Marshall.

The three letters were published in the magazine, followed by a response from Thomas C. Vint, a Park Service planner, followed by a rebuttal from Marshall in which Bob demolished Vint's arguments one by one. Marshall's points were valid, but his tone was more sarcastic than usual. For example, Vint had argued that the new Park Service trails were wider because they were being built by air compressors and tractors. Marshall replied:

> For years trails in the parks were built effectively without machinery. Now that machines have been discovered which can do the job for a lower cost, Tom feels they must be used, even though the job is unsatisfactory. This is like abolishing symphony orchestras because organ grinders can play the music more cheaply. It is like outlawing hand woven rugs because woven rugs are cheaper. It is like getting your illness diagnosed by quacks because good doctors are too expensive.[33]

That same autumn, Marshall wrote an uncommonly sharp letter to his old friend from Priest River, Idaho—Gerry Kempff. Marshall had helped Kempff get a job on the Klamath Indian reservation. Kempff then got himself mired in a personnel dispute in which he received a humiliating demotion after bitterly criticizing Commissioner John Collier. He wrote Marshall asking for "a friend's advice" about what he had done wrong. "I want to know," he said, "where I have been weak enough to merit 'a good swift kick in the pants.'"[34]

Marshall told him bluntly that he had been "extremely intolerant and vituperative about matters in which to say the least you knew only a small fraction of the whole case." He had also, Marshall said, been unreasonably hostile to the lumber companies and he still had "the unfortunate habit" of rising to his own defense "the instant anyone critiques what you have done." It may, Marshall concluded, "be impertinent of me to take the liberty to say such things but in view of the letters which you and Lily sent me I feel that I should." Kempff's immediate reaction is not in the record; but it appears that Marshall's blunt letter finished off their friendship.[35]

Marshall next unburdened himself on an Indian named Ivan Drift, who had written a book titled *America Needs Indians.* Marshall had ordered ten copies of Drift's book, which he received in December 1937, but upon reading it he promptly wrote Drift that he was "very much disappointed" in it. "While you did write interestingly in places," Marshall said,

> it seems to me at least that your book had long sections of terribly dull writing, and immense amount of repetition and at least three times the length for which there was any justification. Furthermore, the small type you used was a preposterous strain on the eyes of people who have far too many strains already.

Marshall went on to predict that most readers would soon "get disgusted" at Drift's "eighth grade smart-Alecky-style." But his only objective in writing so critically, he said, was in the hope that Drift's next work would really be something to help the cause in which they both believed.[36]

And finally there was the Pueblo Agency Superintendent, Dr. S. D. Aberle, a strong-headed woman whom Marshall had come to dislike. Hearing that Aberle had fired a promising Indian employee without notice or justification, he wrote Collier a complaint, accompanied by a poem about Aberle that read as follows:

THE TEMPERAMENTAL TARTAR
OF THE MUDDY RIO GRANDE

There are many Al Capones, there are many William Greens,
There are Wade and Ida Crawfords lurking back of many scenes;
But there is no one to match her on the sea or on the land,
She's the Temperamental Tartar of the Muddy Rio Grande.

She is vague, her thoughts run loosely, and she does not know her
mind,

And you wish that you could kick her just a bit on the behind;
When without the slightest warning she will take a stubborn stand,
And all hell can't budge that Tartar of the Muddy Rio Grande.

She won't talk out problems frankly and she won't coordinate,
She'll make guesses and defend them when they're proven second rate;
The ineptitude of nations one can easily understand
Through the Temperamental Tartar of the Muddy Rio Grande. [37]

Collier, who was on close terms with the Tartar, was not amused. He wrote back, telling Marshall curtly that there was no personnel problem at the Pueblo Agency. "As you are now in Washington," he chided, "I suggest that you well might have inquired about the circumstances of this case before supplying polemics and chant." [38]

Marshall does not explain his uncharacteristic testiness that fall and winter. Strain from some source seems apparent. Perhaps he was worn out from pushing himself so hard. Or maybe his illness in Cody had been more serious than he let on. A third possibility is dissapointment in love.

Marshall had continued seeing Georgia Engelhard occasionally through 1937, but the chart he kept shows that they took their last walk together in December of that year. According to Georgia (Engelhard), the relationship ended because Marshall had become too serious about her. She writes:

> I admired Bob immensely and found him a fine companion not only on the trail, but also at theatres, concerts, and on the dance floor. . . . Our relationship for a long time was mostly platonic. But eventually romance cropped up [although] it remained on a "necking" basis. Eventually Bob asked me to marry him, but despite the many things we had in common I did not love him. . . . And that was the end of that. [39]

Mrs. Cromwell could not remember the exact date of Marshall's proposal, but she thought it must have been in December of 1937, since she and Marshall "did not see each other after that." If so, it

would help explain Marshall's impatience and exceptional combat-
iveness that winter. For he must have been feeling very disappointed and frustrated, besides being worn out and possibly concerned about some illness. He kept this all to himself, not wanting
to be a pessimist or a complainer. His papers, however, show a
Bob Marshall who was less happy than normal in the last couple of
months of 1937.

If Marshall was indeed despondent that winter, he did not let it
affect his major goals of preserving wilderness and liberalizing
Forest Service recreation policies. In late 1937 he drew up a list of
forty-four policy questions, which were distributed by Assistant
Forest Service Chief Chris Granger to other foresters working on
the recreation-policy report. It soon was clear that several of Marshall's proposed policies were controversial. One of the most
revealing had to do with racial and religious discrimination.[40]

Dude ranches and resorts operating in the national forests were
required to obtain special use permits from the Forest Service. It
came to Marshall's attention, however, that among the resorts pos-
sessing such permits were a number that openly practiced discrimination. The Sahnaro Lake Ranch of Arizona, for example, adver-
tised that "the patronage of Gentiles only is desired." Lairds'
Lodge of Montana said: "We cannot accept guests of the Jewish
faith." The H. F. Bar Ranch and Paradise Ranch, both in Wyoming, accepted nobody as guest "against whom there can be the
slightest racial, moral, physical or social objection."[41]

In the southern national forests, which had very few resorts or
dude ranches, the problem was with campgrounds. These were
theoretically open to everyone. But, as Marshall observed, "it hap-
pens that the negroes are scared to use our campgrounds and they
are used only by white people." The solution, some said, was to
build separate campgrounds for blacks. "However," Marshall
noted, "such action, while it probably would bring more practical
benefit to the negroes, would involve having the government
openly recognize the principle of discrimination."[42]

Marshall wanted the Forest Service to adopt a policy saying that
no such discrimination would be practiced by the Forest Service or

any of its permittees. But the recreation-policy committee voted against him, eighteen to one. Such a policy, they said, could never be enforced in the South. Besides, southern Congressmen would cut off their funds in less time than it takes to say Jim Crow.[43]

But Marshall would not give up. Civil-rights work was a Marshall family tradition. He wrote a friend, Roger Baldwin, Director of the American Civil Liberties Union, for advice. "Is there," Marshall asked, "any legal basis for holding that the federal government cannot discriminate against people because of their race, color or creed... ?" And could the Forest Service write clauses into permits barring discrimination? "In trying to get the Forest Service to agree to [these policies], it would obviously be helped if I could show that we were legally required to do so." Baldwin wrote back, suggesting the fifth amendment and some statutory arguments, which Marshall used in his ongoing debate with the committee.[44]

Other matters occupied Marshall as well. In February 1938, the Quetico-Superior Committee, which he had been serving on, published its report to the President. It proposed a treaty between Canada and the United States under which a 175-mile network of lakes would be kept "undisturbed in a state of nature." It recommended a program of government acquisition on the American side, since "unnecessary road building" could be stopped only if the government owned most of the land.[45]

The plan was vigorously opposed by development interests in northeastern Minnesota, and intense struggles over the boundary waters continued for forty more years. No treaty was ever signed, but the establishment in 1978 of the Boundary Waters Canoe Area wilderness adjacent to the already-existing Quetico Provincial Park had much the same effect.[46]

Also that winter, Marshall and another adventurer, H. T. Cowling, formed the Washington Chapter of the Explorers Club. Sixteen members and four guests made the first meeting, held at the Cosmos Club on March 1. Marshall made the arrangements and picked up the tab.[47] Marshall had earlier joined the Explorer's Club, headquartered in New York City. He was not otherwise especially active in it, except that he wrote to Vilhjalmur Stefansson at least twice to express concern about congressional "fascists" joining the club.[48]

A lot of exploration was now being done by plane, which Marshall did not like. "I have developed a particular prejudice against airplane exploration," he said. "The area left in the world where people can get the explorer's thrill is very limited and the slower such areas are used up, the better it will be." Exploration, to Marshall, was chiefly an aesthetic experience. Using a plane, he thought, was "like peeping at the end of a book to see how the plot will come out."[49]

Around the same time, Marshall hosted two parties, one for his liberal adult friends and one for their children. The one for adults was a dinner and dance at the Shoreham Hotel. Among those present was Congressman John M. Coffee of Washington. "It was delightful," said Coffee, laying it on pretty thick "to mingle with your really liberal and truly fascinating friends and also to bask in an atmosphere so stimulating."[50]

Nobody basked more happily than Marshall at these parties—except when the dancing stopped and a floor show came on. Then, according to Gardner Jackson, Marshall would "curse impatiently" at the banality of most of the shows, barely able to sit still until the dancing started again.[51]

A few days later, Marshall hosted a party at Gardner and Dode Jackson's house for his children friends, at which he showed them films he'd taken of four wilderness areas. "We'll have some ice cream and whatever goes with it," Marshall promised, sounding a bit too sweet himself. ". . . You're also invited to invite your mother and father to come with you if you feel like doing so."[52]

By late March, Marshall was dreaming of his upcoming summer travels. He had become, as he said, "an enthusiastic desert fan." When an old Indian Service friend, Bill Zeh, told him of a trip Zeh had recently taken, Marshall wrote back excitedly:

Oh gosh! do you know how delightful it is to be homesick? Well, I haven't been so homesick in a long time as when I [read about] your three-day journey through that Ajo-Yuma Wilderness and boy, my mouth watered so the drool ran right down my chin which, because I have become so soft and sissy living in Washington, didn't even have any whiskers on it to absorb the moisture.

He went on to tell Zeh that he planned to be in Arizona and New Mexico later that year. Perhaps they could plan a wilderness trip together. He listed eight places they might go, including the Mohave and Great Nevada Desert regions. But then he remembered Zeh preferred forests. "Oh gosh," he concluded, possibly setting the single-page *gosh* record, "I forgot you don't like deserts, but even so I've given you plenty else to choose from."[53]

April 1938 found Marshall working hard on Forest Service recreation policies and trying to arrange a weekend with Mable Abercrombie. He had not seen her much, if at all, since their meeting in Missoula the previous July. He wrote to her from his office at 10:34 P.M. on April 21, after working all day on his recreation report. ("I haven't gone out to dinner yet," he said, "but, oh boy, how I will eat.") He then listed twenty-four subjects he was dying to talk with her about, and invited her up to Washington later that spring. (She accepted.)[54]

Meanwhile, Marshall's boss, Ferdinand Silcox, had already approved a new policy on wilderness that Marshall had developed. There were by then some seventy-two primitive areas, covering 13.5 million acres, in ten Western states. But the "L-20" regulation governing these areas was very permissive. In fifteen of the areas, road building was allowed. In sixty-two of them, grazing was permitted. In fifty-nine of them, logging was allowed. In only four areas were all three of these activities prohibited.[55]

The new wilderness policy was much tighter. "The Forest Service," it said, "will preserve substantial areas of wilderness under as many different conditions of topography and forest type as is reasonably possible." These should be closed to all motorized transportation and should exclude "summer homes, resorts, organization camps and commercial logging." There should be two classifications, by size: "Wilderness" areas would be greater than 100,000 acres, and "Wild" areas would be from 5,000 to 100,000 acres. The regions were directed by Silcox to start reclassifying their primitive areas in accordance with this new policy.[56]

Two specific wilderness issues—the Olympic National Park bill and the Kings Canyon National Park bill—were especially hot at this time. In both cases Marshall criticized his own agency for its approach.

In continuing to resist the Olympic park proposal, the Forest Service had published a report stressing the commercial value of the big timber that would be locked up if put into park land. Marshall then wrote a lengthy memo of his own, lambasting the Forest Service report. In particular, he took exception to a statement that recreationists were more attracted to stunted alpine trees than to big timber at lower elevations. He said:

> If the Forest Service really wants to understand what tourists in general feel about big timber they should follow the caravan which travels all year long to see the few small growths of redwood which have been preserved along the Redwood Highway. They should listen to the awed wonder of the hundreds of thousands who go annually to visit the big trees of Sequoia and Yosemite. They should then realize that immense timber does have for hundreds of thousands of American citizens value such as nothing else in the world can supply, and that one sizeable example of the Pacific Northwest immense timber is not exorbitant to leave in order that posterity may continue to delight in its immensity.[57]

(The Olympic Park bill was passed and signed by President Roosevelt on June 29, 1938. Six hundred forty-eight thousand acres were included; with subsequent additions it now totals 896,000 acres, or about 1,400 square miles. The Park Service, despite constant pressure to build roads, has generally preserved its wilderness character.)[58]

Marshall felt his agency was equally myopic in its approach to the Kings Canyon issue. The Kings Canyon country, on the western flank of the Sierra Nevada, is a land of majestic mountain scenery and spectacular canyons. As early as 1881, a large part of it was proposed for national park status. John Muir, the eminent naturalist and wilderness defender, visited the region in 1875 and proclaimed it as fine as the better known Yosemite Valley. Steve Mather dreamed for years about bringing it into the Park Service.[59]

But Mather never did get his Kings Canyon National Park; there were too many sheep grazers, lumbermen, irrigationists, power developers, and Los Angeles water officials interested in the region's resources. But in the late thirties another major push to make it a national park was launched. The Forest Service, which held the land, tried to prevent this by emphasizing what it called "multiple purpose" management. The agency did place a section of the mountains in the High Sierra Primitive Area, but it also proposed to develop the region's two most spectacular gorges, Tehipite Valley and Kings Canyon, for water storage, electricity, irrigation, and "developed recreation." It proposed further to build summer homes, create several artificial lakes, and harvest most of the timber.[60]

Marshall again dissented, arguing that the Forest Service plan was totally self-defeating. "If I were outside the government," he wrote,

> and was shown this plan of the Forest Service, I would swallow all my prejudices against the Park Service and root for a Kings River National Park merely to keep out these commercial desecrations and the roads which will go with them from as glorious a wilderness as remains in the United States. . . .
>
> If the Forest Service wants to keep the Kings River country as a National Forest, I think it should burn this Kings River report and write a radically new one.[61]

But the Forest Service did not burn the report. The agency kept emphasizing water development and Marshall kept telling them their strategy was wrong. "It seems to me," he told Chris Granger, "we might as well face the issue now of whether we will fight the invasion of all our wilderness areas by the Park Service on the basis of needing them for multiple use, or whether we should fight them on . . . the far more logical and reasonable bases, which recognize in such areas the prior claim of recreational values."[62]

While working on the Olympic and Kings Canyon issues, Marshall became acquainted with Rosalie Edge, a militant social reformer and our first nationally prominent female conservationist. She was active first in the women's suffrage movement, then became an avid birdwatcher (804 species on her life list) and finally helped a contentious naturalist, Willard Van Name, form the Emergency Conservation Committee (ECC). Van Name called Edge "the only honest, unselfish, indomitable hellcat in the history of conservation."[63]

Edge may best be remembered for establishing Hawk Mountain Sanctuary in Pennsylvania, where prior to the mid-thirties thousands of migrating hawks were slaughtered each year by misguided gunners. She hated most hunters, trappers, predator poisoners, and the Forest Service. While writing Marshall on the Olympic Park issue, she characterized the agency on various occasions as "greedy," "arrogant," "uncontrolled," and "in disgrace."[64]

Marshall defended the Forest Service and also hunting under certain conditions. Even so, he donated $100 annually for several years to the ECC, which was essentially Edge's organization. Once, he offered to take Edge on a wilderness pack trip.

"I should indeed love to go," she replied, "and would say that, barring things that cannot be foreseen, I will go." But she never did, and in the end asserted that she never trusted Marshall ("though I liked him, and his money").[65]

Marshall continued to have fun in Washington. One Friday evening in early May he went to a party at the Soviet Embassy hosted by a Mrs. Rhea Oumansky. The *Washington Post* covered the event and gave a thrilling account of Mrs. Oumansky's dress. A few days later, Marshall wrote her the following:

Dear Mrs. Oumansky:
Last Friday evening when I had the great pleasure of seeing you

and dancing with you at the delightful party which you had at the Soviet Embassy, I admired the lovely-looking dress you were wearing. Imagine my amazement upon finding the next morning when I read the Post that you were not wearing a lovely blue dress at all but that you were

"gowned in a powder blue chiffon, fashioned with an extremely full skirt, V neckline with shirring at the shoulders, and short pump sleeves. Lining the sleeves as well as the gown itself was an underdress of rose pink taffeta... "

Gee! I refuse to believe you were "shirred at the shoulder" because I've always been taught that only eggs are shirred and as for an extremely full skirt, neither you nor the skirt seemed extremely full but in excellent shape. Anyway, even if you do wear an underdress of "rose pink taffeta" I think you are one of the swellest people in all Washington, and I want to thank you for a delightful evening... [66]

When he wasn't hosting parties, going to parties, or trying to save the wilderness, Marshall concerned himself with social reform. He continued to feel strongly that natural resources should be nationalized; he was greatly alarmed at the spread of fascism in Europe; he was worried about civil liberties in the United States; and he wanted workers to get better wages and working conditions.

Consequently, he continued to give liberally to various civil rights, labor, and socialist organizations. Folders in the Robert Marshall papers at the American Jewish Archives show that he gave to at least eighteen such groups. His gifts included, for example, $2,000 in 1936 to the American Civil Liberties Union; $500 in 1938 to the National Negro Congress; and various amounts to the Socialist Party, U.S.A., the American League for Peace and Democracy, and the Washington Friends of Spanish Democracy. [67]

One of his favorite groups was the Workers Alliance, a national union of WPA workers and unemployed citizens. Marshall gave this group $2,500 in 1938—as much as he gave The Wilderness Society some years. "This is an increase of $500 over my last years's contribution," he noted when he sent the check. "Under no circumstances will I be able to give any additional sum before 1939. I have carefully budgeted my entire estimated income for the coming year (except for approximately fifteen percent for personal expenses) among a great many worthwhile organizations which need it and there will be nothing left over." This, he added, was his largest single contribution. The Workers Alliance was doing a "splendid job." Without it, "the danger of fascism would be greatly enhanced."[68]

In June 1938, Marshall and seven other government officials sponsored a meeting addressed by Vicente Lombardo Toledano, a Mexican politician then leading his government's program to nationalize its oil resources. The *Washington Post* then carried an editorial saying that the American officials, by sponsoring the meeting, had in effect endorsed Mexico's oil program. Such "bungling conduct," said the *Post*, showed how far we still had to go "before we develop a non-political civil service."[69]

Marshall wrote a reply which was never printed but which illustrates the cavalier manner in which he usually responded to such criticism and also his strong belief in free speech. He said:

> Sir:
>   Of course it is more amusing to read about oneself in the newspaper than it is to read about Joe Palooka, so it was fun last Sunday to read on the editorial page of the Post about my "bungling conduct" and also that I am "incompetent to handle technical problems in a truly professional manner... "

He went on to defend his position, then questioned the notion that government workers must act as if their tongues had been removed:

> I cannot conceive why a person working for the public must accept an inferior position as a citizen to one who receives a salary from private enterprise. The real danger to American institutions and American democracy will come, not when government officials participate as citizens in the democratic determination of politics, but when a large body of American citizens who are government workers become permanently muzzled.[70]

It should be noted that Marshall's liberalism was not purely theoretical. He was compassionate toward people less fortunate than he was, and he was often generous toward individuals. For example, he took a strong interest in a Pottawatomie Indian youth, Albert Alloway, who was in jail for a crime committed while he was drunk. Alloway was put in touch with Marshall because he was interested in forestry. Marshall sent him subscriptions to *Conservation* magazine and *American Forests*, then made several inquiries into his case. He learned that Alloway had done so well in classes at the prison that he was given a teacher's position there. After corresponding directly with Alloway, Marshall offered to pay attorney fees to have his sentence reviewed, and he gave Alloway advice on how to get into the Indian Service Forestry Division.[71]

Another time, a Wisemanite went to Yugoslavia to get a wife. When he had trouble getting her back into the United States, Marshall called the State Department and helped expedite the process.[72]

On July 1, 1938, the new recreational policies that Marshall had been working on were issued. In civil rights he had one victory and one defeat: A policy was adopted prohibiting discrimination by Forest Service permittees (western dude ranches), but no mention was made about racial segregation on Forest Service campgrounds. Several other policies were clearly the result of Marshall's work, although they needed the liberal climate of the New Deal to get approved. They included a policy stating that the Forest Service would henceforth build and operate its own resorts as funds allowed; one stating that resorts catering to a "small and exclusive minority" (that is, to the wealthy) were inappropriate on Forest Service lands; and one stating that the Forest Service favored public assistance to help transport underprivileged people to outdoor recreation sites.[73]

Despite these successes, however, Marshall was becoming frustrated with his job. There was no end to the number of reports he had to write, and these were interfering with his plan to revisit Alaska in the summer of 1938. Moreover, the paperwork was keeping him from getting out into the forests to do his job the way he thought it should be done. On July 18, 1938, he sent Silcox a long letter of exasperation. If all his job meant was writing reports, he said, "I don't want it. . . . There are too many other exciting and important things to do. . . . If I'm going to spend most of my time in the city, I want to work on a subject which should be handled in the city and not in the field."

Marshall then asked Silcox to fire him if he disagreed with his position. "I think you and Chris [Granger] are grand bosses, but I can't do a competent or a cheerful job for you if you won't even let me follow what seems to me the fundamentals of good work."[74]

Marshall sent a copy of this letter to his friend Raphael Zon, with whom he had been discussing mutual frustrations. Zon's response is interesting. "Sil cannot afford to let you go," he said. "It would be too much of a blow to his prestige as a liberal chief of a supposedly liberal organization. The matter will be patched up . . . and you will be able to visit your old friends in Alaska."[75]

Zon was right. Three days later Marshall was released from work on a ponderous report. He could now take a leave and go back to the Koyukuk.

239

13

Two Last Flings
(1938–1939)

Let's keep Alaska largely a wilderness!

Bob Marshall

On August 4, 1938, Bob Marshall caught a flight from Ketchikan, Alaska, to Fairbanks. On the plane, some news reporters asked him if he "wasn't afraid of being lynched" in Wiseman. There had been rumors since the publication of *Arctic Village* in 1933 that certain Koyukukers were not pleased with his candid descriptions of their lives. One story even had it that Harry Horton had knocked out Marshall's teeth and blackened his eyes in a Seattle hotel.

But when he landed in Wiseman, Marshall found the people as friendly as ever. Youngsters who hadn't been born when he'd last been there already knew him as Oomik, the Bearded One. They lined up excitedly for his famous piggy-back rides. Adults slapped his back, pumped his hand, and asked him where his whiskers went.

To be sure, there was plenty of discussion about *Arctic Village*. Verne Watts admitted he was "sore as hell" when he first saw quoted his description of Clara Carpenter. Clara, Verne had said, was "so thin that a couple of macaroni sticks would make a pair of drawers for her." And George Eaton told Marshall solemnly, "Of course, Bob, when I was saying how I'd slept with more women

241

than any man in Alaska, I didn't expect you to put it in a book, but I'm a-telling you, it's true."[1]

Jack White, for his part, was delighted with Marshall's treatment of how he, Jack, tore the roof off his own cabin to evict a tenant. Dishoo, an Eskimo girl, was also delighted with parts of the book pertaining to her. She quoted for Marshall verbatim a passage about the way she and her friends dressed.

Less pleasant was the realization that Wiseman had changed in the seven years since Marshall had been there. Two or three planes now flew into Wiseman each week. One hundred fifty tourists had visited during the previous year, whereas only one had come in during Marshall's thirteen-month stay seven years before. And an automobile now hauled men and supplies all summer to the mining operations at Nolan Creek and Hammond River. "One constantly hears [the auto] rattling around the dirt streets of town," Marshall noted.[2]

His sadness at these changes was soon forgotten, however, as he spent the next several days renewing old acquaintances. He danced at the roadhouse, played ball with the Eskimo children, and made plans with three companions for an expedition to Mount Doonerak. He had gotten Ernie Johnson, Jesse Allen, and Kenneth Harvey to go along on this trip. These men, he felt, were "the three outstandingly competent wilderness travelers in the entire Arctic Koyukuk."[3]

On August 10, these four men and two dogs (Judge and Moose) began floating down the Middle Fork of the Koyukuk in an "old tub" they had rented. The wooden tub was thirty feet long and had an outboard motor. It weighed 1,200 pounds by itself. With their gear on it, it weighed well over a ton. They called it "the raft."[4]

They reached the mouth of the North Fork that same afternoon. For the next six days, they motored, pushed, pulled, poled, carried, and dragged the raft against the winding current of the North Fork. Traveling eleven hours a day, they passed through the Gates of the Arctic and finally made a base camp on a low spruce bank two miles below Ernie Creek and 108 miles from the nearest settlement at Nolan Creek.

Marshall and friends before their 29-day 1938 Brooks Range Trip: left to right, Ernie Johnson, Jesse Allen, Bob Marshall, and Kenneth Harvey (Photograph courtesy The Wilderness Society)

They spent the next five days waiting for the heavy rains to stop so that they might climb Mount Doonerak, one of Marshall's biggest dreams. When the weather didn't change, they crossed the Arctic Divide and spent a week or so exploring the headwaters of the Anaktuvuk River. It was still raining on September 3, and so they decided it was time to get out of the mountains. The weather turned cold that morning and it was snowing hard as they loaded the boat. They climbed aboard and floated swiftly downriver—directly into the worst disaster of Marshall's career as an explorer.[5]

They had been on the river a short time as Ernie steered the boat around one of the river's many bends. Ahead of them, they

243

saw that the river was boring a narrow tunnel directly *through* what had once been its gravelly bank. The raft hit the bank with a sickening crunch and the four men were tossed into the frigid water.

Marshall found himself sluicing through the tunnel like a piece of timber being sent to the mill. Everything was pitch dark. "Immediately I felt the overwhelming certainty of death," he recalled in *Alaska Wilderness.* "In a most objective way I was feeling: 'What an easy way to die. Hold my breath for forty, fifty, maybe sixty seconds, trapped in this tunnel, hold it 'til I'm ready to burst, then have to let it out, and it's all over.' "

But then the blackness of the tunnel changed to light. He was popping out the other end. He worked himself into an eddy on the left side. Looking around, he saw Johnson go floating by, still clinging to the shipwrecked raft. Then he saw his two other companions scramble to shore on the opposite bank. Johnson worked the raft over to Marshall's side and jumped out. Both men were shivering uncontrollably. The danger of hypothermia was further increased because the temperature was only in the thirties.

Marshall held a piece of birch bark in his shaking hands while Johnson lit a match to it. The bark ignited and they built a huge fire. The two men on the opposite bank did the same. Had either pair failed in this, they would have died from exposure. The four men spent the next day drying equipment and fixing the raft, and four days later they were back in Wiseman.[6]

Most people would have considered that trip a nightmare: It had rained twenty-seven of twenty-nine days, and Marshall and his companions had failed to climb Mount Doonerak, had lost much of their equipment and most of their photographs, and had very nearly perished. But to Marshall it was fun.

"For a purely good time," he wrote, "without any anti-social by-products it would be hard to beat our four weeks adventure in unexplored wilderness."[7]

While Marshall was exploring the Brooks Range, he was also being discussed in the U.S. House of Representatives. A House committee to investigate unAmerican activities, known as the Dies

Committee, after its chairman, Martin Dies of Texas, made the front page of the *New York Times* on August 18, 1938, by announcing that eight federal officials were contributing to communism. Among the eight were Marshall and Chief Forester Silcox. They aided communism, said the committee, by contributing to such groups as the Workers Alliance and the American League for Peace and Democracy, groups "controlled by Communists." Another of Marshall's offenses was his open support of public ownership of oil lands in the U.S. and Mexico. About a year later, Marshall made the front page again for similar alleged misdeeds.[8]

The business of investigating radicals was becoming a deadly serious game. The Dies Committee, as historian Robert Griffith observes, "pioneered the whole spectrum of slogans, techniques, and political mythologies that would later be called 'McCarthyism'. " The committee soon listed 640 organizations, 438 newspapers, and 280 labor groups as possible communist fronts. The following year its list of government workers who were either communists or "sympathetic with totalitarian ideology" grew from eight to 1,121.[9]

However, in his book *The Communist Controversy in Washington from the New Deal to McCarthy*, Earl Latham estimates that in Marshall's time there were no more than seventy-five communists among a half million federal employees. And their primary goal was not espionage but simply to promote "left tendencies" within their specific agencies. Latham concludes that "there does not seem to have been a planned and premeditated 'infiltration' of the federal agencies, certainly not at the start."[10]

Yet many people took the Dies allegations at face value. Marshall and Silcox were fortunate in that their careers were not ruined, as many others' were, through the expedient of "guilt by association." But their reputations were needlessly tarnished.[11]

Former Chief Forester Richard McArdle, a political moderate, has commented on the accusations against Marshall. "I have heard several times," McArdle writes, "that Bob Marshall was a card-carrying commie. That is not so." McArdle goes on to explain that during World War II, he, McArdle, was selected to review FBI records of various government employees. He apparently came across an old file on Marshall.

As near as I could tell the FBI agents recorded whatever they were told and only occasionally did they try to check these conversations. I never found anything to prove or even hint that Bob Marshall wasn't absolutely loyal to the USA. Sure, he was liberal thinking in many respects but most of his liberal ideas wouldn't be thought at all radical today.[12]

In fact, as McArdle says, there is no reason to believe that Marshall was disloyal. He wanted a much more socialistic economic system, which made him an easy target for politicians looking for headlines. And some of the organizations to which he contributed had active members who were communists—there was a lot of cooperation between communists and other left-of-center interests during the 1930s because they all greatly feared the spread of fascism.

But few people have ever loved their country as Marshall did. He believed fervently in participative government, freedom of speech, press, and religion, and the egalitarian ideals which influenced his country's development. He was a serious student of American history. In all of his thousands of miles of wilderness travel, he never left North America. And, perhaps most importantly, he loved his country from the ground up, starting with the soil and rocks and ferns and trees.

Marshall himself was too busy traveling to respond to the allegations. After leaving the Koyukuk, he spent a week in the Kenai Peninsula and about two weeks on the Alaskan coast, "about half the time studying fox farming." He reached Seattle October 9 and probably looked up Virginia Olmsted—at least that was his habit. Marshall, Olmsted recalled, would make his entrance by somersaulting through the doorway, saying "I just rolled in" as change spilled out of his pockets onto the floor, all to the great delight of Olmsted's young daughter, Pam. Fifty years later, Olmsted recalled how popular Marshall was with her family:

Virginia Olmsted (Photograph courtesy
Virginia Olmsted)

[Pam] still speaks of thinking that Bob was especially hers and that
they shared a secret understanding that excluded all other grown-
ups. I also remember Bob's gentleness to my mother on his visit in
1939 just after my father's death following a long illness at home.[13]

Marshall and Olmsted had a friendly but platonic relationship.
"Irving Clark thought there was something between us," Virginia
says, "but we were never intimate." She goes on to say that Marshall liked her "for the wrong reasons." Her parents had had a hard
time during the depression, and Virginia had helped them out a
great deal. Marshall admired her for this and frequently asked her
"what he could do" for her. She would reply that he could use his
influence to speak for people who didn't have the ability or the
connections that he had.[14]

Marshall liked to tell Olmsted funny stories about people he met
or women he dated. One of his favorites concerned a disastrous
date he once had with a wealthy heiress who had very strict standards of social protocol. Since Marshall had no car, the heiress
picked him up in a limousine driven by a black chauffeur. They

went to a play or concert, but the woman was extremely unhappy with Marshall's choice of seats. She compared him unfavorably with European men, who, she said, knew how to treat a woman correctly.

After the show, Marshall asked her if she'd like to go out for "some ice cream." Being, as Marshall observed, "more hungry than angry," she accepted. But when they reached the ice cream place, Marshall lost her forever by inviting the chauffeur to come in and join them.[15]

After Seattle, Marshall spent time that fall in Washington, Montana, Oregon, Nevada, Utah, Arizona, New Mexico, and California. "It was a grand autumn," he told Jesse Allen back in Wiseman. "One of the outstanding features was a four-day pack-horse trip into the Superstition Mountain wilderness of Arizona, which the Forest Service has just set aside to be forever kept free from roads." That fall alone, he took ten walks of thirty miles or more. The longest was a forty-four-miler through "the terribly overgrazed rangeland just east of El Paso" on Thanksgiving day before sitting down to eat his turkey.[16]

Another place that he looked at—and especially liked—was the North Cascades Primitive Area in Washington, a region so rugged and picturesque that it has been called the "American Alps." These mountains had long been considered a candidate for national-park status, and Marshall's friend, Irving Clark, supported this idea. Marshall, however (despite his disagreements with the Forest Service over the Olympic and Kings Canyon regions) thought otherwise. He told Clark:

> I honestly believe that the Forest Service wilderness areas . . . are far safer then Park Service wilderness areas. Because of this belief, which I entertained long before I came to the Forest Service, I advocated for 6 years that the entire North Cascade country, down to Stevens Pass [an enormous area], should be created as a National Forest wilderness. I know and you know perfectly well that if this area should be made a park it would have roads extended into its heart.[17]

While Marshall wandered around the West that fall, he was, quite literally, homeless. His old landlords, the Blaisdells, had left Washington, and so he had moved out of their house on B Street Northwest. This was not a major problem since, outside of books, some camping gear, and a few scientific implements, Marshall had almost no material possessions. But he would need a place to sleep and occasionally entertain when he returned in November. In October, he wrote to his personal secretary, Dorothy Sugarman, asking her to find him an apartment. He gave her seven criteria to look for. They included no kitchen (wasted space as far as Marshall was concerned); a bathroom "reasonably free from cockroaches"; a living room capable of holding sixteen people; and a "wide bed you don't tumble out of every time you roll over." He was willing to pay whatever was necessary for these requirements, but, he said, "I don't want to pay merely for a stylish neighborhood."[18]

Having room for sixteen people was especially important, for Marshall's parties had become something of a tradition. According to several friends (including Silcox, Catherine Bauer, the Blaisdells, the Jacksons, the Zons, John Collier, and Congressman Coffee), Marshall would "get all kinds of people together—Congressmen, prima-donna braintrusters, professional civil servants, promoters of this or that—hand them a dubious drink, and then insist that they debate seriously and exhaustively on some such topic as the public ownership of resources, Soviet Russia or our refugee policy."[19]

What exactly Sugarman found Marshall for the winter of 1938–39 is not clear from his papers. His assistant at the Forest Service, John Sieker, recalls him staying at the old Roger Smith Hotel. His room there, presumably, was large enough to entertain sixteen people, and he settled in for another winter of work and socializing.[20]

Though he never drank, he was the life of many parties. Stories of his antics circulated widely and perhaps were embellished just a bit along the way. One has him walking on his hands down the steps of the Russian Embassy to protest the "lavishness" of a party. In another, while dressing for a formal dinner party, he discovers that moths have nibbled holes in the seat of his black tuxedo. No problem, he says as he applies black shoe polish to his underwear so it won't show through, pulls on the holey tuxedo, and hustles off to the party.[21]

Marshall also continued to date different women. He sent his sister-in-law, Lenore Marshall, occasional ratings of his top ten girlfriends, whom he referred to as "whiz-bangs." His favorite one may have gotten away, but it was not in his nature to brood over what might have been.[22]

Besides John Coffee, Marshall had two other interesting friends who were members of Congress: Maury Maverick of Texas and Jerry O'Connor of Montana. Maverick, for a time, was the quintessential New Deal lawmaker. Back in Texas, he had made his name defending communist sympathizers and promoting radical schemes to distribute the state's concentrated wealth. He employed the effective if sometimes shadowy services of young Lyndon Johnson to win a congressional seat in 1934. Then he led a spirited group of leftish House upstarts—known as the Mavericks—who met each week in Renkel's Cafeteria. Their main topic was how to sabotage the conservative House leadership.[23]

In 1938, Maverick lost his seat. The following year, when he was elected mayor of San Antonio, Marshall wrote:

> Hurray and congratulations on your election! It is a great event in the liberal development of the South. You deserve the thanks of all liberals for pioneering the way to this development a second time.[24]

Jerry O'Connor, from the first district of Montana, thought a lot like Maverick—so much so, in fact, that he too lost his seat in 1938. Marshall wrote to him and his wife, Mazie:

> We're all three young enough that we'll probably meet many defeats in the next fifty years in the struggle for civil liberties and a decent economic system for this country and for democracy in the world at large. It's even conceivable that when we die we still will not have won the fight. That's happened before to many generations of people who have been working for goals which would make

human beings happier. But win or lose, it will be grand fun fighting and knowing that whatever we do in the right direction will help eventual victory.[25]

That letter illustrates a quality of Marshall's that his liberal friends greatly admired: He had an incredible ability never to seem discouraged, to be constantly exuberant and optimistic. As his friends later observed, "he was the one guy who could always pull you out of the squirrel-cage and make you feel again the excitement, importance and opportunity in what you were trying to do."[26]

Three of Marshall's major concerns at the Forest Service that winter were "fly-by-night mountaineers" in Oregon, discriminative ski policies in Washington, and wilderness everywhere.

The problem with irresponsible mountaineers brought out a dilemma in wilderness management that has never been solved. That is, should people be protected from themselves through extensive rules and regulations governing their actions in the back-country? If too many rules are imposed, then one of the great values of wilderness—freedom—is lost. But if no rules are imposed and users get into trouble, the managing agency may be accused of negligence or, at best, find itself constantly preoccupied with search and rescue operations.

The problem was brought sharply into focus when, in January of 1939, Marshall's office received a memo from a junior forester named Becker, at Mount Hood National Forest in Oregon. Becker wondered what to do about a local adventurer named Bill Lanahan, who had "a complex of some sort" which led him repeatedly to break their mountain-climbing rules. Recently, Lanahan and a friend had attempted to climb the difficult west face of Mount Hood on a stormy day with improper equipment. They got in trouble and barely escaped with all their toes, not to mention their lives.

Several other climbers routinely refused to register with rangers and broke other rules. Yet rangers were expected to risk their own lives in rescue attempts when these bad actors got into trouble. What did the Washington office think should be done?[27]

Marshall's reply reflected his own belief that freedom was an important wilderness value. It also reflected the tendency of Marshall and other foresters to compare themselves to the Park Service. He told Becker that he preferred the slower process of education to the faster expedient of more regulations. The big advantage of national forests over national parks was that national-forest visitors were "not under constant regulation." Bad as the situation Becker described was, Marshall told him that "it would be far worse to make people feel that they are under the same restrictions to freedom of action on the national forests as they are in the national parks."[28]

In another letter on the same subject, Marshall again compared the two agencies. He said: "We don't want [our policies] to have the same bad traits as those of the Park Service, which give people far too much the feeling of constant regulation. After all, regulation is one of the things they seek to escape when they come to the woods." He suggested, instead, posting attractive signs pointing out dangers to climbers and rescuers. "The WPA ought to still have lots of boondogglers in the office who will be glad to make vivid sketches of tumbling mountaineers."[29]

Marshall watched for violations of civil rights like a hungry lynx watching for snowshoe hares. When he saw anything that might suggest favoritism of one group over another, he pounced on it ferociously. One of many such cases occurred when regional forester Buck sent the Washington, D.C., office a copy of some new policies for the Stevens Pass Ski Hut in the Wenatchee National Forest in Washington state. One of the policies said that in case of conflicting applications, "the Supervisor will determine the user and will give preference to winter sports groups, character building, educational, religious, and other organizations."[30]

Marshall objected. "Isn't there discrimination," he asked Buck, "when you specify certain groups who will receive preference, but leave out other equally laudable groups?" It seemed to him "that labor unions, junior unions or farmer groups should have as much preference as the groups you mentioned. Incidentally, in view of the fact that less than half of the American citizens belong to any religious organizations, it does not seem to me that we have any conceivable authority to give preference to this minority as opposed to the majority who are associated with no organized religion. It would be doing violence to the spirit if not the letter of the First Amendment."[31]

Thus Marshall was possibly the first high-level official seriously to fight discrimination in Forest Service recreational policies. On other occasions he argued strongly against summer-home development, "elaborate" resorts, and high fees for ski lifts on national forests, all of which, he believed, were exclusionary and had no place on public lands. Without doubt, many of the foresters with whom he clashed on these issues thought he was a zealot. To Marshall, however, that was immaterial. He may have been wealthy and he may have given up Judaism, but he was still a minority and still the son of Louis Marshall, the great civil-rights activist. He believed, as Virginia Olmsted had reminded him, that he had a responsibility to speak for those minorities who were not as eloquent or as well positioned as he happened to be. And he had long since stopped worrying about whether anybody thought he was fanatical.

Wilderness, of course, was never far from Marshall's mind. In February 1939, he complained to Assistant Chief Granger that the regions were giving him the stone-face treatment on proposed additions. He listed twenty-seven new areas he wanted declared wilderness or wild, plus twenty extensions to existing primitive areas. Since he had returned to the service, Marshall noted, only five new areas had been established—the Anaconda-Pintlar in Montana, the Three Sisters in Oregon, the Sawtooth in Idaho, and the Mazatzal and Superstition areas in Arizona. The worst offenders were regions one (Northern Rockies) and six (Oregon and Washington). "They just say 'no' to all new wilderness areas," Marshall told Granger, "even those which they recommended in the recreation report outline. In these cases it would seem to be your solemn duty under the oath you took to perform the function of your office, to choose between the regional foresters and me." Granger, however, did not feel compelled to arbitrate, and so many of these areas were left for the future aggravation of Richard McArdle.[32]

Public sentiment for wilderness preservation was now growing fast. That winter, a bill was introduced in Congress that would have authorized the President to declare wilderness areas in national parks and national monuments. No hotels, permanent camps, or roads would be allowed in these areas. The Forest Service proposed an amendment to allow the same designation on national forests.[33]

The bill died, but it was among the first of many "wilderness bills" to be introduced in Congress, culminating in the 1964 Wilderness Act establishing a wilderness system of federal lands. Marshall, in a 1939 letter to Kenneth Reid of the Isaac Walton League, said he favored presidential proclamation of wilderness, but not congressional designation. He did not explain why; perhaps he thought congressional approval would be too cumbersome a process.[34]

Spring found Marshall still as liberal and whimsical as ever. In late February he had a luncheon with Eleanor Roosevelt at the White House, to discuss plans for a national recreation conference. She served, as Marshall said, "the worst concoction I have yet been unfortunate enough to taste—baked grapefruit just hot enough to burn your tongue," followed by "a funny mushed-up mixture of vegetables in which only the taste of onions stood out clearly."[35]

Marshall still kept in touch with Gifford Pinchot, one of his all-time favorite liberals. "Of course," he told Pinchot in March of 1939, "I have also tremendously admired what you did for civil liberties in Pennsylvania when you broke a long-established and nefarious coal and iron policy; what you did for the cause of well-run relief in Pennsylvania during your second administration; and as recently as this January, that evening at my house, for the best exposition I have ever heard of what liberals and labor people should do to get elected more consistently."

But the thing he admired most was Pinchot's "pioneer work in

the direction of placing resources under the only type of management which is possible if they are to serve acceptably the public
welfare."[36]

Marshall wished his profession had more people like Pinchot. As
he told a liberal friend who was thinking of leaving forestry:

> I think there is no profession that needs the benefit of liberal people
> in its ranks more urgently than the forest profession. When Gifford
> Pinchot started the profession going, it was about the most left wing
> profession in the country [probably an exaggeration]. Today, as we
> both know to our sorrow, it is exceedingly reactionary and there's
> hardly even a nucleus of good liberals in it. Therefore it seems to me
> that each one of us who is in this liberal category is badly needed in
> the profession.[37]

One day in April, Marshall spotted in the *Washington Post* a
column by sportswriter Shirley Povich that struck his fancy. Povich
had noted that a gold mine of baseball talent was "on the loose"
but being wasted by major league teams. He referred to black
ballplayers, who, under a "gentleman's agreement" among team
owners, were kept out of the big show. Marshall complimented
Povich on his piece:

> Dear Mr. Povich:
>
> That was really a grand article you had Friday morning on Negro
> baseball players. I have been a baseball fan since Christy Mathew-
> son and Honus Wagner were in their prime and I have always won-
> dered why in hell some liberal big league president did not sign up
> an all-Negro team and trim their race prejudice-ridden rivals. Your
> article is the first time I have yet seen this matter in print. Con-
> gratulations![38]

The Wilderness Society, meanwhile, continued to grapple with
the Park Service-Forest Service dilemma. At a council meeting in
April the question arose again in regard to the bill to create Kings

Canyon National Park out of national forest land. According to Marshall, "all the members" agreed with him that the Forest Service was "better equipped" to preserve areas that did not possess important commodity resources. But the Kings Canyon region had valuable timber and hydroelectric potential, both of which, as noted earlier, the Forest Service was inclined to develop. So Marshall urged the Council to "concentrate [its] attack on saving these two magnificent valleys [Tehipite Canyon and South Fork Canyon] which can be properly safeguarded only through the creation of a Park." The Council agreed with him, five to one. The dissenter was MacKaye, who was thoroughly disgusted with the Park Service. Benton, said Marshall, "still felt that the Park Service record in regard to the primitive was so very bad that we ought to state that we were for retention of this area as a national forest."[39]

By June it was time for another grand tour of North America. This time Marshall planned to visit Alaska first and then conduct a long series of national forest inspections from July 26 to October 24. Then, after a brief return to Washington, he would spend another month inspecting forests in the Southeast.

On June 21, he landed in Wiseman for what was to be his final Brooks Range expedition. His primary goal was again to climb Mount Doonerak; he planned also to fill in several more blank spots on the Brooks Range map at the headwaters of the Hammond River and the North Fork.

Kenneth Harvey and Jesse Allen had agreed to join Marshall again this summer. Because Ernie Johnson was busy with mining, they recruited a Kobuk Eskimo named Nutirwik to take his place. Nutirwik was slender and barely five feet tall; his hands were tiny and gnarled. But he was, in Bob's words, "one of the most companionable, competent and considerate of all the fine people around Wiseman." He had given himself a "white man's" name, Harry Snowden; but on wilderness trips he used his Eskimo name, Nutirwik, which meant "blizzard."[40]

Influenced, no doubt, by their bad experience with the previous

256

summer's wooden boat, Bob and his friends decided this time to travel exclusively on foot. To help them carry their supplies, they brought along three dogs.

Summer nights don't get very dark that far north, but they do get cool, and so the adventurers traveled in the evening to get a little respite from heat and mosquitoes. After reaching the North Fork of the Koyukuk they followed it north and on July 1 reached the mouth of Bombardment Creek. There, four miles from the peak of Mount Doonerak, they made a base camp.

For the next two days they tried to climb Doonerak. The weather this time was good, but the summit was simply too steep for their abilities and equipment. To Marshall this was a big disappointment. A couple of weeks later, on another Brooks Range peak, Mount Apoon, he philosophized about it:

> Was our happiness on Apoon diminished because we could not climb 2,000 feet of sheer rock? Is it possible to reconcile oneself to the second best and feel satisfied with the best one can attain? That was the question in everything. One in a million, perhaps, could be a Nobel Prize winner or a President of the United States. The other 999,999 might burden their lives in gnashing their teeth over unrealized ambitions for greatness, or they might adjust to limitations and fate and get the greatest possible happiness out of the North Dooneraks, the Amawks, and the Apoons which they could attain. Perhaps this philosophizing on a windswept pinnacle of rock might seem a little forced, but I could not help it, because I had talked only recently with an assistant manager, an associate professor, and a division chief whose lives for several years had been unhappy because they had not been promoted to head manager, full professor, and bureau chief.[41]

For Marshall, mountain climbing was a metaphor. Each peak represented one of life's challenges. In attempting to climb it, you explored your limitations; and when you found those limitations, you learned to accept them.

Three days later, Marshall and his friends were back in Wiseman. Marshall's career as an Alaskan explorer was over.

257

Marshall on North Doonerak in the Brooks Range, 1939 (Photograph from Alaska Wilderness, *University of California Press; reproduced courtesy of George Marshall)*

Altogether, he spent 210 days exploring the Brooks Range. The map he made covered about 15,000 square miles of the Koyukuk watershed, 12,000 of which had previously been totally blank. The

U.S. Geological Survey maps of the region now include 164 names of mountains, rivers, and other features proposed by Marshall.[42] Many of these names—such as Blackface Mountain and Bonanza Creek—had been used locally since the gold rush days. Others—such as Sillyasheen Mountain and Yenikuk Creek—had been used even longer by the Eskimos. But still many others were originated by Marshall, for there were dozens of features which neither the Eskimos nor the sourdoughs had bothered to name. Consequently, the list of place-names in the northern Koyukuk reads like a who-was-who and what-was-what in the Alaskan life of Bob Marshall. Among the features named after people Bob liked are Big Jim Creek, Ernie Creek, Harvey Mountain, Holmes Creek, Jack Creek, Kupuk Creek, and Snowden Creek. Among the names based on incidents in his travels are Cairn Mountain, Hanging Glacier Mountain, Grizzly Creek, Kinnorutin (You-are-crazy) Creek, Midnight Mountain, Passless Creek, St. Patrick's Creek, and Walkaround Creek. Finally there are the names that evoke vivid images of the features they refer to: Limestack Mountain, Cockedhat Mountain, Gates of the Arctic, and Frigid Crags.

The journals of his last two trips—titled "Doonerak or Bust," and "North Doonerak, Amawk, and Apoon"—were printed and distributed privately by Marshall to his friends and relatives. They now comprise the final two chapters of *Alaska Wilderness*. The mailing list for "North Doonerak, Amawk and Apoon" testifies to Marshall's ever-widening circle of friends, for it contained 504 names.[43]

It would be hard to overestimate the sheer joy that Marshall derived from these explorations. His brother George once wrote that "Bob found in both the wilderness and in the frontier community some of the esentials of freedom of the human spirit for which he fought and which seemed so lacking in the twentieth-century world of the nineteen-thirties."[44]

Bob himself, in the last paragraph of his last Alaskan account, expressed very powerfully these "essentials of freedom of the human spirit." The world, he observed, could never live on wilderness, "except incidentally and sporadically."

Nevertheless, to four human beings, just back from the source streams of the Koyukuk, no comfort, no security, no invention, no brilliant thought which the modern world had to offer could provide half the elation of twenty-four days in the little explored, uninhabited world of the arctic wilderness.[45]

Unfortunately—from Marshall's perspective—there were lots of people who did not think a wilderness little explored and uninhabited was worth much. Ever since Secretary of State William Seward engineered the purchase of Alaska from Russia in 1867, there had been those who could barely sleep at night knowing of all those minerals, all that lumber, all that fur, and all those potential tourist attractions sitting around up there doing nothing for the economy. In the late thirties, still groping for ways to beat the Depression, federal officials were tantalized more than ever by the fabled riches of the Great Land. In 1937, Congress had asked the administration for a comprehensive plan for developing Alaska's resources. Marshall was appointed to a subcommittee charged with developing recreation proposals for the plan.[46]

Marshall felt that *all* of Alaska's resources—recreational, industrial, agricultural—should be developed very, very slowly. Alaska was a unique chance—the last chance—to show that civilization did not have to swarm over its resources like a pack of wolves going after a wounded caribou calf. He wrote an article for *The New Republic* explaining his position. "World history," he observed, still sounding like his father arguing for preservation of the Adirondacks, "for the last hundred years has been the story of the rapid development of untapped resources which represent the accumulated natural processes of eons, yet this opening of new frontiers has seldom brought more than transient prosperity for the vast majority of those engaged in it. The only reason we have as high a standard of living as we do today is that the more primitive people of past ages saw nothing immoral about leaving resources undeveloped."[47]

Marshall argued against settling refugees in Alaska, against rapid resource development, and against a proposed highway from Seattle to Fairbanks. He believed that the goal of recreational planning in Alaska should not be rapid development or "increasing the volume of tourist traffic." It should be to save "the pioneer conditions yet prevailing throughout most of the territory."

Therefore, I would like to recommend that all of Alaska north of the Yukon River, with the exception of a small area immediately adjacent to Nome, should be zoned as a region where the Federal Government will contribute no funds for road building and permit no leases for industrial development.

Alaska is unique among all recreational areas belonging to the United States because Alaska is yet largely a wilderness. In the name of a balanced use of American resources, let's keep Alaska largely a wilderness![48]

The report finally issued—"Alaska: Its Resources and Development"—followed Marshall's advice to a surprising degree. It put a lot of emphasis on preservation, so much, in fact, that Chief Forester Silcox, generally a wilderness supporter, thought it went too far. The report, he said, "simply gives the impression of locking up and maintaining Alaska as a wilderness." After visiting Alaska himself, Silcox thought this was unnecessary.[49]

People in the Alaska territorial legislature agreed. They passed a quick resolution calling for a new study so that "recommendations for restrictatory conservation and reservation proposed by the Alaska Resources Committee [would] not be adopted."[50]

So began the long and bitter struggle between development and preservation interests in Alaska—a struggle that is far from over. Each side has gotten some of what it wanted. Developers got a road to Fairbanks. They also bulldozed—with no public hearing and little public knowledge—a winter road across the Brooks Range by way of Anaktuvuk Pass. The road was being used to cart supplies to the North Slope within a few months after oil was discovered at Prudhoe Bay in 1968. Also built was the eight hundred-mile trans-Alaska pipeline, which bisects the Brooks Range and clashes harshly with the primitive landscape. Much of the tundra north of the Arctic Divide is now littered with oil drums and crisscrossed with Caterpillar tracks.[51]

But there have also been great victories for preservationists. In

1978, President Jimmy Carter set aside an eight-million-acre Gates of the Arctic National Monument, comprising the heart of the country Marshall explored. Two years later, the Alaska National Interest Land Conservation Act made this a national park. In the region north of the Yukon River, the act also designated an additional fourteen million acres as national park and monuments and more than thirty million acres as national wildlife refuges.[52] Bob Marshall's brain child, The Wilderness Society, played a major role in getting these lands set aside.

As hikers in the High Sierra can't help but recall John Muir... as paddlers in the Boundary Waters feel the presence of Ernest Oberholtzer and Sig Olson... as visitors to the Grand Canyon marvel at the epic journeys of John Wesley Powell... so those who come to Gates of the Arctic National Park often feel the spirit of Marshall traveling with them. In some undefined, abstract, but very real way, he is out there with his pioneer friends, having... gosh... a swell time.

After leaving Alaska, Marshall made his tour of western national forests. While doing these inspections, he addressed all aspects of forest recreation. He sent each region a long, detailed report discussing everything from campgrounds to summer homes to the quality of outhouses. But his biggest concern—it goes without saying—was wilderness, and in the fall of 1939, he was as anxious as ever to get some preserved.

In August, Marshall took a twenty-seven mile day-hike in California's Gibraltar Wilderness and spent three days in the Emigrant Basin Wilderness. He congratulated the California region for proposing several wilderness expansions, then discussed the Kings Canyon country. Again bringing up the Park Service threat, he said in his report:

> I hope that simply because of the King's Canyon park bill the proposal which the Forest Service had to extend the High Sierra Wilderness will not be dropped. It seems to me that the best way to retain an area under national forest management is to give it what we

consider the best type of administration and not fear that by designating an area for recreation it will help the Park Service take it over. Actually, the history of national forest areas transferred to the Park Service has been pretty much the story of the public supporting a park because it felt the Forest Service had not done enough for recreation in general and the preservation of the primitive in particular, rather than because it had done too much.[53]

Kings Canyon National Park was finally established on March 4, 1940; it encompassed some 454,000 acres. (The two fine canyons, Tehipite and Kings, were initially left out but were added later.) It was established as a "wilderness" park, and—as in the case of Olympic National Park—the Park Service has kept it almost entirely wild. So while Marshall was right that the Forest Service was using poor strategy in its attempts to retain jurisdiction over wilderness lands, he turned out to be wrong about the Park Service's willingness to keep roads out of wilderness. But he was wrong in part because of his own efforts: The Park Service changed its ways largely in response to pressure which Marshall himself did much to create.[54]

As Marshall traveled, he was constantly on the lookout for potential Wilderness Society members. One day, in a campground in the San Bernardino National Forest, he met a pair of adagio dancers who had just returned from seven years in Europe. When Marshall told them he was a Forest Service official, he said, "they practically became tearful in begging me to do something to stop the advance of roads into all wilderness country." He got their addresses and had Bob Yard send them "something to fight on."[55]

A couple of weeks later, at Elk Lake, in the Oregon Cascades, he met two teen-agers finishing a fourteen-day hike through the Mount Jefferson and Three Sisters wildernesses. The boys told him they had made the trip for eleven dollars apiece. Marshall arranged for them to receive some Wilderness Society material to "see if they did not want to join." Next, in Portland, he had Sunday dinner with a Mr. and Mrs. Woods, who were "enthusiastic defenders of the wilderness." He told them Yard would be in touch.[56]

Around the same time, Marshall was driven one day through a virgin stand of Douglas fir in Oregon's Willamette National Forest. "It was so beautiful," he reported, "that I rode the running board of the car for quite a distance in order to really appreciate the stand." As he rode, his brown hair streaming in the breeze, he contemplated how much more beautiful these forests were than second-growth stands. As a result of that ride, he urged the region to set aside several large sections—five to ten thousand acres in size—"for future generations to enjoy."⁵⁷

Marshall had arranged for an entourage of foresters and friends to take a trip with him into Washington's North Cascades in mid-September. Included in the party were John Sieker, Senator John Coffee, and Virginia Olmsted. The trip convinced Marshall, more than ever, as he later said, "that no part of the whole United States is so well adapted for a wilderness as the country between Stevens Pass and Hart Pass." He found himself arguing—as he had done so often before—that the Forest Service should emphasize non-commodity values in regions like the North Cascades.⁵⁸

But the primitive area was never extended as far as Marshall wanted it, and Route 20 (built by the state of Washington) now bisects the region. In 1968, North Cascades National Park and two adjacent national recreation areas were established, totaling 674,000 acres. The Park Service has preserved a large chunk of backcountry on either side of Route 20—another indication of both the service's and the public's increased sensitivity to wilderness values since the thirties.⁵⁹

While he was in Washington state that September, Marshall won, *in absentia*, a decisive victory in Washington, D.C. On September 19, 1939, the Secretary of Agriculture, Henry A. Wallace, signed Regulation U-1 (governing "wilderness areas") and Regulation U-2, (governing "wild areas"). These "U-Regulations" endorsed the policy developed by Marshall's committee to protect wilderness and wild areas from road building, lumbering, hotels, resorts, summer homes, and the like. The regulations also made the areas more permanent, by requiring a ninety-day public notice and public hearings, if demanded, before establishing, changing, or abolishing them. Passage of the new regulations was an important step in the evolution of Forest Service wilderness policy. They were extremely important because they gave Forest Service wilderness areas more permanence and approval at the cabinet level.[60]

The Forest Service Primitive Area system had grown by that time to nearly fifteen million acres, an increase of about 5.4 million since 1933. At least one article has credited Marshall with "single handedly" bringing about this expansion, and others have implied the same thing.[61] But that is not quite true. There were many other factors, including the competition between the Park Service and Forest Service, increased demand for backcountry recreation, the efforts of Harold Ickes to capture the Forest Service for his "Department of Conservation," the support of Chief Foresters Greeley and Silcox, the work of L. F. Kneipp, and the efforts of many unrecognized local foresters. It is true that Marshall played an important role by calling constant attention to the wilderness issue and by pressuring the Forest Service from both inside and outside the agency.

Marshall's role in the wilderness movement is big enough without having to be exaggerated. Helping to preserve and better manage Forest Service wilderness, moreover, represents only part of his accomplishment. He also kept a seven-year vigil over the National Park Service, saving in the process a major eastern wilderness (the western half of Great Smoky Mountains National Park) from being bisected by a highway, and contributing to the Park Service's increased sensitivity to wilderness values. He was the primary founder of an organization (The Wilderness Society) which has become a leading voice for the preservation of wild lands in the United States. And he stirred up a great deal of public interest through presentations, articles, and his posthumous book, *Alaska Wilderness.*

Marshall was never as eloquent as Thoreau or Muir or Aldo Leopold; and his arguments were not as ecologically sophisticated as Leopold's or Olaus Murie's would later be. He was, however, extremely articulate and pragmatic. And because of these qualities Marshall, far more than the others, made a direct and substantial impact on public policy. Indeed, he personifies the transition between the naturalists of an earlier time who avoided politics as much as possible, and the professional environmentalists like Howard Zahniser and David Brower who came along later. Like Marshall, these latter figures learned to be as much at home in a congressional hearing as on a mountaintop.

Finally—but perhaps most importantly of all—there was Marshall's enthusiasm. With his endless supply of "goshes," "gees," and "swells"; with the humor and freshness that he managed to put into every article, letter, and memo; with the optimism that flowed from him like water from a mountain stream—Marshall not only stirred things up but became a truly inspirational figure.

In this and other respects, the one conservationist that Marshall most resembles is John Muir. Both Muir and Marshall were clearly in a kind of ecstasy in the wilderness; both liked their wilderness on the grandest scale possible; both expressed their enthusiasm in extravagant terms (indeed they both had a penchant for overusing the word "glorious"); both had extensive experience in the mountains before becoming wilderness activists; and both were the primary founders of major preservationist organizations.

But unlike Muir, Marshall couched almost all of his arguments in terms of the human benefits resulting from wilderness preservation. One reason is that he saw wilderness as a legitimate use of land to be carefully and routinely considered in resource planning. Besides, stressing human benefits was the most practical approach. In later years the notion that wilderness should be preserved for its own sake, or as an expression of goodwill to other creatures, began to draw support. Marshall would certainly have liked this concept, but it would not have done him much good in the 1930s.

14

"He Never Rested" (1939)

◆ ──────────────────────────────── ◆

The variable which to me seems to make the difference between a tragic and a normal death is the factor of happiness; a dual factor embracing both the personal happiness of the one who died and the amount he did toward making other people happy.

Bob Marshall

Bob Marshall had a busy schedule—as usual—on Friday night, November 10, 1939. Shortly before seven, he dropped in on Margaret Tyler, Bob Yard's daughter. He talked with her briefly about her parents' shaky financial situation. Marshall was paying Yard $125 a month to run The Wilderness Society, but that was all the income that Yard and his wife had. Marshall told Margaret that her father was a great man and deserved much better. He, Marshall, had a dinner party that night and was then leaving for New York, but upon returning to Washington, D.C., he would talk with her again about ways to help out Bob and Mrs. Yard.[1]

After leaving Margaret Tyler, Marshall went to dinner at Gardner and Dode Jackson's. He seemed to be in fine spirits and good health when he left the Jackson's to catch a midnight train to New York to visit his brothers, George and Jim, but when the train pulled into Pennsylvania Station, Marshall did not get off. A porter found him dead in his berth. He was not quite thirty-nine years old.[2]

267

Marshall's friends and relatives were devastated. "Bob's death shattered me and was the most traumatic event in my life," George Marshall has said.[3]

A letter from Marshall to Virginia Olmsted arrived on November 15, five days after his death. In the same mail came a letter from other friends, saying they'd read of Marshall's death in a Spokane newspaper. Olmsted began making phone calls, vainly hoping to hear there had been some mistake.[4]

Harvey Broome wrote Yard twice in one day after hearing the news. "The word about Bob has made me so tense," he wrote, "I have hardly been able to eat. The only relief I can get is to talk about him with somebody who knew him. . . . "[5]

When the initial shock wore off, Bob's friends began to see that they might not have been so surprised. They recalled his mysterious illness in Cody, Wyoming, in 1937. And they learned that he had suffered a similar illness just after his recent Cascade trip. Virginia Olmsted, in fact, recalled that, while on that trip, Marshall had looked terrible. "He looked very thin and stooped," Olmsted said, "so that suddenly it was possible to imagine what he must have been like as a very little boy and how he would appear as an old man."

Virginia also noticed that Marshall was in pain. She told Irving Clark:

> . . . [O]n the first day's ride up to Buck Creek Pass, I noticed that three or four times his face was twisted into a grimace of real pain and that with both hands he was supporting his weight by pressing against the pommel of the saddle. I asked him if he would care to trade horses, thinking that his saddle must be miserably uncomfortable and knowing that he wasn't fond of riding anyway. The real pain that he showed made me watch him closely for a couple of days, but I soon forgot it when he seemed perfectly comfortable after arriving at that first night's campingplace.[6]

To the other members of the party, Marshall seemed fine. He took a twenty-eight-mile-walk the day after they got to camp, then walked another six or seven miles after supper to stretch his legs.

George, James, and Robert Marshall at New Hope, Pennsylvania, ca. May 1939: their last meeting all together (Photograph courtesy George Marshall)

Said John Sieker: "Throughout the whole trip Bob was in the best of spirits, showed no fatigue at all after long walks, and ate heartily. He gave no sign at all of illness."[7]

Marshall still seemed well when he reached the Cascadian Hotel in Wenatchee, Washington, on September 20. But at 9:30 the next morning, he called Gilbert Brown, a local forester, and said he was sick and needed a physician right away. Brown reached a Dr. Gerhardt, who came quickly. After a short examination, the doctor told Brown that Marshall was "very bad, apparently near death." Brown rushed to the hotel, where he found Marshall "just coming out of what appeared . . . to be an epileptic fit." (One is reminded of Marshall's reference to biting his tongue—which is common during seizures—in the course of his mysterious illness in Cody, Wyoming.) Brown said he asked Bob how he felt. Bob said, "fine," and promptly passed out.

He was rushed to the hospital in an ambulance. There, says Brown, "Bob had one or two more spells . . . , but not so severe."[8]

A couple of days later, Marshall flew back to Washington, D.C., cutting short his western tour. Before leaving, he reportedly had a confidential talk with Dr. Gerhardt. Nobody knows what Gerhardt said. Marshall would only say that he was advised to go home and rest.

Back in Washington, Marshall checked in to the Emergency Hospital. Visitors found him cheerful and looking well. He told them the attack had been sunstroke and that the examination showed nothing serious. John Sieker, however, wondered if this was true. "I had a vague impression at the time," he said, "that [Bob] was making light of the situation and had knowledge of some critical ailment, but Bob would never have let such a condition be known."[9]

Marshall again did not rest long. On October 5, just two weeks after his severe attack in Wenatchee, he left Washington to resume his western inspections. He continued to play down his illness, but his explanations were inconsistent. He told some people it was sunstroke and others it was from "eating something indigestible." To show how healthy he was, he pointed out the long hikes he was again taking. The day before he died, he wrote Virginia Olmsted:

> Oh, yes, I have gotten completely over that sunstroke. In fact, I have traveled around Utah, Wyoming, Idaho, Montana and Missouri for four weeks steadily since then, the jaunt including a 32-mile walk in the country I am hoping to add to the Wind River Wilderness just east of Jackson, Wyoming; a 30-mile walk with Lincoln Ellison over Mt. Ogden near Ogden, Utah; and a really glorious 41-mile walk in the Ozarks of Missouri . . . [10]

Why did Marshall keep driving himself so hard right to the end? *If* he knew he was fatally ill, there are two possibilities: One is that he was following his sister Putey's example and "living life to the

270

full" for as long as possible; the other is that he was in a hurry to complete his life's work. Bob Yard thought the latter was the case. "Doctors no doubt had told him that he might live for years a quiet life at his desk," Yard reasoned. "But that was impossible for him. To achieve his great objective of a wilderness system... and achieve it before his inevitable death, meant work at the utmost of speed. He had also objectives to accomplish in Alaska."

This, however, was entirely conjecture. George Marshall, for one, did not think Marshall knew he was going to die. He had been a hard driver well before the time when he might have been told he was seriously ill.[11]

It is impossible to say for sure, then, whether Marshall knew he was fatally ill. It has often been written that he had a congenital heart problem, but that is mere speculation that has become accepted as fact. George Marshall insists—emphatically—that Bob had no congenital heart problem. A police autopsy suggested that he had myelogenous leukemia and coronary arteriosclerosis (hardening of the arteries). These certainly would have killed him eventually, and perhaps, as Yard speculated, Marshall's unwillingness to slow down speeded up his decline.[12]

In the weeks following Marshall's death, the future of The Wilderness Society was greatly in doubt. The organization had relied so heavily on him that it was unprepared for his absence. He and Yard had conducted the society's business very informally, handling problems as they came up and keeping only casual records. When Marshall died, the society owed $400 in printing bills, and Yard owed the society about $200 for "doctors, druggists and absolutely necessary replacement of personal clothing."[13]

Marshall had promised to pay these debts, but there was no record of his promise. And even if these were paid, where would the money come from to keep the society going after that? A statement by Harvey Broome reflects the way most society councillors felt. "I'm terribly worried about the Society," Broome told Yard, "as much for Bob's sake, as for our own and the cause of the Wilderness. We must find some way of keeping on."[14]

Their worries were eased a little on December 7, 1939, when Yard learned that Marshall had left in his will a substantial fund to help preserve wilderness. Marshall's entire estate, before taxes, was worth $1,534,070. He named just one individual beneficiary: his old friend and guide, Herb Clark, to whom he gave $3,000. The rest he had put into three trusts. One was to educate people about labor unions and to promote "an economic system in the United States based upon the theory of production for use and not for profit." The second was to advance the cause of civil liberties. The third was to be used for the "preservation of wilderness conditions in outdoor America, including, but not limited to, the preservation of areas embracing primitive conditions of transportation, vegetation and fauna." Its trustees were further directed to "use any and all lawful means to increase the knowledge of the citizens of the United States of America as to the importance and necessity of maintaining wilderness conditions in outdoor America for future generations."[15]

This last trust became known as the Robert Marshall Wilderness Fund. As its five trustees, Marshall named Bob Yard, George Marshall, Irving Clark, Olaus Murie, and Bill Zimmerman, an Indian Service Official. All but Zimmerman were Wilderness Society Councillors, and Zimmerman later became one. Thus, as Yard said: "While the Wilderness Society is not mentioned in the will, the personnel of the testamentary trusteeship insures its indefinite use of this money."[16]

Stephen Fox, in a short history of The Wilderness Society, shows how useful this fund has proved to be. The fund, he says, made grants to The Wilderness Society of $12,000 in 1945, $17,900 in 1947, and $28,200 in 1954. In 1959 a three-year grant of $150,000 made it possible for The Wilderness Society to promote vigorously the bill which resulted in the 1964 Wilderness Act. In the 1970s, grants from the fund allowed the society to promote the Alaska National Interest Lands Conservation Act. These were the two biggest wilderness issues of the second half of the twentieth century, and thus Marshall's influence lasted well beyond his lifetime.[17]

Bob Marshall (Photograph courtesy The Bancroft Library, University of California, Berkeley)

On August 16, 1940, Agriculture Secretary Wallace honored the recently deceased Bob Marshall by designating a 950,000-acre roadless area in the Flathead and Lewis and Clark national forests in Montana as the Bob Marshall Wilderness Area. Thus Marshall has had named after him an organization camp in the Black Hills of South Dakota, a mountain in the Adirondacks, a lake in the Brooks Range, and a wilderness in the Northern Rockies. He got around.[18]

Lovers of the Bob Marshall Wilderness like to call it the "Flagship of the Wilderness Preservation System," and boast that it's the most famous Forest Service wilderness. A slight exaggeration, perhaps, but certainly the Bob Marshall Wilderness may have done more than any other single thing to make the name *Bob Marshall* a household word among wilderness enthusiasts. He deserves that recognition, for besides being an extraordinary wilderness traveler, he helped preserve hundreds of thousands of acres of wild land, became an inspiration to a couple of generations of wilderness advocates, and was a founding father of the modern environmental movement. He ranks with John Muir, Aldo Leopold, and a handful of others who taught us that by saving wilderness we also save a vital part of the human spirit.

Marshall was also a humorist, writer, explorer, scientist, and social critic—a kind of da Vinci in high-topped sneakers. His economic ideals were sometimes utopian, even naive—yet they were also consistent for Marshall and his times. He came of age when capitalism was coughing and sputtering like a badly tuned Model A Ford. It saddened him deeply to see people exploited or forgotten: He wanted everybody to have the same shot at happiness that he had had. Though he hated "stuffed shirts," he saw something good in every backwoods mill worker, drunken fire fighter, and destitute Indian that he met. He believed success in life was largely a matter of opportunity.

For all his interests and energy, Marshall was an uncomplicated man. He loved people and he loved the interchange of ideas. Most of all, he loved wildness. When he died, a lot of people had something to say about what he was like. One of the best observations came from his assistant in the Forest Service, John Sieker. In one paragraph, simply stated, Sieker got to the heart of the matter. He said:

> Bob was a man of great energy and enthusiasm. He was scrupulously fair and honest and followed the dictates of his conscience regardless of the consequences. He was friendly to all and interested in all groups of people, but few really understood his inner thoughts. I did not feel that I knew him until after several 30-mile walks in the wilderness during which time he talked about his theories of life, and philosophies. The world has lost a great humanitarian and the Forest Service has lost a conservationist who was willing and able to fight for the principles of true conservation to the end. Those few who really knew him have lost a loyal friend.[19]

Notes

◆ ——————————————————————— ◆

In most cases I have collected the references necessary to a particular paragraph in one note. The full citation is given on the first mention in each chapter. The following abbreviations are used:

Names:
RM   Robert (Bob) Marshall
LM   Louis Marshall

Collections and Publications

AJA	American Jewish Archives, Cincinnati, Ohio
APA Archives	Association for the Protection of the Adirondacks Archives, Adirondack Research Center, Schenectady Museum, Schenectady, New York
Apperson Papers	John S. Apperson Papers, Adirondack Research Center, Schenectady Museum, Schenectady, New York
Carson Papers	Russell M. L. Carson Papers, The Adirondack Museum Library, Blue Mountain Lake, New York
Clark Papers	Irving Clark Papers, University of Washington, Seattle, Washington
FDR	Franklin D. Roosevelt Library, Hyde Park, New York
LMP-AJA	Louis Marshall Papers, American Jewish Archives
MacKaye Papers	Benton MacKaye Papers, Dartmouth College, Hanover, New Hampshire National Archives, Washington, D.C.

275

NA	National Archives, Washington, D.C.
RG 75	Record Group 75 (Indian Affairs)
RG 95	Record Group 95 (U.S. Forest Service)
NYT	*New York Times*
Personnel	Robert Marshall Personnel File, U.S. Office of Personnel Management, Washington, D.C.
R-1 Files	U.S. Forest Service Region 1 files, Missoula, Montana
RMP-AJA	Robert Marshall Papers, American Jewish Archives, Cincinnati, Ohio
RMPB	Robert Marshall Papers, Bancroft Library, University of California, Berkeley, California
RMP-FDR	Robert Marshall Papers, Franklin D. Roosevelt Library, Hyde Park, New York
RMP-SUNY	Robert Marshall Papers, Moon Library, State University of New York College of Environmental Science and Forestry, Syracuse, New York
RSY-WY	Robert Sterling Yard Papers, University of Wyoming, Laramie, Wyoming
TWS-DEN	The Wilderness Society archives, Denver Public Library, Denver, Colorado
TWS-Washington	The Wilderness Society, Washington, D. C.

Chapter 1: The Kind of Vision We Need Today

1. Mable A. Mansfield, "Lighter Moments with Robert Marshall" (typescript of article for *Montana Magazine*).
2. All conversations between Marshall and Schaefer in this chapter are quoted in Paul Schaefer, "Bob Marshall, Mount Marcy, and—the Wilderness," *The Living Wilderness*, Summer 1966, pp. 12–16.
3. Leo A. Isaac, "Douglas Fir Research in the Pacific Northwest,

1920–1956" (Oral interview transcript, Forest History Society, 1967).

4. RM, "The Problem of the Wilderness," *The Scientific Monthly*, February 1930, pp. 141–148.

5. RM, "Adirondack Peaks," *High Spots*, October 1933, pp. 13–15.

6. Schaefer, "Bob Marshall," 14.

7. Ibid., 16.

Chapter 2: An Activist Father

1. RM to "a friend," 11/12/27, in Charles Reznikoff, ed., *Louis Marshall, Champion of Liberty: Selected Papers and Addresses*, Vol. 2 (Philadelphia: The Jewish Publication Society of America, 1957), p. 1174.

2. Ibid.

3. LM to Charles H. Sedgwick, 4/13/14, in Reznikoff, *Champion*, 4. See also Cyrus Adler, *Louis Marshall: A Biographical Sketch* (New York: The American Jewish Committee, 1931); Morton Rosenstock, *Louis Marshall, Defender of Jewish Rights* (Detroit, Wayne State U. Press, 1965); and James C. Young, "Louis Marshall Looks Back," *New York Times Magazine*, 12/12/26, pp. 9–10, 18–19 for biographical material on Louis Marshall.

4. LM to G. Friton, 4/24/29, in Reznikoff, *Champion*, 6.

5. LM to Charles H. Sedgwick, 4/13/14, in Reznikoff, *Champion*, xv, 4.

6. Oscar Handlin, "Introduction" to Reznikoff, *Champion*, x, xi.

7. Young, "Marshall Looks Back."

8. Handlin, "Intro." to Reznikoff, *Champion*, xi.

9. LM to J. Schiff, 10/2/14 in Reznikoff, *Champion*, 6.

10. Handlin, "Intro." to Reznikoff, *Champion*, xiii.

11. LM to R. Medina, 3/9/29, in Reznikoff, *Champion*, 8.

12. Adler, *Biographical Sketch*, 9–10.

13. Rosenstock, *Defender of Jewish Rights*, 25.

14. Handlin, "Intro." to Reznikoff, *Champion*, xiv.

15. Handlin, "Intro." to Reznikoff, *Champion*, xvi; George Marshall interview, New York City, 12/7/82.

16. Handlin, ibid., xviii.
17. Rosenstock, *Defender*, 26; J. Marshall to J. Glover, 10/6/82.
18. Adler, *Biographical Sketch*, 55: George Marshall interview, 12/7/82.
19. Rosenstock, *Defender*, 27.
20. Ibid., 67–68.
21. Handlin, "Intro." to Reznikoff, *Champion*, xxviii.
22. See Frank Graham, Jr., *The Adirondack Park: A Political History* (New York: Knopf, 1978), pp. 65–125.
23. LM to A. W. Knauth, 7/30/29, in Reznikoff, *Champion*, 1062.
24. Ibid., 1063.
25. LM to NYS Gov. Frank W. Higgins, 3/17/05, in Reznikoff, *Champion*, 1014.
26. LM to NYS Forest, Fish and Game Commissioner, 9/25/08, in Reznikoff, *Champion*, 1015.

Chapter 3: A Young Romantic

1. "Bob Marshall's Autobiographical Outline," RMPB; George Marshall interview, 12/7/82; E. Wortis to J. Glover, 2/25/82. See also Benny Kraut, *From Reform Judaism to Ethical Culture: The Religious Evolution of Felix Adler* (Cincinnati: Hebrew Union College Press, 1979); "Ethical Culture School, prospectus for 1905–1906," NY Public Library.
2. E. Wortis to J. Glover, 2/25/82.
3. James Marshall interview, 7/28/81.
4. George Marshall interview, 12/7/82; Neil Hosley, "Bob Marshall, Friend and Roommate," typescript.
5. George Marshall interview, 12/7/82.
6. Ibid.
7. Ibid.
8. Ibid.
9. Ibid.
10. James Marshall interview, 1/5/83.
11. George Marshall, "Robert Marshall as a Writer," *The Living Wilderness*, Autumn 1951, p. 14.
12. Perry Miller, "The Romantic Dilemma in American National-

ism and the Concept of Nature," *Harvard Theological Review* 48 (October 1955): 240. See also Edward Halsey Foster, *The Civilized Wilderness* (New York: The Free Press, 1975); Hans Huth, *Nature and the American: Three Centuries of Changing Attitudes* (Berkeley: U. of California Press, 1957; reprint ed., Lincoln, Nebraska: U. of Nebraska Press, 1972), pp. 30–53.

13. RM, *Alaska Wilderness*, 2d ed. (Berkeley: U. of California Press, 1970), p.1.
14. RM, "Impressions From the Wilderness," *The Living Wilderness*, Autumn 1951, p. 10.
15. Mr. Van Cour (Knollwood caretaker) interview, 6/11/82; James Marshall, "The Man in Shirtsleeves," in Reznikoff, *Champion*, 1151.
16. RM to LM, 8/7/16, J. Marshall personal files.
17. J. Marshall, "Shirtsleeves," 1151.
18. RM, "The Knollwood League, 1916–1923," typescript, p. 10.
19. J. Marshall, "Shirtsleeves," 1149.
20. Ibid.
21. RM, *Alaska Wilderness*, 2.
22. George Marshall, "Adirondacks to Alaska: A Biographical Sketch of Robert Marshall," *Ad-i-ron-dac*, May–June 1951, p. 44.
23. J. Marshall to J. D. Vickery, 11/28/78, J. Marshall personal files.
24. RM to LM, 8/1/16, J. Marshall personal files.
25. See Frank Graham, Jr., *The Adirondack Park: A Political History* (New York: Knopf, 1978), pp. 170–171; Charles Reznikoff, ed., *Louis Marshall, Champion of Liberty: Selected Papers and Addresses* (Philadelphia: Jewish Publication Society of America, 1957), Vol. 2 pp. 1020–1027.
26. RM to W. G. Howard, 1/30/37, RMPB.
27. George Marshall interview, 12/7/82.
28. Reznikoff, *Champion*, 897, 1150; George Marshall interview, 12/7/82; RM to R. Carson, 8/18/36, George Marshall personal files.
29. RM to R. Carson, 8/18/36, George Marshall personal files.

30. RM, "Great Adirondack Guides, No. 4—Herbert Clark," *High Spots* (Adirondack Mountain Club newsletter), October 1933, p. 9.
31. Ibid.
32. Ibid.
33. George Marshall, "Some Reflection on Ampersand," *High Spots*, July 1934, p. 3—4.
34. Quoted in George Marshall, "Robert Marshall as a Writer," *The Living Wilderness*, Autumn, 1951, p. 14.
35. Frank Bergon, ed., *The Wilderness Reader* (New York: Mentor, 1980), p. 188; Frank Graham, Jr., *The Adirondack Park: A Political History* (New York: Knopf, 1978), pp. 65—78, 128.
36. Quoted in Bergon, *Wilderness Reader*, 90.
37. G. Marshall, "Adirondacks to Alaska," 44.
38. RM to LM, 9/10/17, James Marshall personal files.
39. RM to LM, 8/15/17, James Marshall personal files.
40. RM to LM, 3/10/17; RM to LM, 9/7/21: James Marshall personal files.
41. Russell M. L. Carson, *Peaks and People of the Adirondacks* (New York: Doubleday, 1927; reprint ed., Glens Falls, NY: The Adirondack Mountain Club, 1973), p. 14; RM, *The High Peaks of the Adirondacks* (Albany, NY: The Adirondack Mountain Club, 1922), p. 14.
42. G. Marshall, "Adirondacks to Alaska," 44.
43. RM, "Great Guides," 10.
44. George Marshall, "Approach to the Mountains," *Ad-i-ron-dac*, March—April 1955, p. 24.
45. Ibid.
46. Ibid., 25.
47. Ibid., 26.
48. Ibid., 27.
49. RM, "A Day on the Gothics, August 11, 1920," *High Spots*, January 1942, p. 10.
50. Ibid.
51. Ibid.
52. Ibid.

53. Ibid, 11.
54. Ibid.
55. Ibid.

Chapter 4: Pond Seeker

1. RM, "Why I Want to Become A Forester in the Future," typescript, 4/17/18;, RMPB.
2. George Marshall interview, 12/7/82.
3. Nelson C. Brown, "The First Nine Years," in George Armstrong and Marvin W. Kranz, eds., *Forestry College: Essays on the Growth and Development of New York State's College of Forestry, 1911–1961* (Syracuse: SUNY College of ESF Alumni Association, 1961), pp. 30–32; Charles Reznikoff, ed., *Louis Marshall, Champion of Liberty: Selected Papers and Addresses*, Vol. 2 (Philadelphia: The Jewish Publication Society of America, 1957) pp. 1080–1082.
4. Brown, "Nine Years," 32–33; Registrar's Records, SUNY College of Environmental Science and Forestry.
5. George Marshall interview, 12/7/82; RMP-AJA letters.
6. John Shanklin interview, 8/8/81.
7. N. Hosley to J. Glover, 9/17/81; C. Forsaith to J. Glover, undated, summer 1981; Ralph T. King "The Faculty," in George Armstrong and Marvin W. Kranz, eds., in *Forestry College*, 125–126.
8. Neil Hosley, "Bob Marshall: Friend and Roommate," typescript; RM to Captain F. Pernays, 4/20/39, RMPB: George Marshall interview, 12/7/83.
9. N. Hosley to J. Glover, 9/17/81.
10. Ibid.
11. Hosley, "Friend and Roommate."
12. *Empire Forester*, 1924, p. 82; George Marshall, Preface to Russell M. L. Carson, *Peaks and People of the Adirondacks* (New York: Doubleday, 1927; reprint ed., Glens Falls, NY: The Adirondack Mountain Club, 1973), p. xii; RM, "Climbing 42 High Adirondack Peaks," *New York Evening Post*, 7/21/22.

13. "Syracuse Youth Masters Every Adirondack Peak," Syracuse *Herald*, 11/2/21; Hosley, "Friend and Roommate"; *Empire Forester*, 1924.

14. "Bits of Summer Camp History," *Camp Log*, 1922, pp. 13–14.

15. RM, "Weekend Trips In the Cranberry Lake Region," typescript, 1923, pp. 1–3.

16. Ibid., 5.

17. Ibid., 6–8.

18. Ibid., 15.

19. Ibid., 15–16.

20. William M. Harlow interview, 12/28/81; W. M. Harlow to M. Nadel, 1/20/69, TWS - Washington; Al Cline, "The First Marcy Trip," *Camp Log*, 1922, 34–35.

21. RM, "Weekend Trips," 20–21.

22. *Camp Log*, 1922, 55.

23. RM, "Weekend Trips," 23.

24. Ibid., 24–25.

25. Ibid., 35–37.

26. Ibid., 45.

27. Ibid., 48.

28. Ibid., 51.

29. RM, *The High Peaks of the Adirondacks* (Albany, NY: The Adirondack Mountain Club, 1922).

30. Ibid., 7–9.

31. Ibid., 37–38.

32. George Marshall, Preface to Russell M. L. Carson, *Peaks and People of the Adirondacks*, xii.

33. RM, "The Perfect Forester," *Empire Forester*, 1924, p. 43.

34. RM, "Recreational Limitations to Silviculture in the Adirondacks," *Journal of Forestry* 23 (February 1925): 173–178.

35. Roger C. Thompson, "The Doctrine of Wilderness: A Study of the Policy and Politics of the Adirondacks Preserve-Park" (Ph.D. dissertation, State University College of Forestry, Syracuse University, 1962), p. 157.

36. *Empire Forester*, 1924, p. 82; Registrar's records, SUNY College of ESF; G. Marshall to J. Glover, 1/29/83.

Chapter 5: Bee Stings and Broiled Eggs

1. Leo A. Isaac, "Douglas Fir Research in the Pacific Northwest, 1920–1956," (oral history interview conducted by Amelia R. Fry for the Forest History Society, 1967), pp. 57–58.
2. E. E. Carter to RM, 5/6/24, RMPB; C. H. Flory to RM, 5/21/24, RMPB; C. H. Flory telegram to RM, 7/11/24, RMPB.
3. Isaac, "Douglas Fir Research," 59–60.
4. R. McArdle to D. A. Bernstein, 8/31/77, TWS-Washington.
5. Ibid.
6. Ibid.
7. Ibid.
8. RM to Family, 9/4/24, James Marshall personal files; David A. Bernstein, "Bob Marshall: Wilderness Advocate," *Western States Jewish Historical Quarterly* 13 (October, 1980): 29.
9. "The Alumnae," *The Harvard Forest 1907–1934* (Cornwall, NY: Cornwall Press, 1935), p. 8.
10. N. Hosley to J. Glover, 7/24/82.
11. Olmsted quoted in *The Harvard Forest*, 41; Hosley to J. Glover, 8/17/81.
12. "Forest Log" (logbook at the Harvard Forest); RM, "The Growth of Hemlock Before and After Release From Suppression" (Masters Thesis published by Harvard Forest as Bulletin No. 11, 1927), pp. 1–7.
13. "Forest Log"; N. Hosley to J. Glover, 8/17/81.
14. N. Hosley to J. Glover, 8/17/81.
15. "Forest Log."
16. Ibid.
17. Ibid.
18. RM, "Growth of Hemlock," 17, 38–41.
19. RM, "Precipitation and Presidents," *The Nation*, 3/23/27, pp. 315–316.
20. N. Hosley to J. Glover, 3/8/83.
21. George Marshall, Preface to Russell M. L. Carson, *Peaks and People of the Adirondacks* (New York: Doubleday, 1927; reprint

ed., Glens Falls, NY: The Adirondack Mountain Club, 1973), pp. xiv–xv.
22. George Marshall to J. Glover, 3/6/85; idem. *Peaks and People,* xxix.

Chapter 6: Rocky Mountain Greyhound

1. Quoted in Roger C. Thompson, "The Doctrine of Wilderness: A Study of the Policy and Politics of the Adirondack Preserve-Park" (Ph.D. dissertation, New York State College of Forestry, Syracuse University, 1962), p. 307.
2. "Growth of a Forester" (Unpublished arrangement, compiled by George Marshall, of selected letters that RM wrote to friends and relatives while he worked for the Northern Rocky Mountain Forest Experiment Station. This letter dates 6/17/25.)
3. Harold K. Steen, *The U.S. Forest Service: A History* (Seattle: U. of Washington Press, 1976), pp. 138–140.
4. "College Alumni Notes," *The Newsletter* (of the New York State College of Forestry), January 1927, p. 22.
5. RM, "Mountain Ablaze," *Nature,* June–July 1953.
6. "Growth of a Forester," 7/26/25.
7. Ibid.
8. Ibid.
9. Ibid., 8/23/25.
10. Ibid.
11. Ibid.
12. Ibid., 7/26/25.
13. RM, "Mountain Ablaze."
14. RM, "The Work of the Northern Rocky Mountain Forest Experiment Station," *The Empire Forester,* 1927, pp. 12–15; "Growth of a Forester," 8/31/25.
15. "Growth of a Forester," 8/13/25.
16. RM, *Alaska Wilderness* 2d ed. (Berkeley, U. of California

Press, 1970), p. 2; *Empire Forester*, 14; "College Alumni Notes," January 1927, p. 22.

17. "Growth of a Forester," 10/17/25.
18. Ibid., 10/23/25.
19. Ibid., 6/1/27.
20. Ibid., 11/25/25.
21. RM to E. Untermyer, 1/12/27, RMPB.
22. RM, "Howard R. Flint," *Journal of Forestry* 34 (January 1936): 75–76.
23. E. Flint to Mrs. R. Billikopf, 11/14/30, RMPB.
24. Virginia Olmsted interview.
25. Henry A. Peterson, "Early-Day Ranger in the Priest Lake Country," in *Early Days in the Forest Service*, Vol. 4 (USDA Forest Service, Northern Region, Missoula, 1976), p. 250.
26. Kempff correspondence, RMPB.
27. "Growth of a Forester," 1/2/26.
28. RM to L. Whipple, 6/7/33, RMPB.
29. Thompson, "The Doctrine," 307.
30. "Growth of a Forester," 8/27/25.
31. Ibid.
32. Ibid., 2/14/26.
33. Ibid.
34. "Growth of a Forester," 2/25/26.
35. Ibid.
36. Ibid.
37. RM to R. Weidman, 7/29/26, RMPB.
38. R. Weidman to RM, 7/16/26, RMPB.
39. Ibid.
40. "College Alumni Notes," January 1927, p. 22.
41. RM, "Impressions From the Wilderness," *The Living Wilderness*, Autumn 1951, p. 12.
42. Ibid., 13.
43. September 13, 1927 telegram, RMPB.
44. J. Marshall to RM, 8/15/27, RMPB.
45. Charles Reznikoff, ed., *Louis Marshall, Champion of Liberty:*

Selected Papers and Addresses, Vol. 2 (Philadelphia: The Jewish Publication Society of America, 1957), p. 1047.

46. *Adirondack Enterprise*, 11/7/27.
47. RM to Poh (no other name given), 11/13/27, RMPB.
48. Undated announcement, RMPB.
49. Russell M. L. Carson, *Peaks and People of the Adirondacks* (New York: Doubleday, 1927; reprint ed., Glens Falls, NY: The Adirondack Mountain Club, 1973), p. 231.
50. T. V. W. Anthony circular, 12/27/28, Apperson Papers; T. V. W. Anthony to J. Apperson, 7/15/28, Apperson Papers; Chapter 212, Laws of NY, 1929 copy circulated by Anthony; J. Apperson to T. V. W. Anthony, 4/29/29, Apperson Papers.
51. LM to Doctor Hall, 8/3/28, APA Archives.
52. T. V. W. Anthony to "Some Fellow Members," 1/14/28, Apperson Papers.
53. Ibid.
54. T. V. W. Anthony to J. Apperson, 5/17/28, Apperson Papers.
55. See Oscar Handlin, "Introduction" to Reznikoff, *Champion;* Cyrus Adler, *Louis Marshall: A Biographical Sketch* (New York: The American Jewish Committee, 1931), pp. 39–43; Morton Rosenstock, *Louis Marshall, Defender of Jewish Rights* (Detroit: Wayne State U. Press, 1965), pp. 128–200; Albert Lee, *Henry Ford and the Jews* (New York: Stein and Day, 1980); Ernest Volkman, *A Legacy of Hate: Anti-Semitism in America* (New York: Franklin Watts, 1982), pp. 29–43.
56. RM to R. M. L. Carson, 1/23/28, Carson Papers.
57. LM to RM, 2/11/28, in Reznikoff, *Champion*, 1056.
58. Philip G. Terrie, Jr., "Mount Marshall: The Strange History of the Names of an Adirondack High Peak," *Ad-i-ron-dac*, July–August 1973, pp. 73–75, 83.
59. RM, "Contribution to the Life History of the Northwestern Lumberjack," *Social Forces*, December 1929, pp. 271–273.
60. See Dennis Roth, "The National Forests and the Campaign for Wilderness Legislation," *Journal of Forest History* 28 (July 1984): 113–114; also James P. Gilligan, "The Development of Policy and Administration of Forest Service Primitive and Wil-

derness Areas in the Western United States" (Ph.D. dissertation, U. of Michigan, 1953), p. 83.

61. Gilligan, "Development," 86.
62. Ibid., 105.
63. Ibid., 114–116.
64. Ibid., 107–121, 132–173; Russell Lord, Ed., *Forest Outings* (Washington, D.C.: Forest Service, 1940).
65. See Donald F. Cate, "Recreation and the U.S. Forest Service: A Study of Organizational Response to Changing Demands" (Ph.D. dissertation, Stanford University, 1963), p. 49–53.
66. RM, "The Wilderness as a Minority Right," *U.S. Forest Service Bulletin*, 8/27/28, pp. 5–6.
67. "Growth of a Forester," 4/14/28.

Chapter 7: Baltimore Liberal

1. RM to G. and L. Kempff, 3/3/30, RMPB.
2. John C. French, *A History of the University Founded by Johns Hopkins* (Baltimore: Johns Hopkins Press, 1946), pp. 231, 434; RM, "An Experimental Study of the Water Relations of Seedling Conifers With Special Reference to Wilting (Ph.D. dissertation, Johns Hopkins, 1930); RM to G. and L. Kempff, 3/3/30, RMPB.
3. RM to A. Cline, 7/15/30, RMPB.
4. RM to "Helen," 3/12/30, RMPB.
5. League for Industrial Democracy objective quoted from inside cover of RM, *The Social Management of American Forests* (League for Industrial Democracy, 1930); RM to A. Cline 7/15/20, RMPB.
6. Arthur M. Schlesinger, Jr., *The Age of Roosevelt*, Vol. 1: *The Crisis of the Old Order* (Boston: Houghton Mifflin, 1957), p. 130.
7. RM to O. W. Holmes, Jr., undated, RMPB; John Dewey, *Individualism Old and New* (New York: Minton, Balch and Co., 1929), pp. 101–120.
8. See Harold K. Steen, *The U.S. Forest Service: A History* (Seattle: U. of Washington Press, 1976), pp. 173–195.

9. Ibid., 185–195.
10. RM, "Forest Devastation Must Stop," *The Nation*, 8/28/29, p. 218.
11. George P. Ahern, *Deforested America* (Privately published, reprinted as Senate Document No. 216, 70th Cong, 2d Session, 1929).
12. RM, "Forest Devastation"; RM, "A Proposed Remedy for our Forestry Illness," *Journal of Forestry* 28 (March 1930); RM, *Social Management*.
13. RM, *Social Management*, 35.
14. Ibid.
15. See RM, *Alaska Wilderness*, 2d ed. (Berkeley: U. of California Press, 1970), pp. 1–2.
16. Ibid., 3.
17. Ibid., 4.
18. Some good descriptions of the region are also found in David J. Cooper, *Brooks Range Passage* (Seattle: The Mountaineers, 1982); Lois Crisler, *Arctic Wild* (New York: Harper & Row, 1973); and Margaret E. Murie, *Two in the Far North* (New York: Knopf, 1957; reprint ed. Anchorage: Alaska Northwest Publishing Co., 1978).
19. RM, *Alaska Wilderness*, 4.
20. Ibid., 5.
21. Ibid., 5.
22. RM, *Arctic Village* (New York: The Literary Guild, 1933), p. 3; *Alaska Wilderness*, 5.
23. RM, *Alaska Wilderness*, 5.
24. Ibid., 12.
25. Ibid., 25.
26. Ibid.
27. Ibid., 26.
28. Ibid., 26–27.
29. Ibid., 26.
30. RM, "Journal of the Exploration of the North Fork of the Koyukuk by Al Retzlaf and Bob Marshall," *The Frontier Maga-*

zine of the Northwest, January 1931, pp. 169, 173; RM to Family et al, 11/18/30, mimeographed, RMP-SUNY.

31. RM, "Journal," 175.
32. "2500 Pay Tribute to Louis Marshall," NYT, 11/11/29, p. 23.
33. RM to Helen Terry, quoted in Charles Reznikoff, *Louis Marshall, Champion of Liberty: Selected Papers and Addresses*, Vol. 2 (Philadelphia: The Jewish Publication Society of America, 1957), pp. 1173–1174.
34. Ibid.
35. "Son Probates Will of Louis Marshall," NYT, 10/9/29, p. 64.
36. See M. Nelson McGeary, *Gifford Pinchot, Forester-Politician* (Princeton: Princeton U. Press, 1968); also Harold T. Pinkett, *Gifford Pinchot, Private and Public Forester* (Urbana, IL: U. of Illinois Press, 1970).
37. RM to G. and L. Kempff, 3/3/30, RMPB.
38. "A Letter to Foresters," 2/7/30, RMPB.
39. RM to G. and L. Kempff, 3/3/30, RMPB.
40. Ibid.
41. Ibid.
42. RM to O. W. Holmes, Jr., undated, Johns Hopkins U. letterhead, RMPB.
43. RM to A. Cline, 7/15/30, RMPB.
44. George Marshall, "On Bob Marshall's Landmark Article," *The Living Wilderness*, October/December 1976, pp. 28–30; RM, "The Problem of the Wilderness," *The Scientific Monthly*, February 1930, pp. 141–148.
45. Ibid., 143.
46. Ibid., 144–5.
47. George Catlin, *North American Indians: Being Letters and Notes on their Manners, Customs, and Conditions, Written during Eight Years' Travel amongst the Wildest Tribes in North America, 1832–1839* (2 vols. London, 1880), Vol. 1, pp. 288–295, reprinted in Roderick Nash, ed., *Readings in the History of Conservation* (Reading, Mass.: Addison-Wesley, 1968), pp. 5–9; Aldo Leopold, "The Wilderness and its Place in Forest

Recreational Policy," *Journal of Forestry* 19 (November 1921): 718–721; Aldo Leopold, "The Last Stand of the Wilderness," *American Forests and Forest Life* 31 (1925): 602; Aldo Leopold, "Wilderness as a form of Land Use," *Journal of Land and Public Utility Economics* 1 (1925): 398.

48. Quoted in Elizabeth Flint, "Robert Marshall," *Montana Review*, 11/16/1939.
49. See James P. Gilligan, "The Development of Policy and Administration of Forest Service Primitive and Wilderness Areas in the Western United States" (Ph.D. dissertation, U. of Michigan, 1953), pp. 122–130, and Vol. 2 (Appendixes), pp. 1–4.
50. R. Stuart to RM, 3/7/30, RMPB.
51. RM to A. Cline, 7/15/30, RMPB.
52. Ibid.

Chapter 8: Wiseman Winter

1. RM, *Arctic Village* (New York: The Literary Guild, 1933), pp. 57–58.
2. RM, *Alaska Wilderness*, 2d ed. (Berkeley: U. of California Press, 1930), pp. 33–40.
3. Ibid., 41–42.
4. RM to friends and relatives, 9/23/30, RMP-SUNY; *Alaska Wilderness*, 50.
5. RM, *Alaska Wilderness*, 53–54.
6. RM to Family et al, mimeographed letter, 10/6/30, RMP-SUNY.
7. Ibid.
8. RM, *Arctic Village*, 7–8.
9. Ibid., 8.
10. Ibid.
11. RM To Family et al., mimeographed, 10/31/30, RMP-SUNY.
12. Ibid.
13. Ibid.
14. Ibid.

15. RM to Family et al., 10/26/30, RMP-SUNY.
16. Ibid.
17. RM, *Arctic Village*, 364.
18. Ibid., 367.
19. Ibid., 368.
20. RM to Family et al., mimeographed, 1/27/31, RMP-SUNY.
21. B. Cordozo to RM, 3/8/31, RMPB.
22. RM, *Arctic Village*, 87.
23. Ibid., 78–79.
24. Ibid., 80–81.
25. Ibid., 54–56, 295–296.
26. Ibid., 55–56.
27. Ibid., 244.
28. Ibid., 77, 80.
29. Ibid., 53.
30. RM to Family et al., mimeographed, 11/5/30, RMP-SUNY.
31. RM, *Arctic Village*, 307–310; RM to Family et al., 10/31/30, RMP-SUNY.
32. RM, *Arctic Village*, 310.
33. Ibid., 310.
34. Ibid., 95–98.
35. RM, *Alaska Wilderness*, 108; RM to Mrs. B. Livingston, 4/6/33, RMPB.
36. RM, *Alaska Wilderness*, 37–38; RM to friends and relatives, 9/23/30, RMP-SUNY.
37. RM, *Alaska Wilderness*, 62.
38. Ibid., 66.
39. RM to Family et al., 4/10/31, RMP-SUNY.
40. RM, *Alaska Wilderness*, 67.
41. Ibid., xxviii.
42. Ibid., 94.
43. Ibid., 103.
44. Ibid., 108.
45. Ibid., 109.
46. Ibid.
47. V. Olmsted to J. Glover, 8/23/82.

Chapter 9: Writer and Socialist

1. RM to M. Slisco, 1/5/32, RMPB.
2. RM to G. Gratt, 1/3/32, RMPB.
3. G. Pratt to RM, 1/18/32, RMPB
4. G. Pinchot to RM, 1/20/32, RMPB.
5. RM to H. P. Baker, 4/28/32, RMPB.
6. RM to H. Hicks, 10/18/32, RMPB.
7. Frank Graham, Jr., *The Adirondack Park: A Political History* (NY: Knopf, 1978), pp. 195–6; James P. Gilligan, "The Development of Policy and Administration of Forest Service Primitive and Wilderness Areas in the Western United States" (Ph.D. dissertation, U. of Michigan, 1953), p. 192.
8. See, for example, William Glasser, *Positive Addiction* (New York: Harper & Row, 1976); Michael H. Sacks and Michael L. Sachs, eds., *Psychology of Running* (Champaign, Ill.: Human Kinetics Publisher, 1981), pp. 81–82, 115–130.
9. Abraham H. Maslow, "Lessons From the Peak Experiences," *Journal of Humanistic Psychology* 2 (Spring 1962): 9; see also Neil R. Scott, "Toward a Psychology of Wilderness Experience," *Natural Resources Journal* 14 (April 1974): 231–237; Robert Wuthnow, "Peak Experiences: Some Empirical Tests," *Journal of Humanistic Psychology* 18 (Summer 1978): 59–75.
10. RM to E. Clapp, 8/17/32, RMPB; RM to P. Baxter, 5/18/38, Baxter Papers, Portland, ME.
11. Harold K. Steen, *The U.S. Forest Service: A History* (Seattle: U. of Washington Press, 1976), pp. 199–204; Samuel T. Dana and Sally K. Fairfax, *Forest and Range Policy*, 2d ed. (New York: McGraw-Hill, 1980), pp. 168–9.
12. Steen, *Forest Service*, 137–141, 200; RM to G. Marshall, 1/21/33, RMP-FDR, E. Clapp to RM, 7/27/32, RMPB.
13. RM to E. Clapp, 8/17/32, RMPB; E. Clapp to RM, 9/8/32, RMPB; RM to A. Retzlaf, 1/17/33, RMPB.
14. James P. Gilligan, "Development," 80, 133.
15. RM to M. Wolff, 5/17/33, RMPB.

16. Gilligan, "Development," 127.
17. RM to Jim, 6/3/32, RMPB.
18. RM to Ike Spinks, four telegrams sent October 1932; RM to Ike Spinks, 1/25/33.
19. *A National Plan for American Forestry*, Sen. Doc. 12, 73d Cong. I, March 13, 1933, p. 463; RM to G. Marshall, 1/21/33, RMP-FDR.
20. *National Plan*, 467.
21. Ibid., 471–79.
22. Ibid., 487.
23. Ibid., 480.
24. Ibid., 485.
25. Ibid., v–x; Steen, *Forest Service*, 203–204; RM to several newsmen, spring 1933, RMPB.
26. Arthur M. Schlesinger, Jr., *The Age of Roosevelt*, Vol. 1: *The Crisis of the Old Order, 1919–1933* (Boston: Houghton Mifflin, 1957), pp. 166–176.
27. See Schlesinger, *Age*; Otis T. Graham, Jr., *Toward a Planned Society* (New York: Oxford U. Press, 1976), pp. 1–68.
28. RM to anonymous, 4/12/33, RMPB.
29. Ibid.
30. RM to E. Flint, 2/21/33; RM to R. Zon, 1/23/33.
31. RM to G. and B. Marshall, 2/15/23; all in RMP-FDR.
32. RM to E. Flint, RMP-FDR.
33. RM to R. Zon, 1/23/33 RMP-FDR.
34. Ibid.
35. Ibid.
36. RM to R. Zon, 2/27/33, RMPB.
37. RM to R. Zon, 1/23/33, RMPB.
38. Pinchot to FDR, 1/20/33, in Edgar B. Nixon, ed., *Franklin D. Roosevelt and Conservation, 1911–1945*, Vol. 1 (Hyde Park, NY: General Services Administration, 1957), pp. 129–132, 212–216; Steen, *Forest Service*, 225–7; Henry Clepper, *Professional Forestry in the United States* (Baltimore: Johns Hopkins Press, 1957), pp. 147–9.

39. RM to C. McMullen, 3/15/33, RMPB; RM to B. Livingston, 4/19/33, RMPB; RM to M. F. Hyde, 4/6/33, RMPB.

40. RM to L. Ellison, 2/21/33, RMPB; *American Magazine*, May 1934, p. 45.

41. RM, "Walks of Georgia Engelhard and Bob Marshall," RMPB.

42. RM to P. S. Tang, 7/12/33, RMPB.

43. RM to R. Zon, 2/27/33, RMPB.

44. RM to V. Stefansson, 5/26/33, RMPB.

45. John Collier, *From Every Zenith: A Memoir and Some Essays on Life and Thought* (Denver: Sage Books, 1963), p. 277.

46. RM to G. Pinchot, 1/14/33, RMPB; RM to H. Ickes, 3/28/33, RMPB.

47. RM to L. Gannett, 5/2/33, RMPB.

48. RM to V. Stefansson, 5/26/33; RM to H. Smith, 5/26/33; RM to J. A. Davis, 5/29/33; RM to A. Cline, 7/12/33: all RMPB.

49. RM to H. Smith, 5/26/33, RMPB.

50. RM, *Arctic Village* (NY: The Literary Guild, 1933), p. 356.

51. RM to H. Smith, 12/31/36, RMPB; RM to Jesse Allen, 4/4/34, RMPB.

52. V. Neck to RM, 5/5/34, RMPB.

53. Daines Barrington, "An Arctic Middletown," *Saturday Review of Literature*, 5/13/33, p. 589; R. L. Duffus, "Utopia is Tracked Down to the Arctic Circle," *NYT, Book Review Section*, 5/7/33, p. 5; H. L. Mencken, "Utopia in Little," *The American Mercury*, May 1933, pp. 124–126.

54. Mencken, "Utopia," 126.

55. *Ibid.*

56. RM, *Arctic Village*, 219–20, 242.

57. Kenneth R. Philp, *John Collier's Crusade for Indian Reform, 1920–1954* (Tucson: U. of Arizona Press, 1977), p. 117.

58. Personnel.

Chapter 10: The Wilderness Society

1. RM to N. Hosley, 11/4/34, RMPB.

2. Kenneth R. Philp, *John Collier's Crusade for Indian Reform,*

1920–1954 (Tucson: U. of Arizona Press, 1977), p. 24; see also Lawrence C. Kelly, *The Assault on Assimilation: John Collier and the Origins of Indian Policy Reform* (Albuquerque, NM: U. of New Mexico Press, 1983).

3. Graham D. Taylor, *The New Deal and American Indian Tribalism* (Lincoln: U. of Nebraska Press, 1980), p. 6; John Collier, RM, and Ward Shepard, "The Indians and Their Lands," *Journal of Forestry* 31 (December 1933): 905–6.
4. Philp, *Collier's Crusade*, 135–159.
5. Collier, RM, and Shepard, "Indians," 308; RM, "Indians, Forest, and Grass," *Indians at Work*, 1936, Reorganization Number, p. 24.
6. D. Harbison to RM, RMPB.
7. *Wildlife Restoration and Conservation: Proceedings of the North American Wildlife Conference Called by Franklin D. Roosevelt* (Washington: Government Printing Office, 1936), p. 224; unnamed Junior Range Examiner to RM, 11/20/37, RMPB.
8. RM, "Forty-one Miles in the Ozarks," *Service Bulletin* (USFS), 11/27/39; RM to M. Murie, 7/31/33, RMPB.
9. RM to Mrs. Pringel, 6/4/37, RMPB; RM to Editor, *Alaska Miner*, 5/19/39, RMPB; Mable Mansfield, "Lighter Moments With Robert Marshall," typescript.
10. RM to M. Murie, 7/31/33, RMPB.
11. M. Murie to J. Glover, 6/26/81.
12. RM, *The People's Forests* (NY: Smith and Haas, 1933), 21.
13. Ibid., 219.
14. Ibid., 149.
15. Franklin Reed, "The People's Forests" (review), *Journal of Forestry* 32 (January 1934): 104–107.
16. RM to Mrs. H. F. Pringle, 2/15/38, RMPB; RM to H. Smith, 7/31/33, RMPB.
17. RM, "Walks of Georgia Engelhard & Bob Marshall," RMPB; RM to J. R. McCarl, 4/30/35, RMPB.
18. RM to J. R. McCarl, 4/30/35, RMPB.
19. Ibid.
20. Ibid.
21. M. Murie to J. Glover, 6/26/81.

22. RM to F. Dotson, 4/3/36, Personnel.
23. G. Marshall to J. Glover, 6/15/85.
24. A. Harper to RM, 4/16/36, RMPB.
25. T. H. Watkins, "The Terrible Tempered Mr. Ickes," *Audubon*, March 1984, pp. 93–111.
26. Ibid., 101.
27. William Zimmerman, Jr., "Wilderness Areas on Indian Lands," *The Living Wilderness*, July 1940, p. 10; Roderick Nash, *Wilderness and the American Mind*, 3d ed. (New Haven: Yale U. Press, 1982), p. 204.
28. "The Petition of June 13, 1934," *Journal of Forestry* 32 (October 1934): 781–783.
29. RM, "Should the Journal of Forestry Stand for Forestry?" *Journal of Forestry* 32 (November 1934): 904–908.
30. David Montgomery, ed., "Evolution of the Society of American Foresters, 1934–1937, As Seen in the Memoirs of H. H. Chapman," *Forest History* 6 (Fall 1962): 2–9.
31. H. H. Chapman, "Comments on Marshall's Article," *Journal of Forestry* 32 (November 1934): 908.
32. Montgomery, "Evolution," 6.
33. "Walks of Georgia Engelhard and Bob Marshall," RMPB; RM, "Memo: The Range Situation on the Crow Reservation," 1/4/34, NA, RG 75.
34. Minutes, Crow Range Committee, 6/22/34, NA, RG 75.
35. Ibid.
36. RM to J. Collier, 6/26/34, NA, RG 75.
37. G. M. Nyce to J. Collier, 7/10/34, NA, RG 75; Collier telegram, 8/10/34, NA, RG 75
38. File 28432, NA, RG 75.
39. E. Oberholtzer to H. Ickes, 8/25/34, RMPB. For a closer look at the Quetico-Superior issue, see R. Newell Searle, *Saving Quetico-Superior: A Land Set Apart* (St. Paul: Minnesota Historical Society Press, 1977).
40. Roderick Nash, "Historical Roots of Wilderness Management," in John C. Hendee, George H. Stankey, and Robert C.

Lucas, *Wilderness Management* (Washington: USDA Forest Service, 1977), pp. 30–33.

41. Harvey Broome, "Origins of the Wilderness Society," *The Living Wilderness*, July 1940, pp. 13–14; RM to R. S. Yard, 10/26/35, RSY-WY; Lewis Mumford et al. "Benton MacKaye: A Tribute," *The Living Wilderness*, January/March 1976, pp. 7–34; Benton MacKaye, in Foreword to Ronald M. Fisher, *The Appalachian Trail* (Washington: National Geographic Society, 1972), p. 5.
42. Broome, "Origins," 14.
43. Ibid.
44. Ibid.
45. Ibid.
46. Ibid.
47. RM memo to H. Ickes, 8/18/34, RSY-WY.
48. Quoted in RM to B. MacKaye, 2/19/37, McKaye Papers.
49. H. C. Anderson to B. MacKaye, 9/12/34, RMPB.
50. Broome, "Origins"; Stephen Fox, "We Want No Straddlers," *Wilderness*, Winter 1984, p. 5; RM to A. G. Whitney, 5/1/35, RMPB.
51. Broome, "Origins."
52. 7/8/82 interview, Mable (Abercrombie) Mansfield.
53. B. MacKaye to H. A. Slattery, 10/22/34, RMPB.
54. RM to H. Ickes, 5/4/37, RMPB; Harold L. Ickes, *The Secret Diary of Harold L. Ickes*, Vol. 2: *The Inside Struggle, 1936–1939* (New York: Simon and Schuster, 1954), p. 584.
55. Broome, "Origins"; Mansfield interview 7/8/82; RM to J. C. Merriam, 10/25/34, RMPB.
56. RM to H. C. Anderson, 10/24/34, RMPB.
57. R. S. Yard to J. C. Merriam, 3/29/34 and 4/6/34, RSY-WY; R. S. Yard to B. MacKaye, 10/26/34, RMPB; R. S. Yard to RM, 10/30/34, RMPB; H. C. Anderson to RM, 11/11/34, RMPB.
58. Mansfield interview, 7/8/82.
59. Ibid.; MacKaye to RM, 12/1/34, RMPB.

60. RM to M. Abercrombie, 4/27/36, 2/9/36, and 4/21/38, M. Mansfield personal files; G. (Engelhard) Cromwell to J. Glover, 3/14/86.

61. Biographical notes, Clark Papers.

62. I. Clark to RM, 1/7/35, Clark Papers.

63. RM to I. Clark, 1/26/35, Clark Papers.

64. RM to I. Clark, 3/19/35, Clark Papers.

65. Arthur M. Schlesinger, Jr., *The Age of Roosevelt*, Vol. 1: *The Crisis of the Old Order* (Boston: Houghton Mifflin, 1957), p. 140; Schlesinger, *Age*, Vol. 2: *The Coming of the New Deal*, p. 51.

66. "The Wilderness Society," four-page printed statement.

67. Ibid.

68. Ibid.

69. RM to H. Ickes, 2/14/35, RMPB.

70. RM to H. Broome, 2/28/35, RMPB.

71. Ibid.

72. A. Leopold to RM, 4/3/35, RMPB.

73. "Robert Sterling Yard," *The Living Wilderness*, December 1945, pp. 1–4; Donald C. Swain, *Wilderness Defender: Horace Albright and Conservation* (Chicago: U. of Chicago Press, 1970), pp. 42, 67; Robert Shankland, *Steve Mather of the National Parks* (New York: Knopf, 1951), pp. 95, 167; Stephen Fox, *John Muir and his Legacy: The American Conservation Movement* (New York: Little, Brown, 1981), pp. 203–205; Henry Ward, "Yard, the Dreamer and Builder," *The Living Wilderness*, December 1945, p. 11; R. S. Yard to C. F. Truitt, 1/18/38, RMPB.

74. R. S. Yard to RM, 9/22/37, RMPB.

75. RM to C. R. Dion, (quoting back the remark, which was originally Dion's), 12/8/38, RMPB.

76. B. MacKaye to RM, 12/12/35, Paul Oehser personal files.

77. R. S. Yard to H. B. Ward, 12/26/39, TWS-DEN.

78. RM memo to Mr. Moahan, 2/14/34, NA, RG 75; Mansfield interview, 7/8/82.

79. Mable Mansfield, "Lighter Moments With Bob Marshall," typescript, Mansfield personal files.

80. *Congressional Record (House)*, Vol. 79, Part 1, 1/28/35, pp. 1089–90.

81. "Federal Officials Accused as Reds," NYT, 2/2/35, p. 5.
82. RM to H. Fish, 4/2/37, RMPB.
83. RM, "Memorandum to Secretary Ickes: Immediate Problem of Wilderness Preservation," 4/25/35, RMPB.
84. Ibid.
85. RM, "Memorandum to the Secretary, Proposed Green Mountain Parkway," received 3/29/35, RMPB; RM memo to H. Ickes, 6/6/35, TWS-DEN.
86. RM to J. Collier, 6/16/34, NA, RG 75; Zimmerman, "Wilderness Areas," 10.
87. RM to W. Zimmerman, 6/22/35, NA, RG 75.
88. Ibid.
89. RM to F. Silcox, 6/24/35, RMPB.
90. RM, "Memo on Proposed Restoration of Uncompahgre Reservation to the Utes," undated, early 1935, NA, RG 75; L. W. Page to J. Collier, 6/28/35, NA, RG 75; RM telegram to J. Collier, 7/17/35, NA, RG 75; J. M. Stewart to J. Collier, 7/15/35, NA, RG 75; RM telegram, 7/17/35, NA, RG 75; see also Wil son Rockwell, *The Utes: A Forgotten People* (Denver: Sage Books, 1956), p. 257.
91. RM to M. Abercrombie, 8/13/35, RMPB.
92. RM to R. S. Yard, 9/6/35, RMPB.
93. *The Living Wilderness*, Fall 1935; RM to R. S. Yard, 6/29/35, TWS-DEN.
94. Aldo Leopold, "Why the Wilderness Society," *The Living Wilderness*, January/March 1976 (reprinted), p. 8.
95. RM to M. Abercrombie, 8/13/35, RMPB; RM to I. Clark, 10/26/35, Clark Papers.
96. Gilligan, "Development," 182–3; RM to L. F. Kneipp, 1/29/36, TWS-DEN.
97. See John Ise, *Our National Park Policy: A Critical History* (Baltimore: Johns Hopkins U. Press, 1961), p. 383; Robert L. Wood, *Trail Country: Olympic National Park* (Seattle: The Mountaineers, 1968), pp. 1–42; Ben W. Twight, "The Tenacity of Value Commitment: The Forest Service and Olympic National Park," (Ph.D. dissertation, U. of Washington, 1971).

98. B. MacKaye to RM, 5/10/35, RMPB; R. S. Yard to C. F. Truitt, 1/18/38, RMPB.
99. RM to I. Clark, 3/19/35, Clark Papers.
100. RM to I. Clark, 12/27/35, Clark Papers.
101. RM (signed by Yard), 12/28/35, RSY-WY.
102. RM, "Statistical Study of the Manual Support to the Heads of Supreme Court Justices in Action," RMPB.
103. B. Cordozo to RM, 12/26/35, RMPB.
104. Lithgow Osborne, "Truck Trails in the Adirondacks?" *American Forests*, January 1936, pp. 3–6; RM, "Fallacies in Osborne's Position," *The Living Wilderness*, September 1935, p. 4.
105. Raymond H. Torrey, "Truck Trails in the Adirondacks," *The Living Wilderness*, September 1935, p. 3; RM, "Fallacies"; Osborne, "Truck Trails?"; RM, "Comments on Commission's Truck Trail Policy," *American Forests*, January 1936, pp. 6, 43.
106. RM, "Fallacies," 4–5.
107. RM to F. Yardley, 2/21/36, TWS-DEN; R. Torrey to RM, 10/28/35, Apperson Papers.
108. "Minority Report of the Committee Appointed by Governor Herbert H. Lehman on the Problem of Forest Fire Truck Trails," James Marshall personal files; Frank Graham, Jr., *The Adirondack Park: A Political History* (New York: Knopf, 1978), p. 195; RM to F. Yardley, 2/21/36, TWS-DEN.
109. Graham, *Adirondack Park*, 195.

Chapter 11: Indians and Wilderness

1. RM to M. Abercrombie, 2/9/36, M. Mansfield personal files.
2. E. Oberholtzer to C. Kelly, 3/19/36, RMPB; RM to M. Abercrombie, 2/9/36, Mansfield personal files.
3. "The Cult of the Wilderness," *Journal of Forestry* 33 (December 1935): 955–957.

4. Leopold letter to the editor, *Journal of Forestry* 34 (April 1936): 446.
5. RM letter to the editor, Ibid., 446–448.
6. RM to M. Abercrombie, 4/27/36, M. Mansfield personal files.
7. Ibid; Minutes of APA board meeting, 5/11/36, APA Archives.
8. RM, "Statement on Behalf of The Wilderness Society on the Proposed Mount Olympus National Park," RMPB.
9. RM to F. Silcox, 6/3/36, TWS-DEN.
10. Memo to Mr. Granger and Mr. Keplinger, 6/12/36, Personnel; C. Granger to RM, 8/26/36, RMPB; H. Ickes to H. Wallace, 8/5/36, Personnel.
11. H. Ickes to H. Wallace, 8/5/36, Personnel; RM to G. Nyce, 5/14/37, RMPB.
12. RM to Mable Abercrombie, 6/16/36, Mansfield personal files.
13. Quoted by Mable Mansfield in "Lighter Moments With Bob Marshall," typescript.
14. RM to R. M. L. Carson, 8/18/36, George Marshall personal files.
15. Ibid.
16. Ibid.
17. Ibid.
18. E. Oberholtzer to RM, 10/15/36, RMPB; RM and Althea Dobbins, "Largest Roadless Areas in United States," *The Living Wilderness*, November 1936, pp. 11–13; RM, "Maintenance of Wilderness Areas," in International Association of Game, Fish, and Conservation Commissioners, Proceedings, 13th Convention, 8/31/36, p. 30.
19. James P. Gilligan, "The Development of Policy and Administration of Forest Service Primitive and Wilderness Areas in the Western United States" (Ph.D. dissertation, U. of Michigan, 1953), p. 185.
20. Ibid., 133, 185.
21. RM to J. Collier, 11/2/36, NA, RG 75.
22. H. Howarth to RM, 11/3/36, NA, RG 75.
23. RM to R. K. Tiffany, 11/23/36, NA, RG 75; M. Smith to P. W. Mathias, 5/6/37, NA, RG 75.

24. N. O. Nicholson to J. Collier, 5/24/37, NA, RG 75; N. R. Garrett (Wash. DOT) to J. Glover, 12/17/84.
25. RM to H. Smith, 12/31/36, RMPB; RM to H. Smith, 1/14/37, RMPB.
26. RM to S. B. Franklin, 5/12/37, RMPB.
27. "Meeting of the New York Members of The Wilderness Society," 1/27/37, TWS-DEN.
28. Quoted by RM in letter to B. MacKaye, 2/19/37, MacKaye Papers.
29. Ibid.
30. RM, "Secretary Ickes on Speedways," RMPB.
31. RM to E. Oberholtzer, 3/23/37, RMPB.
32. Searle, *Saving Q-S*, 139.
33. RM to E. Johnson, 3/3/37, RMPB.
34. RM to J. Allen, 3/28/37, RMPB.
35. J. Collier to RM, 4/13/37, Personnel; E. Loveridge to Ag. Secretary, 4/20/37, Personnel; C. Granger to All Divisions, Wash. Office, 5/16/37, Personnel.
36. R. S. Yard to H. Broome, 2/14/35, RMPB.
37. George Marshall, "The Wilderness Society's Council, 1935–1945," *The Living Wilderness*, Winter 1965–66, p. 25; RM to B. MacKaye, 2/24/37 and 3/25/37, MacKaye Papers.
38. RM to B. MacKaye, 2/24/37, MacKaye Papers.
39. R. S. Yard to G. Marshall, 11/28/39, TWS-DEN.
40. William Zimmerman, Jr., "Wilderness Areas on Indian Lands," *The Living Wilderness*, July 1940, p. 10.
41. "Wilderness Now on Indian Lands," *The Living Wilderness*, December 1937, pp. 3–4.
42. RM to W. Zeh, 11/18/37, RMPB.
43. John Collier, *From Every Zenith: A Memoir and Some Essays on Life and Thought* (Denver: Sage Books, 1963), p. 272; RM to J. Collier, 1/24/39, RMPB.
44. Jack M. Hession, "The Legislative History of the Wilderness Act" (Masters Thesis, San Diego State College, 1967), pp. 48–51; Collier, *Zenith*, 118.
45. Collier, *Zenith*, 272–273; Hession, "Legislative History," 118.

46. Kenneth Philp, "Termination: A Legacy of the Indian New Deal," *The Western Historical Quarterly* 14 (April 1983): 180; Richard White, *The Roots of Dependency* (Lincoln: U. of Nebraska Press, 1983), pp. 212–323.

47. Donald L. Parman, *The Navajos and the New Deal* (New Haven: Yale U. Press, 1976); Lawrence C. Kelly, "The Indian Reorganization Act: The Dream and The Reality," *Pacific Historical Review* 44 (August 1975): 312.

48. RM to G. Nyce, 5/14/37, RMPB.

Chapter 12: Back to the Forest Service

1. Memo, "Various Major Accomplishments by the Forest Service, 1933–1940," NA, RG 95.

2. RM memo, "Recreation for Low Income Groups," 12/37, NA, RG 95.

3. RM, "Three Consecutive Days," typescript 5/21/37, RMPB.

4. RM "An Evening With Professor Einstein," typescript, 9/7/36, RMPB.

5. John Ise, *Our National Park Policy: A Critical History* (Baltimore: Johns Hopkins U. Press, 1961), p. 214; RM letter to the editor, *Journal of Forestry*, 36 (February 1938): 263.

6. RM to H. H. Chapman, 4/28/37, RMPB.

7. H. H. Chapman to RM, 6/18/37, RMPB.

8. RM to H. H. Chapman, 8/25/37, RMPB.

9. RM to H. H. Chapman, 3/25/38, RMPB. For Marshall-Chapman *Journal of Forestry* debate, see Chapman, "The Colorado-Big Thompson Reclamation Project: A Test Case," 35 (October 1937): 897–904; Chapman, "The National Conservation Employees Association: A Study in Objectives," 35 (October 1937): 954–957; "Wilderness Areas," 36 (May 1938): 469–474. RM letters to editor: 36 (February 1938): 262–265; 36 (November 1938): 1173–1174.

10. C. Bauer to RM, 6/1/37, TWS-DEN.

11. RM to R. S. Yard, 8/24/37, RMPB.

12. Olaus Murie, "Wilderness is for Those Who Appreciate," *The Living Wilderness*, July 1940, p. 18.
13. RM to H. Broome, 1/20/38, TWS-DEN.
14. RM to F. Silcox, 7/18/38, Personnel.
15. Richard E. McArdle with Elwood R. Maunder, "Wilderness Politics: Legislation and Forest Service Policy," *Journal of Forest History* 19 (October 1975): 178–179.
16. Ibid.
17. "Maintenance of Recreation Values in the High Sierra," *Sierra Club Bulletin* 23 (no. 5, 1938), p. 85.
18. Ibid., 86–87.
19. RM to S. Olson, 7/3/37, RMPB. A closer look at Olson may be found in Frank Graham, Jr., "Leave It to the Bourgeois: Sigurd Olson and His Wilderness Quest," *Audubon*, November 1980, pp. 28–39.
20. Sigurd Olson, "Quetico-Superior Elegy," *The Living Wilderness*, Spring 1948, p. 6.
21. Ibid., 10.
22. Ibid., 10.
23. Ibid., 12.
24. L. C. Merriam, Jr. "A Land Use Study of the Bob Marshall Wilderness Area of Montana" (Forest and Conservation Experiment Station, Montana State University, Bulletin No. 26, October 1963), pp. 26–29; Regional Forester Kelley to FS Chief, 7/8/37, R–1 files; Charlie Shaw, *The Flathead Story* (Kalispell, Mont.: USDA Forest Service, Flathead National Forest, 1967), p. 67.
25. RM to E. Koch, 7/27/37, R-1 files; E. Koch to RM, 8/7/37, R-1 files; RM to Regional Forester Kelley, 9/7/37, R-1 files.
26. RM to Kelley, Ibid.
27. Don Schwennesen and Steve Woodruff, "Bob Marshall Wilderness Complex," *Missoulian*, 9/27/84, p. 22.
28. McArdle with Maunder, "Politics," 170–178; James P. Gilligan, "The Development of Policy and Administration of Forest Service Primitive and Wilderness Areas in the Western

United States" (Ph.D. dissertation, U. of Michigan, 1953), pp. 204–225; John Sieker interview, 6/30/81.

29. Sieker interview, 6/30/81.
30. RM to M. Wolff, 10/7/37, R-1 files.
31. H. Gisborne to RM, 10/2/37, RMPB.
32. R. S. Yard to I. Clark, 11/13/39, Clark Papers.
33. "Women Members Protest Against Elaborate National Park Trails," *The Living Wilderness*, December 1937, pp. 8–12.
34. G. Kempff to RM, 9/5/37, RMPB.
35. RM to G. Kempff, 12/23/37, RMPB.
36. RM to I. Drift, 12/31/37, RMPB.
37. RM to J. Collier, 11/11/37, NA, RG 75.
38. J. Collier to RM, 11/13/37, NA, RG 75.
39. G. Cromwell to J. Glover, 3/14/86. Marshall's papers—at least those made available for this biography—show nothing about his proposing to Engelhard.
40. RM, "Recreation Policy Questions to be Determined in Connection With the Recreation Report," typescript, NA, RG 95.
41. RM to R. Zon, 3/3/38, RMPB.
42. RM to R. Baldwin, 3/7/38, RMPB.
43. RM to R. Zon, 3/3/38, RMPB.
44. RM to R. Baldwin, 2/11/38, RMPB; RM to R. Baldwin, 3/7/38, RMPB.
45. "Report to the President of the United States on the Quetico-Superior Area by the Quetico-Superior Committee," 1938.
46. See R. Newell Searle, *Saving Quetico-Superior: A Land Set Apart* (St. Paul: Minnesota Historical Society Press, 1977), p. 232.
47. N. T. Cowling memo to members, 3/2/38, RMPB.
48. RM to V. Stefansson, 6/21/39, RMPB.
49. RM to F. V. Coville, 2/8/35, RMPB; RM, *Alaska Wilderness*, xxxiii.
50. J. Coffee to RM, 3/4/38, RMPB.
51. Gardner Jackson, typescript of Marshall eulogy for *The Nation* (this part was not published), Jackson papers, FDR Library, Hyde Park, NY.

52. RM to children friends, 3/1/38, RMPB.
53. RM to I. Clark, 10/26/35, Clark Papers; RM to W. Zeh, 3/7/38, RMPB.
54. RM to M. Abercrombie, 4/21/38 and 1/24/39, M. Mansfield personal files.
55. Gilligan, "Development," 192–3.
56. Ibid, 194; memo: "Basic Policies Governing National Forest Recreational Management," distributed 7/1/38, NA, RG 95.
57. RM, "Dissenting Opinions on the Forest Service's Report on the Proposed Mount Olympus Nation's [sic] Park Bill," RMPB.
58. Ise, *Park Policy*, 389; *The New America's Wonderlands: Our National Parks* (Washington, DC: National Geographic Society, 1980), p. 284.
59. Ise, *Park Policy*, 402–3; Robert S. Yard, "Most Wonderful of Wildernesses—Kings Canyon National Park," *The Living Wilderness*, December 1942, pp. 3–11.
60. "The Problem of the Kings Wilderness," *Wilderness News* (Wilderness Society Newsletter), 2/20/39, pp. 1–4; RM, "Memorandum for Mr. Granger," 6/4/38, NA, RG 95; RM, "Comments on the Region 5 Report of December 1936," NA, RG 95.
61. RM, "Comments on the Region 5 Report of December 1936 Entitled, The Kings River Unit, A Problem in Integrating Public Wild Land Management With Requirements of a Dependent Civilization," NA, RG 95.
62. RM to C. Granger, 6/4/38, NA, RG 95.
63. Stephen Fox, *John Muir and His Legacy: The American Conservation Movement* (New York: Little, Brown, 1981), p. 181.
64. R. Edge to RM, 2/17/37, RMPB; R. Edge to RM, 1/14/38, RMPB.
65. R. Edge to RM, 11/28/37, RMPB; Fox, *Muir*, 212.
66. RM to Mrs. Oumansky, 5/10/39, RMPB.
67. RMP-AJA.
68. RM to Dave and Herb, 12/19/37, RMP-AJA.
69. "Out of Their Role," *Washington Post*, 6/26/38.

70. RM to *Washington Post*, 6/38, RMP-AJA.

71. Correspondence, 1938–'39, RMPB.

72. I. Clark memo "Notes: From Conversation With Bob Marshall—July 12, 1937," Clark Papers.

73. Memo, "Basic Policies Governing National Forest Recreational Management," distributed 7/1/38, NA, RG 95.

74. RM to F. Silcox, 7/13/38, Personnel.

75. R. Zon to RM, 7/20, 38, RMPB.

Chapter 13: Two Last Flings

1. RM, *Alaska Wilderness*, 2d ed. (Berkeley: U. of California Press, 1970), pp. 110–115.

2. Ibid., 114–115.

3. RM, *Doonerak or Bust* (privately printed, 1938), pp. 6–7.

4. RM, *Alaska Wilderness*, 115.

5. Ibid., 115–128.

6. Ibid., 128–140.

7. Ibid., 140.

8. "High Federal Aides Are Linked to Reds at House Hearing," NYT, 8/18/38, p. 1; "WPA Union Called Communist Plan," NYT, 4/18/39, pp. 1, 3.

9. See William Gellerman, *Martin Dies* (New York: Van Rees Press, 1944); David Oshinsky, *A Conspiracy So Immense: The World of Joe McCarthy* (New York: The Free Press, 1983), pp. 91–95; Robert Griffith, *The Politics of Fear* (Lexington: U. of Kentucky Press, 1970), p. 32.

10. Earl Latham, *The Communist Controversy in Washington from the New Deal to McCarthy* (Cambridge, Mass.: Harvard U. Press, 1966), pp. 149–150.

11. Silcox was especially vilified by certain elements of the lumber industry. The *Southern Lumberman* castigated him cruelly, George Jewett compared him with Hitler, and Frank H. Lamb claimed he had "all the traits of Naziism." See Steen, *The U.S. Forest Service*, 233.

12. R. McArdle to D. A. Bernstein, 8/31/77, TWS-Washington.

13. RM to J. Allen, 12/12/38, RMPB; V. Olmsted to J. Glover, 5/26/85.
14. Virginia Olmsted telephone interview, February 1986.
15. Ibid.
16. RM to J. Allen, 12/12/38.
17. RM to I. Clark, 11/12/38, Clark Papers.
18. John Sieker interview, 6/30/81; RM to G. Jackson, 11/9/39, Jackson Papers; RM to D. Sugarman, 10/38, RMPB.
19. Catherine Bauer et al., "Gap in the Front Lines," *The New Republic*, 12/27/39, p. 289.
20. Sieker interview, 6/30/81.
21. V. Olmsted to J. Glover, 8/23/82; James Marshall interview, 7/28/81.
22. James Marshall interview, 7/28/81.
23. See Robert A. Caro, *The Years of Lyndon Johnson: The Path to Power* (New York: Knopf, 1981, Vintage Books Edition, 1983), pp. 276–277.
24. RM to M. Maverick, 5/12/39, RMPB.
25. RM to J. and M. O'Connor, 11/10/38, RMPB.
26. Bauer et al., "Gap."
27. M. E. Becker to District Ranger Engles, 1/10/38, NA, RG 95.
28. RM to Regional Forester Buck, 1/29/39, NA, RG 95.
29. RM to F. V. Horton, 12/16/38, NA, RG 95.
30. 12/16/38 press release, NA, RG 95.
31. RM to Regional Forester Buck, 1/20/39, NA, RG 95.
32. James P. Gilligan, "The Development of Policy and Administration of Forest Service Primitive and Wilderness Areas in the Western United States" (Ph.D. dissertation, U. of Michigan, 1953), pp. 195–6.
33. HR 3648, 76th Cong, 1st Sess.; Ag. Secretary to V.P. of U.S., undated (1939), NA, RG 95.
34. RM to K. Reid, 2/17/39, RMPB.
35. RM memo "Conference With Mrs. Roosevelt at the White House to Discuss Desirablility and Purpose of a National Recreation Conference," 2/28/39, NA, RG 95.
36. RM to G. Pinchot, 3/29/39, RMPB.

37. RM to anonymous, 3/14/39, RMPB.
38. RM to S. Povich, 4/10/39, RMPB.
39. RM to I. Clark, 4/12/39, Clark Papers.
40. RM, *North Doonerak, Amawk and Apoon* (privately printed, 1939), p. 102.
41. RM, *Alaska Wilderness*, pp. 142–163.
42. George Marshall, "Introduction to The Second Edition," in RM, *Alaska Wilderness*, xi.
43. Mailing list used by Dorothy Sugarman, RMPB.
44. RM, *Alaska Wilderness*, xxiii-xxiv.
45. Ibid., 165.
46. FDR to H. Ickes, Mimeographed memo, 8/30/37, NA, RG 95; C. Rochford to RM, 10/8/37, NA, RG 95.
47. RM, "Should We Develop Alaska?" *The New Republic*, 1/8/40, p. 50.
48. "Alaska—Its Resources and Development," U.S. Cong., House Doc. no 485, 75th Cong. 3d Session, 1938, Appendix B, p. 213.
49. F. Silcox to Region 10, 8/23/39, NA, RG 95.
50. "Senate Joint Memorial No. 3," NA, RG 95.
51. See George Marshall, "Introduction to the Second Edition," in RM, *Alaska Wilderness*, xiii-xix.
52. P.L. 96–487 (12/2/80, 94 Stat pp. 2371–2393). The national park lands include Kobuk Valley N. P., Noatak National Preserve, Bering Land Bridge National Preserve, and Cape Krusenstern National Monument. Wildlife refuge lands include the Arctic, Selawik, Kanuti, and roughly two-thirds of Yukon Flats national wildlife refuges.
53. RM, "Inspection of Recreation and Lands Activities, Region 5, August 12–September 5, 1939," NA, RG 95.
54. John Ise, *Our National Park Policy: A Critical History* (Baltimore: Johns Hopkins Press, 1961), pp. 402–403; P.L. 89–111 (8/6/65, 79 Stat, 446).
55. RM to R. S. Yard, 11/7/39, RMPB.
56. Ibid.
57. RM, "Inspection . . . Region 6," 11/10/39, NA, RG 95.

58. Ibid.
59. Michael Frome, *National Park Guide* (Chicago: Rand McNally & Co., 1985), pp. 111–113; *Wonderlands*, 287–292.
60. Gilligan, "Development," p. 197 and Vol. 2, 6–7.
61. Ibid., 198–200; also, see Peter Wild, "Bob Marshall, Last of the Radical Bureaucrats," *High Country News*, 3/9/79. In an otherwise excellent article, Wild says that Marshall "single-handedly added the immense figure of 5,437,000 acres to the government's preserve system."

Chapter 14: He Never Rested

1. M. Tyler to R. S. Yard, TWS-DEN.
2. "Marshall Dies; U.S. Forestry Official Was 38," *NY Herald Tribune*, 11/12/39, p. 34; J. Sieker to R. S. Yard, 12/20/39, TWS-DEN.
3. G. Marshall to J. Glover, 11/16/82.
4. V. Olmsted to Mr. and Mrs. Yard, 11/27/39, TWS-DEN.
5. H. Broome to R. S. Yard, 11/13/39, TWS-DEN.
6. V. Olmsted to I. Clark, 11/21/39, Clark Papers.
7. J. Sieker to R. S. Yard, 12/20/39, TWS-DEN.
8. G. Brown to R. S. Yard, 1/20/40, TWS-DEN.
9. J. Sieker to R. S. Yard, 12/20/39, TWS-DEN.
10. Sieker to Yard, Ibid.; RM to V. Olmsted, 11/10/39, RMPB.
11. R. S. Yard to V. Olmsted, 12/14/39, TWS-DEN.
12. J. Le Cron to R. S. Yard, 11/16/39, TWS-DEN; "Autopsy," City of New York Office of Chief Medical Examiner, 12/11/39.
13. R. S. Yard to J. Le Cron, 11/17/39, TWS-DEN.
14. H. Broome to R. S. Yard, 11/13/39, TWS-DEN.
15. "Last Will and Testament," 7/12/38. See also Richard Neuberger, "He Was a Millionaire Who Walked Himself to Death," *The Sunday Oregonian*, 3/1/42, p. 2; "Marshall Bequest to Preserve Wilds," *NYT*, 12/1/39, p. 14.
16. R. S. Yard to H. Broome, 12/18/39, TWS-DEN.
17. Stephen Fox, "We Want No Straddlers," *Wilderness*, Winter, 1984, pp. 14–17.

18. See Meyer H. Wolff, "The Bob Marshall Wilderness Area," *The Living Wilderness*, July 1941, pp. 5–6; *Alaska Wilderness*, 152n.
19. J. Sieker to R. S. Yard, 12/20/39, TWS-DEN.

Index

◆ ——————————————————————— ◆

Abercrombie, Mable, 176–180,
    184, 197, 198–199, 201,
    226, 232
Aberle, S. D., 227–228
Adams, Mount (Adirondacks), 3
Adirondack Enterprise, 17
Adirondack Forest Preserve,
    13–14
Adirondack Mountain Club, 5,
    27, 50, 91, 206
Adirondacks:
    Marshall's childhood in, 20–24,
        26–36
    Marshall's hikes in, 3, 27–36,
        41, 42–50, 66, 142–143, 188
    preservation of, 12–14, 24
    truck trail issue in, 194–195
Adler, Cyrus, 10
Adler, Felix, 15
Agassiz, Louis, 29
Ahern, George P., 103, 112–113
Alaska National Interest Lands
    Conservation Act, 262, 272
Alaskan development, 260–262
Alaska Wilderness (Marshall), 107,
    244, 259, 265
Alatna River (Brooks Range),
    130, 137
Algonquin, Mount (Adirondacks),
    32
Allen, Jesse, 208, 242–244, 248,
    256–257
Alloway, Albert, 238
American Civil Liberties Union,

152, 180, 185, 230, 236
American Forestry Association,
    141–142, 176, 201
American Forests, 141, 194, 238
American League for Peace and
    Democracy, 236, 245
American Planning and Civic
    Association, 217
Ampersand, Mount
    (Adirondacks), 27–29
Anaconda-Pintlar Wilderness, 253
Anderson, Harold, 116, 174,
    176–178, 181
Anthony, Theodore Van Wyck,
    88–91
Apoon, Mount (Brooks Range),
    257
Appalachian Mountain Club, 94
Arctic Johnny, 129
Arctic Village (Marshall), 5, 19,
    120, 131, 133, 155–157,
    162, 205–206, 241–242
Association for the Protection of
    the Adirondacks, 87,
    194–195, 205–206, 241–242
As You Like It, 16
Atlanta, Georgia, 197
Autobiography of a Curmudgeon
    (Ickes), 166

Baldwin, Roger, 230
Barrett, L. A., 209
Basin Mountain (Adirondacks),
    35

313

Bauer, Catherine, 218
Beard, Charles A., 101
Becker (junior forester), 251–252
Belyea, Harold, 41
Bernard, John, 207
Bettles, Alaska, 138
Bible, 22, 23
Big Jim, 129–130, 146
Billikopf, Ruth Marshall (sister)
    (*see* Marshall, Ruth;
    "Putey")
Blake, Mills, 88–89
Blaisdell, Thomas and Mrs., 199,
    249
Bob Marshall Wilderness, 84, 94,
    201, 223–224, 273
Bolero (Ravel), 126–127
Boreal Mountain (Brooks Range),
    107
Boundary Waters Canoe Area
    Wilderness (*see also* Quetico-
    Superior Committee), 94,
    230
Brandeis, Louis, 153–154
Brooks Range, 117
    developments in, 261
    Marshall's explorations in,
        104–109, 120–122, 134–139,
        242–244, 256–260
Broome, Harvey, 174–176, 178,
    181, 268, 271
Brower, David, 266
Brown, Gilbert, 269–270

Cagle, Ed, 26
Cammerer, Arno B., 176–177,
    186, 188–189, 206
Camp Log (1922 Sophomore camp
    yearbook), 46
Carlsbad Caverns National Park,
    94
Carlson, Floyd E., 67, 79
Carpenter, Clara, 241
Carson, Russell M. L., 51, 66,
    88–89, 92

Carter, Jimmy, 262
Catlin, George, 116
Champlain, Samuel D., 18, 29
Chapman, H. H., 168–169,
    216–218
Clapp, Earle H., 68, 144
Clark, Herb, 1–3, 25–36, 41, 66,
    88–92, 272
Clark, Irving, 180, 189–191, 209,
    218, 248, 272
Clark, John, 33
Clarke-McNary Act, 102–103
Clear River (Brooks Range),
    107–109, 134–139
Cline, Al, 45, 62, 117
Clingman's Dome (Smokies),
    174–175
Coeur d'Alene National Forest,
    80
Coldfoot, Alaska, 126–127
Coffee, John M., 231, 264
Collier, John, 177, 226
    description of, 157–158
    and Indian policy, 154, 160,
        170–171
    on Marshall, Louis, 154
    relationship with Marshall, 154,
        227–228
    and wilderness, 209–212
Columbia University, 8–9, 38
Colvin, Verplanck, 29–30
*Communist Controversy in
    Washington from the New
    Deal to McCarthy* (Latham),
    245
"Contribution to the Life History
    of the North American
    Lumberjack" (Marshall),
    92–93
Coolidge, Calvin, 94
Cooper, James Fenimore, 23
Copeland Report (*see also National
    Plan for American Forestry*),
    144, 146–148, 163
Copeland, Royal, 144

Cordozo, Benjamin, 129n, 152, 193–194
Cranberry Lake (Adirondacks), 42–43, 45, 48
Cowling, H. T. 230
Crater Lake National Park, 94
Crow Indian Reservation, 169–171

Dawes General Allotment Act of 1887, 160
"Dawn in the Woods" (Marshall), 51
Dearborn Independent, 90
Deforested America (Ahern), 112
De Soto, Hernando, 18
Dewey, John, 101–102
Dewey, Melvil, 11–12
Dickens, Charles, 23
Dies, Martin, 245
Dies Committee, 244–245
Dishoo, 242
Dobbins, Althea, 203–204
Doonerak, Mount (Brooks Range), 207, 242–243, 256–257
"Doonerak or Bust" (Marshall), 259
Drift, Ivan, 227

Eaton, George, 241–242
Edge, Rosalie, 235
Einstein, Albert, 11, 216
Ekok, 130, 133–134, 138
Emergency Conservation Committee, 235
Emerson, Ralph Waldo, 29
Emigrant Basin wilderness, 262
Engelhard, Georgia, 152–153, 164, 169, 179–180, 226, 228–229
Ernie Creek (Brooks Range), 120, 242
Eskimos of the Koyukuk, 129–134

Ethical Culture School, 15, 17, 38
Explorer's Club, 230–231

Fairbanks, Alaska, 105, 241
Fish, Hamilton, 185
Fisher, Richard T., 61
Five Ponds region (Adirondacks), 47–48
Flathead National Forest, 273
Flint, Elizabeth and Howard, 77
Ford, Henry, 90
"Forest Devastation Must Stop" (Marshall), 103
"Forest for Recreation" (Marshall), 146
Forest Service, U.S. (*see also* National Park Service: competition with Forest Service), 112
    Marshall in, 55–60, 67–97, 215–216, 219–225, 229–230, 232–235, 238–239, 251–254, 262–265
    and research, 68
    wilderness preservation in, 93–95, 116–117, 145–146, 191, 204, 219–220, 232–233, 253–254, 264–265
Forever Wild (concept in Adirondacks), 21–31
Forsaith, Carl, 39
Forty-Sixers Club, 66, 91–92
Fox, Stephen, 200n, 272
Frank, Bernard, 176, 197
Franklin, Susan, 206
Frigid Crags (Brooks Range), 107
From Every Zenith (Collier), 210

Gates of the Arctic (Brooks Range), 107, 242
Gates of the Arctic National Park and Preserve, 107, 262
Georgia Appalachian Trail Club, 197
Gerhardt (physician), 269–270

Gibraltar wilderness, 262
Gila National Forest, 93
Gila Wilderness, 93
Gilligan, James P., 143
Gisborne, Harry, 225
Gothics Range (Adirondacks), 34–35
Grand Canyon National Park, 94
Grand Portage Indian Reservation, 187, 207
Grand Teton National Park, 94
Granger, Chris (C. M.), 200, 229, 234, 239, 253–254
Grass Pond (Adirondacks), 44
Grass Pond Mountain (Adirondacks), 44
Graves, Henry S., 68
Graves Peak (Adirondacks), 43
Great Bear Wilderness, 224
Great Depression, 111, 148
Great Smoky Mountains National Park, 172, 174–176, 186, 206–207, 265
Greeley, William B., 94, 265
Green, Vaughn, 119–120
Green Mountain Parkway proposal, 186
Griffith, Robert, 245
Grizzly Creek (Brooks Range), 120
Guggenheimer, Randolph, 9

Hammond River (Brooks Range), 137
Handlin, Oscar, 10
Harper, Allan, 166
Harrison, Benjamin, 9
Harvard Forest, 60–66
Harvard University, 60
Harvey, Ken, 208, 242–244, 256–257
Haslem, Pete, 128
Hawk Mountain Sanctuary, 235
Haystack Mountain (Adirondacks), 34

High Peaks of the Adirondacks (Marshall), 50
"High Peaks" region (Adirondacks), 32, 41, 45
High Sierra, 94, 220–221
High Sierra Primitive Area, 234
High Spots, 5
Hildebrand, Joel, 220–221
Holmes, Oliver Wendell, Jr., 114
Hood, Mount (Oregon), 60, 251
Hoover, Herbert, 148
Horton, Harry, 241
Hosley, Neil, 39, 44, 61–62, 66
Houghton, Augustus, 195–196, 199
Hunter College, 9

Ickes, Harold L., 265
    description of, 166–167
    relationship with Marshall, 167, 171, 177, 185–186, 200–201, 208
    urges Marshall to decline Wilderness Society presidency, 182
    as wilderness supporter, 167, 206–207, 209
Indian New Deal:
    description of, 159–161
    Marshall in, 159–162, 169–171, 188, 204–205, 213
    successes and failures of, 212–213
Indian Reorganization Act, 160–161
Individualism Old and New (Dewey), 102
Industrial Workers of the World, 75
Intelligence of Northern Koyukukers, 130–132
Iroquois, Mount (Adirondacks), 32
Isaac, Leo A., 55–56
Isaac Walton League, 94, 175, 254

Jackson, Cleveland, 205
Jackson, Dode (Dorothy), 181,
    209, 231, 267
Jackson, Gardner, 181, 185, 231,
    267
Jewish Tribune, 11
John River (Brooks Range), 137
Johns Hopkins Liberal Club, 101
Johns Hopkins University, 97
    Marshall at, 99–104, 117
Johnson, Ernie, 134–139,
    207–208, 242–244
Jones, Bobby, 126
Journal of Forestry, 103, 160, 163,
    198, 217–218
    Marshall's criticism of, 168–169

Kaniksu National Forest, 69, 74
Katahdin, Mount (Maine), 144
Kellecker, Pat, 125–126
Kelley, Evan, 223–224
Kelly, Lawrence, 213
Kempff, Gerry, 78, 100, 226–227
Kempff, Lily, 78, 100
Kings Canyon National Park,
    233–235, 255–256, 262–263
Kinnorutin ("You Are Crazy")
    Creek (Brooks Range), 137
Klamath Indian Agency, 164, 201
Kneipp, L. F., 117, 145, 204, 265
Knollwood, 20–24, 45, 155
Knollwood League Baseball,
    21–22, 31–32
Knoxville, Tennessee, 172–174,
    176–178, 197
Koch, Ellers, 224
Koyukuk Region (*see* Brooks
    Range; Marshall, Robert:
    Arctic adventures of)
Krutch, Joseph Wood, 109

Lacy, Frank, 75
Lanahan, Bill, 251
Latham, Earl, 245
League for Industrial Democracy,

101, 103
Lehman, Herbert, 195
Leopold, Aldo:
    as wilderness proponent, 93,
        96, 116, 265, 273
    as Wilderness Society co-
        founder, 176–177, 182
    as Wilderness Society
        defender, 189, 198
"Letter to Foresters" (Marshall *et
    al.*), 113
Lewis and Clark, 17, 56, 67
    Marshall on, 19–20, 74, 82
Lewis and Clark National Forest,
    273
Lewis, John L., 216
Limestack Mountain, 120
Livingston, Burton E., 97, 100
Living Wilderness, 189, 194, 218,
    225
Loon Creek (Brooks Range), 137
Lowenstein, Benedict
    (grandfather), 9
Lowenstein, Sophia Mendelson
    (grandmother), 9
Lower Saranac Lake
    (Adirondacks), 1, 14, 20, 23,
    26, 27, 33
Lynch (friend), 101

MacIntyre, Bob, 126
MacKaye, Benton, 116, 172–174,
    176–178, 181, 184, 192, 256
Marcy, Mount (Adirondacks),
    1–2, 5, 32, 45
Marshall, Florence Lowenstein
    (mother), 9–11, 24–25, 77
Marshall, George (brother), 10,
    25, 206
    climbs with Marshall, Bob, 3,
        27–36, 41, 66
    on Marshall, Bob, 17, 259, 268,
        271
    and Mount Marshall issue,
        88–92

and Robert Marshall
   Wilderness Fund, 272
as Wilderness Society officer,
   209
Marshall, Jacob (grandfather), 7–8
Marshall, James (brother), 10, 21,
   23, 25, 86, 202
   on Marshall, Bob, 18, 23
Marshall, Lenore (Mrs. James),
   201, 250
Marshall, Louis, 7–14, 20, 23, 29
   and baseball, 17–18, 21
   and botany, 24
   as civil rights defender, 11–12
   death of, 110–111
   and forestry, 52–53
   influence on Bob, 7, 10, 24, 38,
      52, 86, 111
   as Jewish spokesman, 9, 11–12
   law career of, 8–9, 10
   and Mount Marshall issue,
      89–91
   and New York State College of
      Forestry at Syracuse
      University, 38, 142
   protectiveness of, 86
   and Pueblo Indians, 154
   as wilderness defender, 12–14,
      24, 86–87
Marshall, Mount (Adirondacks),
   88–92
Marshall, Robert (Bob):
   and aesthetics, 29, 48, 116,
      126–127
   agnosticism of, 109
   on Alaskan development,
      260–261
   Arctic adventures of, 104–109,
      119–140, 241–244, 256–260
   athletic pursuits of, 17, 18,
      41–42, 143–144
   awkwardness of, 48, 57, 84
   bequests of, 272
   birth of, 14

childhood of, 15–36
and children, 77, 78, 231
and civil liberties, 79, 152, 237
and civil rights, 229–230, 238,
   252–253, 255
and clearcutting, 64
on Collier, John, 154, 159
Communist allegations against,
   185, 244–246
cooking ability, 58–60
and dancing, 133–134, 178,
   197, 231
on death, 110
death of, 6, 267–268, 271–272
on deforestation, 102–104,
   112–113, 141–142, 150–151,
   163–164
distance hikes of, 1, 2–3, 5, 56,
   62, 67–68, 79, 84, 87–88,
   143–144, 206
exploration interests and
   philosophy, 18, 44, 104,
   137–138, 231
feistiness of, 188, 216–218,
   225–228, 237, 239
feuds with Comptroller
   General, 164–166
financial independence of, 111
as fire fighter, 69–73
and forestry, 52–53, 64, 73–74
and frontier values, 128, 156
generosity of, 146, 238
and grizzly bears, 85–86,
   121–122
on happiness, 110–111
history as an interest of, 39, 47,
   62
homes of, 61, 75–76, 99,
   122–124, 141, 144, 199, 249
housekeeping of, 76, 123–124
humor of, 2, 16–17, 18, 40–41,
   62–64, 76, 83, 166,
   188–189, 193–194, 235–236
illnesses of, 83, 155, 225,

268–271
Indian names as an interest of,
162
and Indian Service wilderness,
186–187, 209–212
inspection trips of, 161–162,
219–225, 256, 262–264, 270
liberal activities and
inclinations of, 74–75,
101–102, 152, 215–216,
236–238, 250–251, 254–255
on Mount Marshall issue,
90–91
on the National Park Service,
180–181, 248, 252
as New Dealer, 148–149
at New York State College of
Forestry at Syracuse
University, 37–53
at Northern Rocky Mountain
Forest Experiment Station,
67–97
optimism of, 213, 251
on Pinchot, Gifford, 114,
150–151, 254–255
photography as an interest of,
31
physical characteristics of, 2, 77
rankings of, 30–31, 39–40,
50–51, 78
as reader, 78–79, 109, 123, 155
and recreation, 144–148,
200–201
romanticism of, 18–20, 132,
146, 157
shyness of, 15, 38, 77, 81–82
on sister "Putey," 25, 202–203
as socialist, 5, 78, 149–150, 151
social life of, 114, 184, 231,
235–236, 249–250
as social scientist, 117–118,
122–134
and solitude, 74
statistics of, 35–36, 57, 64–66,

193–194
underdogs as concern of,
71–72, 74–75
on urban places, 99
wilderness depletion as concern
of, 3–4, 48–49, 82–83, 87
as wilderness manager,
220–221, 251–252
as wilderness preservationist, 4,
5–6, 51–53, 142, 145–146,
167–168, 185–188, 191,
203–204, 206–207, 219–220,
223–224, 232–235, 253,
262–266, 273–274
as Wilderness Society co-
founder, 172–178, 265
as Wilderness Society
defender, 198, 217–218
Wilderness Society
dependence on, 271
as Wilderness Society financial
contributor, 182, 184, 209,
271, 272
as Wilderness Society policy-
maker, 191–193, 199–200,
208–209
as Wilderness Society recruiter,
218, 263
and women, 77, 100–101,
114–115, 133–134, 151,
152–153, 178–180, 228–229,
247–248, 250
work habits of, 184, 219
writings of, 5, 50–51, 65–66,
92–97, 103–104, 115–116,
146–148, 155–157, 163–164,
189
Marshall, Ruth (sister) (see also
"Putey"), 10
Marshall, Zilli Straus
(grandmother), 8
Maslow, Abraham, 144
Mather, Stephen T., 94,
171–172, 183, 234

Maverick, Maury, 250
Mazatsal Wilderness, 253
McArdle, Richard, 56–60,
    219–220, 245–246
McCarl, J. R., 164–165
McCarthyism, 245
McClure, David, 12
McIntyre, Mount (Adirondacks),
    45
Mencken, H. L., 156
Merchant of Venice, 8
Metropolitan Museum of Art, 10
Miller, Perry, 19
Modern Temper (Krutch), 109
Morning Moon, 21
Mountaineers, The, 94, 180
Mount Hood National Forest, 251
Mount Jefferson Wilderness, 263
Mud Lake (Adirondacks), 44
Muir, John, 175, 234, 262,
    265–266, 273
Munns, E. N., 113
Murie, Mardy, 162
Murie, Olaus, 162, 209, 218–219,
    265, 272
Murray, Jim, 74–75

Nakuchluk, 129–130
Nation, 103
National Association for the
    Advancement of Colored
    People, 11
National Audubon Society, 175
National Conference on Outdoor
    Recreation, 94
National Industrial Recovery Act,
    151
National Parks Association, 183,
    217
National Park Service, 265
    competition with Forest
        Service, 94–95, 191–192,
        215, 233–235, 262–263
    roads as an issue in, 171–172

    trails as an issue in, 225–226
National Plan for American Forestry
    (*see also* Copeland Report), 5
Navajo Indians, 161, 210–211
Neck, Victor, 156
Ness, Albert, 119–120
New Republic, 260
New York (city), 7–8, 9–10, 12,
    267
    Marshall in, 15–20
New York State College of
    Forestry at Syracuse
    University, 52, 61, 142
    Bob Marshall at, 37–63
    Louis Marshall as influence on,
        38
New York State Constitutional
    Convention of 1894, 12, 29
New York State Constitutional
    Convention of 1915, 24
New York State Court of Appeals,
    9
New York Times, 185, 245
Nick's Pond (Adirondacks), 47
Normal College, The, 9
North Absaroka Wilderness, 94,
    223–225
North Cascade region, 94, 248,
    264
North Cascades National Park,
    264
"North Doonerak, Amawk and
    Apoon" (Marshall), 257
Northern Rocky Mountain Forest
    Experiment Station, 68
    Marshall at, 67–97
North Fork of the Koyukuk
    River, 105, 107–109, 242,
    257
Nutirwik (*see also* Snowden,
    Harry), 256–257

Oberholtzer, Ernest, 176–177,
    197–198, 203, 262

O'Connor, Jerry, 250
Olmsted, Frederick Law, 61
Olmsted, Harry, 78, 139
Olmsted, Virginia Boutelle, 78,
    139, 160, 180, 189, 264
    on Marshall, 78, 246–247, 268
Olson, Sigurd, 221–223, 262
Olympic Mountains, 94
Olympic National Park, 191–193,
    199–200, 233
Olympic Peninsula, 180
Opalescent River (Adirondacks),
    3
Osborne, Bill, 43, 48
Osborne, Lithgow, 194–195
Oumansky, Mrs. Rhea, 235
Oxadak, 129

Panther Gorge (Adirondacks), 2,
    34, 35
"Perfect Forester" (Marshall), 51
People's Forests (Marshall),
    163–164, 180
Philp, Kenneth, 212
Pinchot, Gifford, 112–114, 142,
    150–151, 216
Pioneer Boys of the Great Northwest,
    19–20
Porcupine Creek (Brooks Range),
    127
Poser, Carl, 32
Postlethwaite, Poss, 126
Pratt, George D., 141–142
"Precipitation and Presidents"
    (Marshall), 65–66
"Problem of the Wilderness"
    (Marshall), 19, 115–116
"Proposed Remedy for our
    Forestry Illness" (Marshall),
    103
Protocols of the Elders of Zion, 90
"Putey" (sister) (*see also* Marshall,
    Ruth), 25, 77, 202–203, 270

Quetico Provincial Park, 230
Quetico-Superior Committee,
    176
    Marshall serves on, 171, 198,
    203, 221–223
    recommendations of, 230
Quinault Indian Reservation,
    204–205

Rainier, Mount (Washington
    state), 60
Reed, Franklin, 163
Reid, Kenneth, 254
*Report of the Topographical Survey
    of the Adirondack Wilderness*
    (Colvin), 30
Retzlaf, Al, 105–109, 120–122
Rice, Walter Channing, 27
Robert Marshall Wilderness
    Fund, 272
Rocky Mountain National Park,
    94, 209, 217
Rocky Mountain Tunnel,
    216–218
Roger Smith Hotel, 249
Roosevelt, Eleanor, 254
Roosevelt, Franklin D., 148–151,
    160
Roosevelt, Theodore, 112
Ruger, William C., 9

Saddleback Mountain
    (Adirondacks), 35
San Bernardino National Forest,
    263
Sanderson, Wilford E., 45
Sawtooth Wilderness, 253
Schaefer, Paul, 1–6, 206
Schlesinger, Arthur, Jr., 101–102,
    181
Scientific Monthly, 3, 115
Selway-Bitterroot Wilderness, 82,
    84–85

Service Bulletin, 93, 95
Shenendoah National Park, 172, 186
Shepard, Ward, 112–113, 160
Shoshone National Forest, 224
"Should the Journal of Forestry Stand for Forestry?" (Marshall), 168
Sieker, John, 224–225, 249, 264
    on Marshall, 224–225, 269, 274
Sierra Club, 94, 175, 220–221
Silcox, Ferdinand:
    Communist allegations against, 245
    disagrees with Marshall on Alaskan development, 261
    recruits Marshall for Forest Service, 200
    relationship with Marshall, 187–188, 239
    as wilderness supporter, 191, 232, 265
Skylight, Mount (Adirondacks), 34, 45
Slisko, Martin, 107, 119, 122–123
Smith, Harrison, 205
Smith, Herbert A., 198
Snowden, Harry (*see also* Nutirwik), 126–127
Social Forces, 92
Social Management of American Forests, 103
Society of American Foresters, 112, 168–169, 217
Sophomore Summer Camp (Marshall's), 42–50
Southern Navajo Indian Agency, 161
South Meadows (Adirondacks), 33
Sparhawk, W. N., 113
Spinks, Ike, 146
Stanford-Binet intelligence test, 130

Stanich, Obran, 127–128
Stanich, Sam, 127–128
Stefansson, Vilhjalmur, 154, 231
Stuart, Robert, 116–117
Suckik, Jennie, 146
Sugarman, Dorothy, 249
Superstition Mountain Wilderness, 248, 253
Syracuse Herald, 41
Syracuse, New York, 8, 9

"Temperamental Tartar of the Muddy Rio Grande" (Marshall), 227–228
Teton Wilderness, 94
Thackeray, William, 23
Thompson, Manly, 95
Thompson, Roger C., 52
Three Sisters Wilderness, 253, 263
Torrey, Raymond, 194, 206
Tyler, Margaret, 267

Uncompahgre Ute Indian Reservation, 188
Untermyer, Samuel, 9

Van Name, Willard, 235
Veblen, Thorstein, 101

Vint, Thomas C., 226
Wallace, Henry A., 264, 273
Warm Springs Indian Agency, 201
Washington Post, 235, 237, 255
Watson, Mount, fire of 1925, 69–73, 75
Watts, Verne, 119–120, 126, 241
Weekend Trips in the Cranberry Lake Region (Marshall), 50
Weidman, Robert, 83–84
Wenatchee National Forest, 252
Whiteface Mountain (Adirondacks), 32, 86–87
Whipple, Leon, 79
White, Jack, 242

White Mountains (New Hampshire), 94
Wilderness Act of 1964, 254, 272
"Wilderness as a Minority Right" (Marshall), 95–97
Wilderness Society, 5, 116, 162, 194, 236
  actions of, 255–256
  Adirondack contingent of, 206
  and Alaska, 262
  criticisms of, 198, 217
  development of, 189, 199–200, 208–209, 218–219
  formation of, 172–178
Willamette National Forest, 264
Wind River Forest Experiment Station (Washington), 56
Wind River Range (Wyoming), 201
Wiseman, Alaska,
  changes of, 242
  dances in, 107, 132–134
  description of, 105
  Marshall in, 119–120, 122–134, 241–242, 256
Wolff, Meyer, 145, 225
Wood, Hattie, 33
Wood, Mrs. W. K., 33
Workers Alliance, 236–237
Wortis, Ethel, 15
Württemburg, Bavaria, 7

Yard, Robert S.:
  conservatism of, 218
  description of, 183
  and Green Mountain Parkway, 186
  on Marshall, 225, 271
  as National Park Service critic, 183
  relationship with Marshall, 183–184, 267
  as Robert Marshall Wilderness Fund trustee, 272
  as Wilderness Society co-founder, 177–178, 181
  provides Wilderness Society headquarters, 184
  as Wilderness Society secretary, 192, 199–200, 208, 263, 271
Yellowstone National Park, 87–88, 94, 223
Yellowtail, Robert, 170
Yosemite National Park, 94

Zahniser, Howard, 266
Zeh, Bill, 231–232
Zimmerman, William, 187, 272
Zon, Raphael, 112–114, 160, 168 239
Zurich, Switzerland, 110

Ul